Working at Leisure

BARRIE SHERMAN

METHUEN

By the same author

Freedom from Work
The New Revolution

(*with Clive Jenkins*)

Computers and Unions
Collective Bargaining
The Collapse of Work
White Collar Unions
The Leisure Shock

First published in Great Britain 1986
by Methuen London Ltd
11 New Fetter Lane, London EC4P 4EE
© 1986 Barrie Sherman
Printed in Great Britain

British Library Cataloguing in Publication Data

Sherman, Barrie
    Working at leisure.
    1. Industrial sociology   2. Technology——
    Social aspects
    I. Title
    306'.36   HD6955

ISBN 0–413–58440–2
ISBN 0–413–58460–7 Pbk

Contents

Acknowledgements

In common with most other books this one has been written with the help of many other people, some of which was given wittingly, some inadvertently. I would like to thank Clive Jenkins with whom I wrote *The Collapse of Work* and *The Leisure Shock*, both of which contain ideas which underpin this book, for his good wishes and indeed for his share of those ideas. I must also thank Diana Gilhespy and Seona McKinnon for their perceptive comments and corrections, and both Alex Bennion and Ann Mansbridge of Methuen and Bill Hamilton for theirs.

Preface

Change is always with us. We grow older, as institutions – sometimes nations – rise, decline and then disappear; the seasons themselves condition us to an annual cycle of change. Very occasionally the rate of change becomes dramatically faster and the change itself more fundamental. We have reached one of these periods today. The changes that stem from the application of electronic, microelectronic and other technologies are altering the ways in which we work, where we work and who does the work. But that is far from all. They are also amending the methods by which we communicate with each other, and as a result social patterns are changing too.

This is a worldwide change. Nothing like it has been seen before in this century. It is another industrial revolution, and like the previous one it will trail behind it the most massive social, economic, political and demographic changes. We can see some of these happening today, though the revolution is still in its infancy. If compared with the history of manned flight from the Wright brothers to the space shuttle *Challenger*, then we have barely reached the point when Blériot first flew across the English Channel.

The changes are all-embracing on two distinct levels. Their consequences are felt on a global basis; all countries, whether industrialised, industrialising, or underdeveloped, are affected – although the changes wrought by the technologies in each of these will be different. The other level concerns the wide range of effects on individuals, families and communities. It is not only employment and work that are changing, but how and where we spend our leisure periods, and when and what these may be. Social mores evolve or regress as technological advances point up moral dilemmas ranging from the privacy of the individual to the sanctity of life itself. The barriers are being lowered in some areas and raised in others, whilst overall the boundaries of achievement are being extended in all directions.

In 1979, 1980 and 1981, when Clive Jenkins and I were writing *The Collapse of Work* and *The Leisure Shock*, these matters were not talked about widely. *Collapse* was one of the first books of its type and in a real sense set the agenda for much of the debate that has followed. *The Leisure Shock* was an attempt to arrive at some sort of solution to a problem which too few people recognised at the time. This situation has now changed in some respects, but many of the arguments in these books still hold true today. Unemployment has become the major political and social issue across Europe and in parts of the USA and Canada, as we predicted it would back in 1979. On the other hand there have been attempts by many authorities to treat leisure and training as a substitute for employment. Each generation throws up its own buzz words and the mid-eighties have spawned 'leisure' and 'flexibility' in connection with this, the second industrial revolution. However mistaken or vague these ideas may be, they give an indication that some people are starting to think what used to be the unthinkable as regards work and free time.

When the previous books were written we had experienced neither the monetarist policies of Mrs Thatcher's Conservative government nor the latest world recession, nor the effect of both of these on jobs. Clearly, political actions and philosophies have a profound effect on what happens to workstyles and lifestyles, yet most of the current theorising on the subject tries to avoid this conclusion. This does not mean that the debate should be conducted only in terms of UK party politics; the subject transcends too many boundaries for that to be sufficient. However, proper thought must be given to asking the right political questions. Why do we work? Do we really like work? Where will new jobs come from? Would life be better in industrialised countries if we all worked less? What is the most appropriate technology and work as far as developing countries are concerned? Each of these questions conceals a plethora of fundamental political choices.

This book starts from the position we find ourselves in at present – not where we would like to be. It deliberately challenges the attitudes to work, leisure and indeed life held by many state institutions and the Establishment. In challenging some accepted wisdoms I am not suggesting that one overall plan will solve all the problems of an industrialised state or the inequalities between states. To do so would be a combination of arrogance and foolhardiness for a variety of reasons, not the least being that the new technologies will challenge fundamentally both capitalist and Marxist theory and practice.

If the book makes people think about the profound differences between this new set of changes and others that have taken place this century, and stops them from using remedies which assume that everything is the same as in the past, then it will have done its work. Things are not the same – and they never will be again.

Barrie Sherman
London 1985

1 The working-go-round

The man, dressed neatly in a dark suit and holding a briefcase, sits forlornly on a park bench on a mild Tuesday mid-morning. This may read like a stage direction and it is quite appropriate that it should; the reason he is there is the stuff of which good theatre is made. He is one of many men who cannot bring themselves to tell their families that they have lost their jobs. He leaves home in the mornings, ostensibly to go to work, but in reality to eke out the hours of the day in miserable fashion. His tragedy is that he has fallen off the working-go-round. He cannot get back on, yet is unable to face himself, or others, with this simple truth.

Industrial societies are dedicated to the working-go-round. At any given time there are new people getting on and others getting off, whilst some are changing their seats. This less than merry-go-round is the central feature of these societies. Success and failure are measured by whether you have a seat, and if so then by what sort of seat it is. No other feature of life, save sex, approaches this in importance. In recent times there have been far too many people for them all to get on at the same time with safety; some have to sit on the side and watch for long periods. There may be other pleasures in the fair, but these are only tolerated for short spells by most people.

What is it about work that can explain this preoccupation, this craving? Withdrawal of work appears to have the same sort of effect on people as the withdrawal of narcotics from a drug addict. There are physical and psychological manifestations and an apparent inability to enjoy any of the things that life has to offer. The difference is that after a period of time the drug addict, if lucky and determined, recovers, while for the long-term unemployed the symptoms get worse over time and the remedy is only too often out of their hands. We, that is most people in the industrialised world, are hooked on work. We dignify this by calling it the work ethic or 'Protestant' ethic.

Work used to be about survival. The earliest people hunted

and made primitive clothes and shelters to survive, and picked fruits, roots and grains to keep starvation away. Childbearing and rearing provided an alternative work pattern for women and, overall, work was concerned with the art of staying alive and ensuring the survival of the next generation. The farmers who tended the land, and gathered livestock together, came later, although their nomadic existence and poor techniques meant that they too had to work in order to live.

Whilst this is patently no longer the case in most of the industrialised world, work is still seen by some as a matter of survival, and an article in *Executive Post* (a magazine circulated to job-seeking executives) carried the message that lack of work has to be tackled in military style, using survival techniques similar to those used behind enemy lines. Unemployment is seen by many people as threatening their existence, as though we had suddenly reverted to the Stone-Age reality of work equalling life. In the less developed countries, however, work and mere existence are all too often still synonymous – as the awful horrors of the Sahel and Ethiopia, where the drought has made it impossible to work, have shown over recent years. The work 'ethic' is a luxury in these nations and their problems are of a different magnitude entirely.

In the Stone and Iron Ages work was only undertaken out of necessity; it was not seen as something good to do in its own right. Work was done in preparation for other work – the making of tools, for example – and there was little specialisation until society started to settle into steady communities. The elderly became the tool-makers; the women became the food-preparers and clothes-makers and did much of the farming; the men hunted, fished and fought. New types of work and new specialisations came along with each technological breakthrough. The wheel created wheelwrights, then cart-makers and tool-makers. The use of iron and bronze created metal producers and workers. Family units and small communities ceased to be self-sufficient, as barter and then other forms of trade revolutionised the way people lived. This continual division of labour allowed some people to absorb power to themselves; to acquire land, possessions, kingdoms and priest-doms. As a result of this and the wars that accompanied it, slavery was born – slaves were the first of the working classes.

The slave-owners did not feel unduly damaged by having

others do their work for them. Given the apparently indolent lives that many of these Etruscan, Greek and Roman patricians led, the work ethic was not much in evidence. The slaves of course needed no such ethic to keep them working: they had no choice. The development of money, and the need to utilise the different skills of people who were not slaves, led to people being 'employed'.

The effects of this were dramatic. Self-sufficiency applied to fewer and fewer people. People had to earn money to buy the things that they had previously made for themselves. The employed workers, often skilled, congregated into discrete settlement areas, and small villages and towns grew up, some into important and large centres. At the same time, however, the working practices on the land were reverting to forms of semi-slavery, and these formed the basis of many Central and South American societies like the Mayan or Inca civilizations.

Both the Old and New Testaments contain many aphorisms about this link between work, or the necessity to work, and a satisfying life. One goes so far as to say: 'If any would not work, neither should he eat' (Thessalonians 3.10). This was written at around the time that Britain was occupied by the Romans, and waves of Viking and Norman invasions added their own cultural elements, such as feudalism, during the following thousand years. In Europe the economic pattern of market towns, ports and feudalism lasted until the Black Death. The labouring population was so decimated by this that workers became valuable commodities and the feudal system faded away in Britain. The first laws against vagrancy, designed to help the landowner retain workers on his lands, appeared. In Britain the mercantile economy grew apace, initially based on wool and minerals, and lasted through the Wars of the Roses and the era of the Tudors and Stuarts until the mid-eighteenth century.

There were massive changes during this period. Specialisations at work became more complex and guilds were formed to protect the mysteries of crafts and enable craftsmen to regulate their activities. The complex needs of cities had to be met, and public services like rudimentary refuse disposal or fire services developed along with the coffee houses, theatres and taverns, the wig- and dress-makers, the shop-keepers and the builders. Hierarchies emerged amongst the workers: apprenticeships led

3

to journeyman and then master-craftsman status, whilst some jobs were more highly prized than others.

This shifting and volatile mass started to rigidify in the Tudor period. The land-owners and the aristocracy were at the apex of the new pyramid, and if the dramatists of the time are accurate in their portrayals, they did little work but missed it not at all. The majority of people still worked on the land, and mining, mineral extraction, metal and woodworking were based in small centres. The motive power for any manufacturing or distributive process was human or animal muscle, wind and water. There were limits to growth, which were imposed by technological shortfalls. And then, quite suddenly and startlingly, it all changed.

It was the steam engine (and the inventors and entrepreneurs who exploited it) that made the first industrial revolution possible. This single technological breakthrough liberated manufacturing and distributive industries across Britain. Textile mills, engineering works, woodworks, metalworks – everywhere power was needed the steam engine was used. The railways and steam-powered ships distributed the goods that had been made by these new processes. New, hitherto unthought-of products emerged and new levels of finish and reliability were built in. No longer did mill- or factory-owners have to position their works on a site near a stream or with a windy aspect, and within thirty years the demographic map of Britain had changed.

The new towns and cities were populated by people from the countryside, now working in the new industries. But it was not a move of desperation; although the steam engine was starting to take jobs from rural areas, few people were actually starving. Every ten years or so the harvest failed, or an epidemic struck the livestock, resulting in a substantially increased number of deaths amongst the very young and the aged. Wages for agricultural labourers were appalling and in times of glut often fell; but these were *incentives* to move from the farms to the towns, rather than imperatives.

The new workers were not used to the disciplines of a mill or factory, and they brought rural habits to the towns – especially those associated with alcohol and timekeeping. A working day of fixed hours, rather than a day geared to the tasks at hand, was novel. It was the first radical change in work practices for

4

countless generations. The links with the land, the impact of nature and the seasons, were broken, and nothing replaced them. The ability to supplement meagre incomes with home-grown produce vanished with the move to the cities; people now had to work for money to live. Men, women and children were all pressed into service and were overwhelmed by the changes.

The towns and the conditions at work added to the confusion of these new workers, and the arduous and long working day (often as long as 14 hours) left them exhausted. The city offered little in the way of recreational activities of a healthy kind; the only anaesthetic was drink. Drink, however, ruined the pro-duction processes. Whilst, in the countryside, it was acceptable to drink as much as you liked and then sleep it off, this could not be done in a mill. The main recreation of the British people was proving to be a blight on productivity and a health hazard. Every time a tipsy person fell into the machinery the down time cost the owners a great deal of money. In the end the problem was solved by religion.

The temperance movements were all based firmly in the Christian religion, and it was the employers who 'endowed' the clergy and built the large churches that now grace the corners of our towns and cities. Sermons on the evils of drink were aimed at gin, rum and other spirits, but permitted the drinking of beer. The brewers and the employers made common cause. If beer was there to dull the ache of the drudgery then religion existed to console the spirit. The preaching turned to the desirability, indeed the essentialness, of work to improve the soul. The difference was that the preachers were no longer referring to work, as it had previously been understood.

A new definition of the work ethic had been invented. Work itself was no longer sufficient, but *paid employment* was the only way to fulfil oneself. This changed definition is the one we still use today. The original work ethic, that is the biblical ethic which continued unchanged up until the start of the nineteenth century, was based on a wide definition of work. It was about labour; repairing one's own home would satisfy that definition, as would growing fruit or vegetables in the garden. Paid employment was part of work but by no means all of it. Work was defined on the basis of doing something to meet a need, either one's own or someone else's; doing something *useful* was the important factor. Today we use the word 'work' to describe employment whether or not it is useful or meets a need.

The paid employment ethic replaced the wider definition of work because labour in factories was so unpleasant that something more than money needed to be offered as a reward and inducement for workers to stay. The new steam-based production systems were labour intensive and 'burnt out' the workers very quickly. The clergy from their pulpits, the magistrates from their benches, the Establishment from Parliament or from their big houses, all preached the same message. It later came to be associated with Victorian Britain but in fact began some fifty years earlier. 'Work is good for the soul', 'the devil makes work for idle hands', 'the poor are blessed', 'work saves' – these were the mottoes that forged the change in attitudes.

There is a great deal of work which does not attract a wage yet is hard, tiring, emotionally draining and skilled. Because the definition of the work ethic changed, housework became non-work and the job of the housewife became a non-job; it simply did not attract a salary and thus by the new definition had to be something other than work. Housework and childrearing is a skilled and tiring occupation, yet it is not work as defined by the employment ethic. Voluntary work falls into the same category. It can be demanding and useful, it can absorb a vast amount of time, but it does not fulfil the employment ethic. Gardening, do-it-yourself of all descriptions, hobbies, physical exercise – all can be very hard work yet none of them fulfil, or get anywhere near fulfilling, the employment ethic. That man on the park bench could do any of these things but would still feel as defeated as he does now.

So there are really two work ethics. The old one based on work as a socially useful factor and the new one which I shall refer to as the employment ethic from now on. Many of the problems facing society today will occur because of this shift of emphasis, which was valuable in the first industrial revolution but is counterproductive for this, the second industrial revolution.

More than two centuries of usage have reinforced the employment ethic as *the* work ethic. In the nineteenth century work became very important as a good thing in itself, the workhouse being an interesting example. It was not sufficient to remove the indigent from circulation, or to give them charity;

these unfortunates had to work, for the sake of their own souls and not as a punishment. The work had to be hard, boring and unpleasant so as to impress the message more firmly. At the other end of the social and financial scale the wealthy landed gentry claimed to do 'good works' or work according to their duties and responsibilities to others, and in either case the word 'work' was needed. For the rich the old work ethic with its wide definition remained, while the poor were using or being forced to use a brand new shiny employment ethic. To be fair, the early entrepreneurs and many of the later Victorian middle classes worked very hard, often founding the fortunes of those who do not need to work today.

There are many ways in which the existence of the employment ethic can be verified. Ask a stranger what he is – it does not matter whether this is at a party or by pushing a camera and microphone at him on a street corner – and the odds are that the answer will be in the form of a job title, whether he is working or not. The question does not even have to be, 'What do you do?' How many people that you know would say that they were a nice person or a good dancer, or give a similar non-work description? Identity is intimately bound up with a job title.

We perpetuate this with our children. An aunt or uncle's favourite question is, 'What do you want to be when you grow up?' and we expect to hear something like 'a nurse' or 'a brain surgeon' in reply. We do not want the child to reply 'clever' or 'beautiful'; both the questioner and the recipient know that it is a coded question. The entire education system is still seen, rather quaintly, as a preparation for a job and youngsters are taught, from a very early age, that their time will be spent trying to get a job and then working at it. Is it any wonder that the amended work ethic has been so influential?

Different job titles, not the people or even the actual jobs, signal to us whether we should mix with a person socially. Why does 'a doctor' or 'a surgeon' sound so much better than 'an insurance clerk', let alone 'a dustman'? It's not just the financial element – indeed there are times when low-status jobs attract far higher remuneration than the high-flying ones. Job titles are part of our identity, so that they are being refined continually to impart some fresh vanity. 'Rat-catchers' become 'rodent operatives', 'computer operators' transmute into 'programmers' at

7

the drop of a floppy, whilst 'secretaries' have emerged from their chrysalis and turned into 'administrative assistants'. It is not unusual for a person to become forthcoming about what it is that they do at work only after one of these changes in job title. The previous title clearly did not reflect the image that they had of themselves and they did not wish to identify with it.

If paid employment imparts an identity, and the job title confirms this identity, then the loss of a job can have disturbing psychological implications on an individual. These are compounded by the reception that society gives to the unemployed. Research in both the USA and Britain suggests that unemployment is bad for the health, both physically and mentally.

Dr Harvey Brenner of Johns Hopkins University led a research project for the Joint Economic Committee of the Congress of the United States in 1976, which covered a thirty-three-year period from 1940 to 1973, including one particularly high unemployment year in 1970. The research uncovered a series of diseases which appeared to have a positive correlation with unemployment but *only after a five-year lag*. These were based on seven medical and social indicators of social stress which were well represented statistically over this period. The time-lag is important. It means that we cannot see the full effects of today's unemployment until five years have passed.

The indicators ranged from changes in total mortality statistics to deaths from murder, suicide, cirrhosis of the liver, cardio-vascular and renal diseases through to changes in the numbers admitted to state prison and mental institutions. Harvey Brenner then developed a 'stress change indicator' which showed the increase in each of these areas resulting from a 1 per cent increase in unemployment five years earlier. The results appear to be significant. Murders rose by 5 per cent, mental hospital admissions increased by 4.3 per cent for men and 2.3 per cent for women, there were 4.1 per cent more suicides and a 4 per cent increase in prison admissions. Deaths from heart, liver and kidney malfunctions and indeed all deaths rose by 1.9 per cent. A separate study was made into the effects of the increase in unemployment of 1.4 per cent in 1970 and these confirmed the estimates which resulted from the 'stress change indicator'. An attempt was also made to estimate the cost of these increases in stress-related effects, and this came to $2.15 billion in 1970.

Other studies have been made, the latest of which was centred on Liverpool and was headed by Dr Alex Scott-Samuel in 1984. This study shows an increase in heart and lung disease and strokes amongst some of the unemployed, whilst stress, mental illness and attempted suicides were all increasing. The illnesses were mainly alcohol- and cigarette-related, the consumption of both of these increasing markedly amongst the unemployed. Other research which links crime increase and joblessness (especially amongst the young) confirms this research. Employment clearly is, like fibre, good for the health. Although there have been reservations about some of the methods used by Harvey Brenner, the basic results have not been disputed; indeed they have been confirmed by most other researchers.

The ultimate cost of not working is death. For some men retirement removes the very reason for their staying alive. A retired man who lives through the first six months of retirement is likely to live well beyond the average life expectancy, yet so many fail to survive this first period. The removal of paid employment for some men is the removal of their entire personality, importance and status. Without these there is little or nothing left to live for. This applies to retirees who had plans to garden, go round the world, or see people that they had neglected for years as much as it does to people who had no plans.

There are four major reasons why employment is regarded so highly. Firstly, a paid job not only defines a person's position in society, it also gives that person a stake in society; it makes the person feel wanted, needed and useful. Work itself, in our original definition, cannot do this today, although before the industrial revolution it could and did. The other reasons are the opportunity employment provides for meeting people, the structure it gives to the day and, of course, the financial reward. But the first reason is perhaps the most important.

Everyone wants to feel needed – it establishes a sense of worth in oneself. Everyone wants to contribute in some way or another towards whatever group they choose, and it is this that gives a person a stake in society or, more often, their local community. As we shall see later in the book, this can lead both to intense local difficulties and to possible solutions in the longer term.

We live in an Alice-in-Wonderland world in Western Europe. The era of the 'quasi-job' is with us at precisely the time when people's needs are rising and are increasingly unmet. A person doing a quasi-job is not registered as unemployed but is also not doing an ordinary job. The remuneration is low and the person concerned is generally on a government-supported scheme which purports to train him or her for a proper job. Youth or other training schemes, or six-month stints on 'community projects' (which tend to be rather anodyne in order to get the backing of both unions and businessmen), are seen by participants as second best. They know they are less fortunate than their mates who have proper jobs. A quasi-job may give some satisfaction (we shall see later that there are a few excellent Youth Training Schemes), but it cannot provide that coveted stake in society which only a job can do.

Quasi-jobs do, however, allow people to meet each other. We are living in societies where it is increasingly difficult to contact others. For example, supermarkets have replaced many of the older shops where people could have a chat and which often acted as unofficial letter boxes; supermarkets do not have the atmosphere for such leisurely confidences. More people now drink at home than in the pub and, overall, the home has become the major leisure centre. The increase in home ownership has made DIY much more widespread, which means that you no longer need to call in a plumber or electrician very often, so the only people you meet at home are those you know already. At the same time it is getting more difficult to meet new people.

The workplace has traditionally been a place where friendships are made and broken, and today this is more important than ever. If the other sources of contact are decreasing then the workplace has to take up the slack. The dole queue or the street corner foster friendships made in mutual depression, rather like those made in hospitals, and as we all know these rarely last. Employment or even quasi-employment is essential to socialisation as things stand at the moment.

Both employment and quasi-employment meet another twentieth-century need. They structure the day. They provide the landmarks which mark the day from breakfast to evening. The disciplines imposed in school and much of tertiary education have, particularly in Britain and France, trained us to believe that such a system is inevitable and, what is more, desirable. One of the great shocks that almost all students find on reaching university is the freedom that they are given. It is not repeated in many employment situations and nor indeed are students equipped to deal with it by any of their previous experiences.

The retired and the unemployed often find the lack of discipline and structure that confronts them very difficult to cope with. Increases in smoking and drinking, late rising, sloppy appearance and general lack of interest – all common symptoms of prolonged unemployment – are a result of not having an imposed discipline. The inability, far too often evident amongst the unemployed, to plan out a programme for the day is the result of not having an imposed structure. Most people have structure and discipline imposed upon them at work, often without finding it irksome and often without even realising its existence. There has never been an attempt to encourage people to organise their own work pattern. If they had been allowed to do so the conditions of work might be totally different and power might be in very different hands.

People without work might succeed in structuring their days and meeting other people, but, if there is little or no money, the end result will still be unhappiness and disenchantment. Many of those who are unemployed or retired share a common problem of lack of money. In today's industrialised societies this is often a great handicap.

In industrialised states there are few people who fall through the safety net provided by state or private institutions into the abyss of death or starvation. Nevertheless, there are families and individuals in both North America and Europe who find it difficult to eat properly, who get neither adequate shelter nor proper clothing and whose children suffer from nutritional deficiency diseases. Their misfortunes stem from a lack of money because they cannot find a job. This can start a vicious circle: poor nutrition often leads to inadequate brain development and this, combined with the acceptance of low standards, can lead to generations of unemployed within the same family.

Money buys things. A simple enough observation but conveniently forgotten when discussing the poor. We live in a society *dedicated* to buying things; consumer goods are the holy grail of the late twentieth century. The visible manifestations of one's status, one's job and one's income and wealth are what other people can see you acquiring, wearing, driving or living in. All industrialised countries are really consumer states. Keeping up with the Joneses or the Calfins has become *the* way of life, and as such money has become ever more important. There has never been a better time to be moderately well off – there have rarely been worse times to be poor. And, as most people do not inherit much money, or are not lucky enough or criminally-minded enough to get it in other ways, they have to work for it.

This has ever been the case. The difference is that never before has the failure to earn a reasonable wage been so apparent in the public arena. It is not sufficient to wear decent clothes. Designer 'gear' with this month's fashionable name attached is a must for the average pre-teenager, let alone fashion-conscious adolescents. A trip to an inner city school where uniforms are not worn will show the intense competition amongst youngsters to wear 'in' clothes, despite the likelihood that neither they nor their families can really afford them. Pride in these matters is intense and not easily forgone. Think, then of the children whose parents cannot afford anything other than hand-me-downs – they suffer at least as much from the scorn of their classmates as do those who get free school dinners or milk. The need to keep abreast if not ahead of potential rivals starts at an early age. It does not appear to abate with age.

The advertising industry exists solely to persuade people to buy, rent or spend money on various things – and it is a very large industry. We are continually told that our sex life will improve if we use the right mouthwash, that managers drink up-market wines and eat special mint chocs when successfully entertaining the boss to dinner, and that husbands will be loving and generous when their clothes are washed in a certain front-loading, space-age washing machine. Different types of cars are supposed to reflect the image of the person driving, and some appear to come with an attractive woman (or man) as an optional extra! Owning a house is better than renting, in the current philosophy, and the house itself is important as an image projector. The right type of front door, painted the right colour, in the best of neighbourhoods is the aim.The gossip columns celebrate the deeds of the rich and obscure and the ordinary person is asked to envy them because they have a lot of money. But most people can never get anywhere near such wealth; the unemployed certainly cannot.

From time to time campaigns are mounted in some British newspapers which brand the unemployed as 'scroungers' or 'spongers on the state' and suggest that they are not only responsible for their own predicament but that they are all potential criminals as well. Over the last few years these campaigns have fallen away slightly, but not much. There was an attempt in 1984 by a Conservative MP, Matthew Parris, to live on the dole for a week, recorded by TV cameras, in order to prove how well the unemployed can live on social security payments. He failed, yet this was only in the tradition of innumerable articles concerning hordes of mythical people who were earning more being unemployed than they were when they were at work. On the contrary, research by groups specialising in the problems of the low paid, like the Low Pay Unit, suggest that well over 80 per cent of the unemployed get less than three-quarters of their previous salary and over half get less than 60 per cent. Being unemployed is not a lucrative profession. The retired are worse off because the maximum occupational pension allowed is two-thirds of final earnings, whilst youngsters on Youth Training Scheme placements earn on average less than half the wages they might have expected had they been able to find a job in the south-east of England. So the pressure to get a job is intense on financial grounds alone.

However, there are other factors at work. There are a few people who can indeed get more money being unemployed than they can by working, and these are generally the very low paid, often women with dependent families. Many of them do nevertheless choose employment because, they say, they feel that they need to get out to go to a job. They *need* paid employment, but not only for the pay. The employment ethic is so strong that it can persuade people to be illogical; the official watchword is that it is better to have any job, even an awful one, than no job at all. Is the employment ethic a natural preoccupation of mankind? In many of the less developed countries the old work ethic prevails. Neither the Aboriginals in Australasia or Papua New Guinea, nor indeed the bushmen around the world or the Indians and Inuits in South, Central and North America appear to have a 'paid employment' ethic. Nor indeed do many of the tribes in Africa, where farming in villages rather than for cash crops is the rule. These people seem not the slightest bit discomfited because they do not have a job in the formal sense. They relax when their tasks are done. Looking busy is not in their social vocabulary. There *is* a strong work ethic, however; social groups are bound together by the fact that one set of people can rely on others to do the work they are supposed to do. Survival and continuity are thus ensured.

The Kuwaitis, who import labour to do most of the work tasks in their economy, have clearly shunted the paid employment ethic aside too, though in very different circumstances. The Japanese have an employment ethic that is intimately entwined with feudal duties and responsibilities, precisely opposite to the jet-setters who are famous for not working at all (let alone having jobs), although from time to time one of them might attempt to take a photograph or two. Not too many of *them* have given interviews bemoaning their lack of jobs. High society in Europe has never pretended to aspire to jobs, although charity 'work' has been high on the list of priorities, especially amongst the women. It is quite different in the USA, where fortunes were made in more recent times and where both the work and the paid employment ethics are stronger. Another factor in the difference may be the strength of Low Church Christian religions in the USA as compared with their relative decline in European countries. It is from these churches that the employment ethic sprang.

There are other small, perhaps aberrant, groups who have no time for a paid employment ethic. There are a few genuinely idle people. There are larger numbers of criminals. There are a small number of eremites and some dedicated vagrants. Most of the rest of us need a job.

In recent times there have been a few graphic illustrations of what work means to people. The miners' strike in Britain was about retaining work within the mining communities, not only for today's miners but also for their children. The depth of feeling can be gauged by the length of the dispute in the light of poverty, hardship and hostile media coverage. Twenty years ago those self-same miners, or their fathers, were saying loudly that under no circumstances would they let their sons go down the pit – *they* would have something better. The communities meant little then, but widespread long-lasting unemployment has completely changed attitudes. Miners in Britain were not just being 'bloody-minded', however. French miners and steel-workers in Lorraine struck when redundancies and closures were announced in the early eighties, and the violence in defence of their jobs was far worse than anything seen in Britain. The French government was forced to delay some closures but, more importantly, had to promise to bring new jobs to the affected areas. A slogan used in the fight against the closure of the Corby steel works sums up the argument: 'These are not your jobs to give away.'

Workers in St Helena and New York stevedores seem odd bedfellows, yet they show another manifestation of the paid employment ethic. St Helena is famous for being Napoleon's last prison, and for little else. There were, however, several flourishing businesses until five years ago when the staple trade in jute and hemp was finally wound up. The island's inhabitants, all of whom were used to jobs, have had to adapt to joblessness and cannot cope. The education system turns out bright youngsters with British-style O and A levels, but there is no work for them. Desperate for jobs, they fight for the few places on road repairs funded by the British government as a job creation scheme. The entire community is running downhill at an alarming rate, not just in terms of money but in terms of morale.

The New York stevedores lost their jobs in different circum-stances. An agreement between the employers and the union has resulted in several hundred stevedores being paid for not going to work, and – they hate it. Boredom, aimlessness and alcohol abuse have all set in. They feel as desperate as the St Helenans. Both sets of workers want to go to work. The difference is that on St Helena the people are now very poor, while the New York stevedores are very well off – but they still feel that they have lost almost everything with the loss of their jobs.

In capitalist societies jobs are created as a consequence of the need for goods and services. Immediately after the Second World War both Britain and the USA attempted to introduce legislative and constitutional changes to guarantee all citizens the right to a job. These attempts failed. The Soviet Union and other communist countries have a totally different approach to jobs and work. Marx valued products, although not services, in terms of human labour, and so in order for the state to place a value on goods people must be working. The product or service is then secondary to the job. This can lead, indeed does lead, to gross inefficiencies within the economy. The paid employment ethic is institutionalised in these countries, and this can lead to what in Western capitalist eyes are absurdities.

If the state values products in terms of labour then, when people are not at work, they have no value in themselves, and indeed can be considered to be anti-state. At times this has resulted in those not working being treated as criminals in various communist countries. However, there is no doubt that work is provided one way or another for everyone, and this may have strange consequences. One large Soviet hotel had electronic eyes installed at the approach to the doors at the end of its corridors. A woman with a table-tennis-like bat was employed to stand near the doors and wave it across the magic eye when people approached, to open the doors for them. In the West this would be thought of as a complete waste of technology and resources.

This raises a fundamental question. Why work if it serves no useful purpose? It is the mirror image of the old work ethic. The ancillary question to this is why do we have unemployed people doing quasi-jobs or silly jobs when the needs and demands of so many people around the world have yet to be met. Work has always been about being useful to others as well as oneself; a 'job' need not fulfil this basic requirement.

The man we left sitting on the park bench is a victim. He suffers from his own self-disgust, he suffers from living a lie and he suffers from cowardice. Why? He is, or was, a perfectly normal, balanced man. *The reason is that industrialised societies in the West have not made being unemployed a criminal offence, but they have made it a social crime.* Somehow the man, and many of his fellow jobless, feel that they are responsible for their own plight, that it is their own fault. British society, as reflected by the prevailing middle-class ethic, has little time for the unemployed. Whilst this is not as marked a tendency as in other countries, the work ethic is still deeply ingrained and the employment ethic even more so. This inevitably means that an unemployed person is treated as an outsider – he (it is not yet as strong in the case of she) is not a member of the club and is excluded from its rites and rituals. In some quarters there appears to be an irrational fear that unemployment is contagious, and so social contacts decline, often with dramatic illogicality.

Given these strong ethics, all the symptoms of stress and illness that can follow not having a job and indeed the fact that opinion polls have consistently shown unemployment to be by far the most urgent concern felt in Britain, one would suppose that going to work is a popular pastime. Nothing could be further from the truth. At best the majority of people tolerate their job, at worst they dislike it. Most people dislike having to cope with the morning and evening rush hours – in the large commercial centres commuters can spend up to four hours a day travelling to and from work. Work itself is often perceived as boring and repetitive. It neither fulfils nor stretches the person who does it. Of course there are people who enjoy their jobs, but these tend to be those who have most control over their working lives. Doctors, lawyers, senior managers and artists, for example, have challenging jobs and many thrive on them. Sadly, others do not. Craftsmen aside, most manual jobs are repetitious and often done in the most noisy, dirty and hazardous of conditions. The majority of clerical jobs are straightforward and for the most part entail putting into practice the orders of other people.

There is a dignity in the concept of work and there is a dignity in the concept of paid employment, but there is precious little dignity in many of the jobs that we ask people to do. Those who claim to see the dignity of labour everywhere are most unlikely to have got nearer to a typing pool or chemical plant, let alone a hospital laundry or production line, than the last reference book they read. It is not surprising that the people who have to do these jobs look forward to the times when they are not at work. A job is a curious thing. People desperately want to have one, yet when they get one they don't really like it. It is similar to castor oil – taken to do you good, but something that no one enjoys.

It is interesting that leisure time is called free time. This presupposes that the time spent in employment is unfree. In turn this means that we want, indeed need, to be unfree or at least do not mind if this captive or coercive element is a feature of a job. The freedom of the weekend is awaited with varying degrees of desperation, whilst the advent of each Monday is cursed and each Friday welcomed. Leisure is the time we spend when not actually working in employment. It is defined by employment. It is the residual time after employment. The unemployed, the retired or the chronically sick do not think of themselves as having unlimited leisure – indeed they do not feel that they have any leisure at all. Modern society believes that leisure has to be earned through employment. It is the reward for doing something unpleasant like the sweet given to a child after the castor oil.

This was not always the case. In pre-industrial times work and leisure were blurred, especially in the countryside. Certainly there were pleasure gardens, taverns and theatres in the cities, and these were frequented after work-time. For the most part, however, work was performed until the job was done, a person did not have to put a pitchfork over a shoulder to look busy if it was raining. The man on the park bench represents the fact that nowadays people feel that they have to be seen to be doing something, even if they are not.

Leisure is important. Without it the modern industrial state could not have developed. The money spent by individuals on goods and services for the times when they are not working has been the stimulus to large economic growth of the type that has sustained the developed countries. Yet leisure is a relatively disregarded thing. It has generated little by way of academic study, and is taken for granted by one and all. It is, however, becoming ever more important. As the number of hours not spent in the workplace increases, so the need for other things to do increases. Some commentators have envisaged leisure as a substitute for employment – a mistake which, as we shall explore later, could be costly. Others have seen the concept of service to others (the old work ethic) as worth reviving, but then appear to want to make it compulsory in some form of national social service. The fact that these matters are being discussed in newspapers as august as *The Times* is significant in itself. We want to work; we need to work; but it is becoming increasingly clear that this work will not be readily available. That the work is there but the jobs are not is a better and more accurate way of putting it. For societies based on employment this is a damaging prospect, one that will be the main political thorn in the flesh of governments of all political persuasions over the coming thirty years, or so.

Not too long ago the working-go-round was free for

everyone. True, there were far fewer options then, but regardless of status the central attraction, work, was always available. Now a change has taken place. It is now an employment-go-round and not everyone can get aboard. This book will try to analyse why this is so, whether it is important, what to do about it and whether we are moving in the right direction.

2 Not enough to go round

It is a mistake to think that high unemployment is an aberration. This is in fact the reverse of the truth. It is a sustained period of full employment that is at odds with history, our values today being conditioned by the extraordinary circumstances of the 1950s and 1960s. Since the start of the industrial revolution in the 1780s and the consequent rapid growth of paid employment there have been more years of relatively high, high and very high unemployment than there have been of full or near full employment.

The cause of these periods of unemployment has traditionally been ascribed to periods of depression in the trade cycle. Trade cycles were known well before the industrial revolution and there were periods when employment was less than full amongst those who had paid jobs. There were a variety of reasons for this sort of unemployment. Natural disasters, floods, droughts and epidemics, for example, drove people off the land and into the towns. For a time these people had no jobs, although they later added to the demand in the towns and helped to create employment. Depressions caused by the debasing of coinage in mediaeval times created unemployment, as did the economic mismanagement wrought by the physiocrats just before the French Revolution, or frauds on the grand scale like the 'South Sea Bubble'. The connection between unemployment and the trade cycle, however, did not emerge properly until the start of the industrial revolution.

Waves of industrialisation began to occur from the late eighteenth century, after the development of the steam engine. Each of them brought in more workers and each of them gave a stimulus to new trades and jobs. Towns grew rapidly. The boom period, however, would last for but a short period, to be followed almost immediately by a slump caused by overproduction, followed in turn by unemployment. Each time this happened there were more workers in the towns and unemployment consequently increased. Each new wave ushered in new systems with new companies replacing those which had gone bankrupt in the previous slump. Productivity rose, output increased, demand could not keep pace and the cycle from boom to slump was foreshortened.

Everyone was forced into the labour market, including women and children who worked in the mines and heavy industry in the most abysmal of conditions. The new towns and cities added to the social upheaval, and unemployment at regular intervals resulted in anger and political unrest. In Britain the Chartists came near to fomenting the first (and only) political revolution whilst Europe's 'year of revolutions' in 1848 was by no means the only symptom of discontent. The British political reform acts which gradually expanded adult male suffrage were a response to the rapid and deep-seated changes of that time, not the least of them being the combination of the employment ethic with high and regular unemployment. This happened despite the lead Britain had over the rest of the world in manufacturing capability, its control of the sea routes and world trade and the Empire which provided cheap food and raw materials as well as acting as a captive market for finished goods.

Throughout the nineteenth century and the start of the twentieth, new products, systems and machines poured from the minds and factories of entrepreneurs all over the world. The engineering feats of that era still command respect – even awe – today. The railway systems of much of the world were put in place, steam ships took much of the physical risk from international trade, and new inventions for consumers and new machines to make them with were weekly occurrences. Ingenuity flourished. Electricity and the electric motor came into use in the productive processes by the end of the century, thus increasing the range of goods that could be made as well as the rate of productivity.

There were continual swings from over- to underproduction coupled with a tendency to follow Say's Law and believe that the supply of goods would create its own demand. This, strangely enough, is probably more true today, given market research techniques, than it was then. Consumer goods became more important as an increasing number of countries industrialised and incomes grew, both in real terms and in aggregate. The infrastructure of the new towns and cities was laid down; roads, public buildings, parks, water and sewage systems and the construction of each of these drew in more people to work.

By the late 1870s it had all crumbled into the deepest depression that either Britain or Europe has ever known. Productivity had risen to the extent that existing markets could not support production, and the politicians of the day urged emigration as the answer – they had no other. The USA, Canada and Australia received most of the émigrés; it was an unpleasant end to what was in many ways an unpleasant century. It is a sobering thought, however, that it was the work done in that era that allows us the freedom and the relative prosperity that we live in today.

The great slump ended with a war, as did so many in the nineteenth century – the Boer War. During the nineteenth century Britain was at war with, at one time or another, America, France, Russia and South Africa. Twenty-one years out of the hundred were spent by Britain actively engaged in major hostilities. The Europeans fared even worse, with the Franco-Prussian Wars, the Balkan and Austro-Hungarian conflicts and Russian and Japanese skirmishes. And none of this takes into account the massive colonial push by the French, Germans, Dutch and Belgians, or the British colonial wars in India and elsewhere. In the USA, the South American and Cuban expeditions and the Civil War took their toll.

It is worth looking at the US wholesale price index and comparing the performance of the economy with external factors. There were peaks in 1812 (internal wars), a small peak in 1846 (the Mexican War), a large peak in the Civil War of 1861–5, and peaks in the First World War as well as the Korean and Vietnamese wars. So it is clear that war has played a vital part in the development of the American economy, and, by inference, on others.

Wars have a dual impact on employment. Some people are killed, so that the labour force is diminished, whilst others are put to making arms and other essential goods. The economic multiplier effects of war create employment too; after almost every major slump the stimulus to recovery has come from war. This is as true for the twentieth century as for the nineteenth. In both 1914 and 1939 there was high and long-term unemployment with no real end in sight until both of the world wars arrived. The interventionist policies of the 1930s were having only a minimal effect.

Early unemployment statistics are difficult to come by. The British did not keep them until the 1860s (and even then they were unreliable) and as the British were leaders in this statistical field it follows that there are no real data for this period anywhere in the world. We do know, however, that there were many economic troughs starting from the 1780s and carrying on throughout the nineteenth century. There were three major ones and over twenty minor ones. We also know through the writings of the historians, dramatists and novelists of the day that living and working conditions for most people were dreadful and even worse during the slumps, with jobs very difficult to find unless starvation-level wages were accepted. The deepest troughs were in 1790, 1840 and 1880.

For those who had it, work was unpleasant. Health and safety regulations were non-existent, pensions and sick pay unheard-of, the hours long and holidays minuscule and unpaid. Early in the century there was considerable ferment about the de-skilling of jobs, and the Luddites destroyed some machinery as a form of protest. They have had such a bad press in history that 'Luddite' is now a term of abuse, but they were not simply trying to save jobs – they were protesting that new technology was making their skills redundant. Henceforth, they would have to work as unskilled machinists. This early pattern was repeated throughout the century as employers replaced skilled workers with unskilled cheaper female and child labour as each new machine was developed. As we shall see, history is repeating itself today.

The twentieth century continued on the nineteenth-century pattern. The recovery after the Boer War in Britain was short-lived, and before the first decade was out high unemployment had re-emerged. Technological changes came thick and fast: The chemical industry grew mightily, the internal combustion engine and then the aeroplane made their appearance, radio replaced the telegraph, the telephone revolutionised communications and the typewriter transformed the office. Old industries, skills and techniques started to disappear. Then the First World War began, after political unrest over most of Europe.

The causes of the war were in essence the 'old' politics, but this political unrest was mainly caused by the 'new' politics based on the ideas of Karl Marx, amongst other radicals. Marx had written about the conditions of the working people in the nineteenth century and believed that the miseries they suffered would exist in the nineteenth-century form for ever. Marx believed that there would be a 'reverse army of labour'. This theory, which suggests that capitalism would *need* a large number of unemployed people to operate efficiently, received the unexpected support of Conservative minister Nicholas Ridley recently.

In some respects the First World War proved to be a watershed in terms of employment. For the first time for over fifty years women entered the labour force in great numbers and proved that they could do 'men's work'. And because so many working men lost their lives in the trenches employers continued to employ some of these women after the war. When unemployment rose again the men faced stronger competition from their more lowly paid wives and sisters. The war stripped many of their remaining illusions away from working people. Having been promised a land fit for heroes, they found themselves in the same familiar soup-kitchen line, with the same lack of money, amenities or prospects. In Germany the armistice settlements proved to be so severe as to destabilise completely the economic and political life of the country. Nevertheless, whilst other European countries failed to rebuild their economies, Germany, Italy and Spain embarked upon Fascism and expansion. The Russian revolution was a watershed too; the new Soviet Union provided a focus for political discontent in other countries and remained an example of what could be done.

The unemployment rate in this period swung sharply. In the USA it reached almost 10 per cent in 1916 and 12 per cent by 1922 but fell as low as 2 per cent in 1907 and 3 per cent in 1918. Britain followed a similar pattern, although the data are very incomplete. As the twenties and thirties wore on, it became increasingly clear that neither the old *laissez-faire* economics of Adam Smith, modified by a myriad of economists, nor the more interventionist approaches of Keynes were succeeding in maintaining anything like full employment. To be fair, however, the Keynesian theories tried out by British and US governments during the thirties did not have much chance to succeed before the Second World War intervened. In Britain unemployment stood at 17 per cent in 1921, 12.5 per cent in 1926 and, apart from 1927 (when it was 9.7 per cent), it did not fall below 10 per cent until the Second World War. Other countries had similar patterns although the Scandinavians had the highest unemployment rates of all.

The twenties and thirties were decades of considerable industrial and social change. The middle classes expanded and consolidated, whilst professional people became increasingly affluent. The Taylorist theory of mass production, promoted and used by Henry Ford, became the dominant method of manufacture. The large capital-intensive chemical plants developed, and industries sprang up around the new products. The development of the motor car spawned jobs in the building and repairing of roads, in the petrol industry, in the accessories market and in the haulage industry. Radio and cinema employed hundreds of thousands of people, as did the new public transport systems and the growth of the consumer durable market. Yet unemployment was still high and variable. In the thirties it became high and static.

Although the stockmarket 'Great Crash' occurred in 1929, unemployment did not rise dramatically until 1930. The unemployment of the thirties is now a part of British, American and French mythology, as is the Weimar Republic inflation in Germany. Unemployment in Britain rose to more than one in five, in the USA to one in four, in Germany to almost half the population who were eligible for work, and in Scandinavia to one in three. The superb portrayals of this period from John Steinbeck and Upton Sinclair, and films from around the world, are enduring reminders that the twentieth century could provide hardship and unemployment to match that of the previous one. Although the levels of unemployment were falling slightly by 1939 under the impact of the 'New Deal' in America and rearmament and Keynesian policies in Europe, the decline was extremely slow. It took the Second World War to halt and then reverse unemployment.

The war had several consequences. It destroyed the last vestiges of British economic suzerainty over world trade, it moved the USA into a position of pre-eminence in the West, it hastened the end of the British Empire, it divided Europe into two political and trading blocs, it tested and released a pent-up series of technological breakthroughs and it changed the composition of the labour force. Once again women did what was traditionally considered to be 'men's work', and skilled craftsmen who had completed long apprenticeships were replaced by people with but six months' training. The most important change of all, however, came from the destructive nature of the new weapons. Vast tracts of European cities and factories, mines, steelworks, railways and roads, housing and shops, public buildings and parks had been obliterated. Europe needed rebuilding.

With hindsight Britain was unfortunate in that more of its working capital was preserved than in Germany, Belgium or France. This meant that Britain had to muddle through with older and more outdated machinery than did her former allies, as well as enemies, in the later post-war years. At the same time the USA had not only emerged unscathed from the war but had recovered from the thirties in major style and was now a creditor to most of the world, having money to burn. There then followed the only period of sustained full employment in the developed world since the industrial revolution started in the 1780s.

The instrument was the Marshall Plan. This consisted of American money provided for the rebuilding of Western Europe, although initially it was offered to Eastern Europe as well. It was not an entirely altruistic act on the part of the American government; there were political and defence strings attached to the receipt of the monies. But although it did reinforce the division of Europe, the Marshall Plan had an extraordinary effect. It allowed investment and consumer demand to forge ahead at the same time. Before this time, investment had only taken place through savings at the expense of consumption, so that at any one moment either growth or consumption was sluggish. The effect of the Marshall Plan was that of a windfall.

Towns and cities had to be rebuilt, refugees had to be resettled, capital had to be renewed or replaced, the transport networks had to be revived. The armed forces returned home with new skills and confidence, and on top of this the war in Korea started adding to demand. The terms of trade were very much in favour of the industrialised nations, and all the new technologies were put to civilian use: penicillin and then artificial antibiotics, plastics and synthetic fibres, advances in radio, television and radar. Aeroplanes were almost unrecognisable from those flying five years earlier, and cars, lorries and buses were all better developed and equipped. More and more consumer goods were invented, and mass-produced and processed foods made popular. Growth rates in the key economic sectors were enormous. The engines of overall economic growth – motors, household consumer durables, petrochemicals, engineering, machine-tool manufacturing and artificial fibres – all grew at 10 or even 15 and 20 per cent every year. And it lasted.

Not only was there little unemployment – there was actually a labour shortage. The first waves of West Indian immigrants came to Britain at this time (indeed, London Transport opened recruiting offices on St Vincent, so desperate were they for workers). Poles worked the mines in France and Britain, and some former German POWs were induced to stay behind to fill vacancies. Frictional unemployment, or people not working because they were between jobs or moving, was the main contributor to the very low unemployment figures – along with a tiny percentage of people who either could not or would not work. For twenty-five years it was a workaholic's dream.

When Harold Macmillan stated baldly in 1957 that 'most of our people have never had it so good', few people objected or disagreed. Few people would have had a right to do so – the age of the mass consumer had begun. Rising incomes added to a new-found security, created by the welfare state in Britain and its equivalents overseas; a new sense of confidence permeated European societies. Once the immediate post-war restrictions like rationing had gone there was a buoyancy in the air. School-leavers knew they would be able to get jobs, and a new wave of well-educated sons and daughters of the working class created a combination of upward social mobility and a more flexible and erudite work force. In turn, this enabled new techniques and products to be developed and used. High public spending on housing programmes, on the health services, on the new schools and later the new universities and polytechnics, also created jobs.

The aspirations of ordinary workers suddenly extended far beyond mere survival. Radio, then the black and white TV, the colour TV and the car, the washing machine and the spin drier;

27

each of these became normal rather than luxury goods. Holidays with pay stimulated the British holiday resorts and later the continental ones, and workers had plenty of money to spend when they arrived. People were living longer, were healthier and appeared to be enjoying life more than ever. Before long, a form of amnesia started to set in – the thirties were forgotten and a whole generation emerged who knew only full employment. It was assumed that the problem of unemployment had been beaten for ever.

It was not only the public who assumed this to be the case – some politicians wrote entire books based on this precept. In Britain Tony Crosland, a senior Labour party politician and theorist, wrote such a book, entitled *The Future of Socialism*. It took full employment for granted and argued that the main problem facing politicians concerned the distribution of income and wealth. This book affected not only the Labour party but a substantial number of the Tory party too. These ideas were also echoed by the French and Italian Social Democrats. They all believed that, given government intervention on the demand side of the economy, either by the use of expenditure or taxation, the economy could be managed and full employment maintained for ever more. Few politicians or others were disposed to challenge this comforting theory – the fact that it was mainly due to the economic equivalent of a good fairy waving her magic wand escaped them. Charitably, one can argue that they were too close to the action at the time.

The post-war decades were very different from each other. The forties, or what was left of them after the war, were austere in Europe, but far less so in the USA. The fifties were drab and decent. The sixties were full of fresh hope, with visions of societies built on the 'Beatles' culture and the new classlessness. They were also important in another respect. Young people felt confident enough to opt out of the work-oriented society in relatively large numbers. They set up communes, they dropped out and they went on treks to Katmandu. Where previous generations had feared that employment might not be available at all times, the young believed that jobs would always be there if they wanted them and, in reaction to their parents' obsession with this seemingly omnipresent commodity, decided to reject it. But the early years of the seventies saw a welter of recriminations about the excesses and the failures of the sixties; the universities settled down and employment became respectable for all generations once again. However, the economic bubble burst too, and the manageable economy suddenly turned nasty.

The very high growth rates were slowing in Britain by the late sixties and the early seventies in the rest of Europe. Rates of 4 and 5 per cent were the norm now. Markets were becoming saturated and the spur to production given by the formation of the European Economic Community was becoming weaker. The 'social limits to growth' arguments proposed by Fred Hirsch were playing their full part now. Replacement had become the major component of demand. The only other growth areas were provided by young people coming into the market with high incomes and demands for fashions and other goods which were guaranteed built-in obsolescence.

The US economy, fuelled by the Vietnam War and the space race, with its trade deficit funded by the rest of the world, continued to grow, with only the occasional minor hiccough – for example, the slump of 1969–70. The European slow-down, which gave little cause for concern at the time, was over-shadowed by what followed. The price of oil soared in 1973 and those who, in 1972, thought that OPEC was a cough sweet knew differently from then on. The effects on all economies were catastrophic; prices rose and the balance of payments of the oil-importing nations dived into the red. To compensate, several governments retrenched. They cut their spending and tried to cut their imports, but inflation roared ahead to histori-cally high levels. The economic wizards tried new spells, but few of them worked. One sect decided to disinter some old spells and monetarism returned to fashion. When this last held sway in the 1920s unemployment was epidemic in the industrialised world at approximately four-yearly intervals. It would seem that its magic is still potent.

The fat, if aberrant, years lasted from 1945 until 1978 – by far the longest period of sustained full employment the industrialised world has ever known. There were small slumps and periods when it was not possible to get a job immediately (the periods 1957–8, 1967–9 and 1975–8 are examples) but until the last of these 3 per cent was thought to be a high unemploy-ment rate. The lean years starting in 1978 showed the analysis which had underpinned the philosophies of full employment to be little more than wishful thinking. Unemployment since then has surged forward, often against all expectations and government policies. In France, President Mitterand and the government were elected on a platform built around the reduction of unemployment. But despite an initial spurt in government spending, stringent exchange controls and more direct methods like 'solidarity contracts' (discussed later), unemployment has continued to rise. Inflation, on the other hand, has fallen.

In Britain unemployment passed the million mark in 1975 for the first time for thirty years. By the time the Conservative government took office in 1979 it had reached 1.5 million, much of this increase due to a severe restriction of the economy in response to high inflation and a sterling crisis. In the next six years unemployment more than doubled to 3.3 million. It cannot, however, be said that governmental policies in Britain have been designed to reduce unemployment; nearly all of them have had the objective of reducing inflation and as a result decreasing employment.

The unemployment data for 1975 and 1979 are not strictly comparable, however, and indeed both underestimate the extent of the problem. Since 1979, school-leavers have been removed from the figures, nor are the increasing numbers of young people on Youth Training Schemes, and other quasi-job arrangements, included. The registration arrangements for men over sixty have also changed, so that far fewer of them are now counted. For comparability with 1975, the 1985 figure should therefore be adjusted up to about 3.7 million. However, both figures are affected by the method of collection. A person has to actively register as unemployed to be counted, and many women, many early retired men and some youngsters do not register as they do not want, or qualify for, benefits. Most responsible estimates made by bodies such as the TUC or the Institute of Manpower Studies put the *real rate of unemployment nearer to 4.3 million*.

The question of what are the real rates of unemployment bedevils international comparisons. The Organisation of Economic Cooperation and Development (OECD) standardises unemployment data in an attempt to overcome the problem. There have been times, however, when the figures suddenly changed for no apparent reason – at least none was given when an answer was requested – so that the standardised data should be treated with circumspection. In the USA and

France unemployment figures are collected in different ways from that of Britain, whilst the Germans are sending their 'guest workers' home so they are not counted at all. Greece claims that its unemployment rate is less than 2 per cent, which seems rather unlikely, whilst Belgium's is nearer 20 per cent and it is estimated that a similar percentage are employed in the informal economy in Italy who may, or may not, be counted as unemployed. What one can say is that unemployment is high (for the post-war period) in absolute and percentage terms in a number of industrialised countries today. At the beginning of 1985 Britain had 3.2 million or 12.2 per cent out of work, France 2.5 million or 11.1 per cent, Italy 2.9 million or 13.2 per cent, America 10 million or 7.6 per cent, and even Japan had over 1 million or 2.5 per cent unemployed.

Unemployment amongst the young is, as we shall see later, the factor which most worries governments around the world. It is extremely high in some countries: Spain has two out of every five youngsters unemployed, Italy one in three, Britain one in four, France one in five and the USA one in six. If quasi-jobs were excluded from the British figures, then unemployment would be nearer to one in two for the sixteen- and seventeen-year age groups. Almost as worrying is the increase in the number of people who have been unemployed for more than one year; nearly one-third of all the unemployed in the UK fit into this category, accounting for over 1 million people.

It is clear that this is an international problem. There has been a slow-down in world trade but it is not at all clear that governments wish to expand trade dramatically. The additional oil crises of the eighties, which quintupled fuel costs, were one of the principal reasons why monetarist policies were adopted in several countries simultaneously. Germany, America, Britain, France (as a late convert), Italy and Belgium have all cut government spending and attempted to reduce the money supply in the last five years. The primary theory is that inflation is directly and positively related to the amount of money circulating in the economy at any one time, so that by reducing this money supply inflation is reduced too. The secondary theory, which affects employment, is that in the longer term either companies will recover or new ones spring up to take advantage of the incentives created by low taxation, weak trade unions and diminished employment legislation. If all else fails, we just have to wait long enough for wages to fall, rather like during the period from the nineteenth century up until the 1930s. How long will we have to wait? As Keynes put it so succinctly, 'in the long term we are all dead'.

If government economic policies were the only reasons for the lack of jobs, there would be little cause for concern over the longer period. Sooner rather than later governments would be elected on platforms of expansionary policies and for a time unemployment would fall. However, many commentators believe that this would be temporary and that for a variety of reasons unemployment would soon start to climb again. Short-run economic difficulties, inflation, balance of payments deficits and bottlenecks of all descriptions are amongst the reasons most often cited. They have all afflicted the UK for the last forty years, especially at times of rapid growth, and there is every reason to suppose that attempts to reduce unemployment by massively increased spending would have to be curtailed within eighteen months as one or other of the economic parameters went 'sour'. The loss of productive capacity in the UK over the past ten years reinforces this likelihood.

A different set of reasons as to why unemployment levels may stay high is based on factors such as the changing nature of world trade, the impact of technology and long-run cyclical theory. There are others, myself included, who believe that a combination of all the above factors, structural and short term, will make it very difficult for full employment to be attained for at least thirty years, if ever again. It is of course possible to change the definition of employment or indeed full employment in an attempt to disguise the truth. The counting as employed of those in training or in quasi-jobs in UK statistics shows how easy this is – indeed after the 1985 budget the London Business School claimed that over 350,000 jobs would be created in the financial year. When analysed, nearly all of them were in the YTS or community schemes, so it was a misleading statistic.

That the patterns of world trade are changing is undeniable and indeed unremarkable. Change is continually occurring – the trade performances of countries ebb and flow, and the areas of expertise and comparative advantage vary with them. The late twentieth-century novelty, however, is the rise of the newly industrialising countries (NICs) along with the emergence of

Japan as an economic superpower. Japan has risen from being what some considered merely a maker of shoddy imitations to a high-growth, high-quality manufacturing nation within a thirty-year period. In cars and other motor vehicles, in consumer electronics and in products as varied as oil tankers and pianos Japanese goods have become the world leaders. At a time of sluggish world trade these expansions were made at the expense of products made in other countries. There is virtually no European shipbuilding industry left, Britain has no motorcycle-manufacturing capability, Switzerland has only a remnant of its former watch industry: the list is a long one. In each of the affected industries jobs have been lost in the older industrialised countries, but jobs in the new electronically based industries have not taken up the slack. On the contrary, these jobs have gone to the NICs as well.

The newly industrialising countries have been using the same technologies and techniques as the Japanese, and indeed are proving to be a threat to some of the Japanese industries and companies themselves. Countries like Taiwan, South Korea, Brazil, Indonesia and Singapore are competing with the world's best in several products. At one time it was believed that a country had to go through all the traditional stages of industrial development, with textile and clothing industries being followed by metal and engineering industries, in order to become fully industrialised. It is now possible to short-cut this lengthy procedure by the use of, and the concentration on, the newer electronic systems and products. The large transnational company has proved to be both the instigator and beneficiary of this movement, and the NIC itself may reap but an indirect and temporary advantage.

A common feature of most of the NICs is that there has been a combination of relatively cheap labour, politically repressive regimes and the lack of free trade unions or observance of the International Labour Organisation's conventions. The combination of a low cost, captive or quiescent, well-educated labour force has proved to be irresistible to many companies. They have for some time been opening plants in NICs for the manufacture and assembly of parts for their products, and it did not take long for both the transnational companies and the governments concerned to realise that they could be making the finished product as effectively as anywhere else, but more cheaply. There is now a stream of television sets, hi-fis, video recorders, cars, ships, silicon chips, steel, computers and robots pouring out of these countries. The older, maturer industrialised countries cannot compete on NIC terms. Even Japan is not protected from this attack; its steel, TV and car industries are all under increasing pressure, whilst its ship-building industry is not meeting the challenge. Given the social arrangements in Japan, the resulting stresses could provoke very severe responses of a most destabilising nature.

The providers of raw materials and commodities pose a potential threat to the existing patterns of world trade too. The Organisation of Petroleum Exporting Countries (OPEC) cartel is an example of what can happen when determined producers band together. It is conceivable that the iron-ore producers, the rare-metal mining countries and perhaps the coffee- or cocoa-growing countries could attempt the same form of coup. Whilst they may be unsuccessful or at the best have a limited short-term victory, it is clear that industrialised nations depend upon the terms of trade being in their favour and on security of supplies. The old colonial empires were designed to secure these forms of stability, and since their dismemberment life has become that much more precarious in the industrialised countries. These changes in trading patterns threaten many jobs in the older manufacturing countries like Britain and the other EEC states.

Nikolai Kondratiev was the Director of the Business Conditions Institute in Moscow in the 1920s. In 1926 he published an article entitled 'The Long Waves in Economic Life', in which he postulated the existence of deep economic cycles every fifty years. The ideas in the article were buried and forgotten along with its author, who was executed in the Soviet purges, until other economists like Schumpeter in the thirties and Kuznets in the seventies attempted to develop the theory. The spur to the research in both cases was an economic depression. Both the Kondratiev cycles and the shorter Kuznets variations fit in quite well with the facts.

Kondratiev's theory is based on technological change. In the periods of the downswing there would be 'many important discoveries and inventions', but these would only be applied at the beginning of the next upswing – having lain 'dormant' until then. The development and use of these new technologies would then become the engine of growth for the boom until, inevitably, the impetus ran down and the downswing started once again. Kondratiev's first postulated wave was steam-engine driven and lasted from 1789 until 1849, with the upswing ending in 1814. The second wave's upswing ended in 1873 and was fuelled by, amongst other things, the electric motor, electricity and, the chemical industry; the downswing lasted until 1896. He had only time before his death to identify the next upswing, which went on until 1920. Using this cyclical theory as a basis for extrapolation, the cycle would have ended its decline in 1945 whilst the next upswing would have been from 1945 to 1970 and the downswing from 1970 to 1995. This is clearly, up to 1985, corresponding with the facts, but it does not mean that the future will correspond in precisely the same way.

Kuznets identified the periods of rapid growth differently, although there are some similarities. For him, 1775 to 1800 was the period of industrial revolution; 1828 to 1857 was the era of the entrepreneur; 1886 to 1911 was the age when scientists and inventors were applying themselves to basic research and the manufacturing processes; 1948 to 1973 was the age of rising expectations. The next Kuznets upswing should begin around now and be based on high technology and the move to the 'post-industrial society', lasting to around 2010. In order to make this correspond with Kondratiev's theories a simple and plausible adjustment can be made. If the next cycle is based on fifth-generation computers, which should be in operation by 1995, the cycles would then be in harmony.

Whilst there is something inherently superstitious in believing rigidly in cyclical theory (it is like relying upon Nostradamus for your forward planning), the concept of pent-up technological changes bursting upon the world has a credible ring to it. It is the sort of theory that depends as much on the reading of collective psychology for its verification and explanation as it does on economic theory. As this element is so clearly missing from modern economics it might explain the attractiveness of the Kondratiev–Kuznets theories to the lay-man, and the lack of interest shown by the economics profession in general.

Up to this point I have assumed that economic growth and the creation of jobs go hand in hand. A boom means jobs, a slump means unemployment. From now onwards, however, this book will challenge that position. It will argue that Kondratiev's theory of technological unemployment after a twenty-five-year interval needs to be revived and reworked in the light of a unique twentieth-century technological change. No longer will the link between economic growth and the growth of jobs be automatically positive. No longer will increases in productivity automatically translate themselves into jobs, as conventional wisdom would have it.

We have reached one of the watersheds in the history of the world. We are faced with a quantum leap, a discontinuity, every bit as dramatic as that caused by the steam engine and the first industrial revolution. That gave the world new towns and cities, new visions and horizons, a new politics and the employment ethic. This one, which also deserves to be called a revolution, will instigate far-reaching changes too.

3 The new technologies

The distinguishing feature of a fundamental technological change is the magnitude of the effect that it has on matters outside its dedicated field. The use of fire, the wheel, gunpowder, steel, the compass, steam power, electricity, the internal combustion engine, the aeroplane, antibiotics and nuclear power are among such developments. Individually each has changed the way that things have been done, collectively they make up a large part of the developmental pattern of the world. Kondratiev's argument that technological changes come together in clumps would appear to be vindicated by the evidence so far produced during the eighties, although many of the new developments have nowhere near reached their maturity yet.

Molecular biology, genetic engineering, cryobiology, nuclear fusion, hydrogen as an alternate fuel source, astrophysics and microelectronics are a few of the major areas of intensive research being undertaken at present. Of these, genetic engineering carries with it the most chilling of possibilities. The cloning of a slave or military caste, or the manufacture of unpredictable and potentially harmful organisms, are only two of the capabilities of this technique and neither belong solely to the realms of science fiction. Indeed, a bacterium to eat the sludge in oil pipes has been developed but what would happen if it escaped. Would it live? Could it thrive? But this rather frightening technological advance also has the capability of meeting the demands of hunger in the world and of providing great advances in medicine. As with so many of the really important inventions, people have to decide whether it will be used for good or evil.

Microelectronics, however, is the most likely of all the new technologies to create major changes in the medium term. Not only is it more advanced and proven than the others, but it has a rare quality – it is a *ubiquitous* technology. It is difficult to think of an area in the formal economy which will not be affected by microelectronics. It is popularly known as the 'new technology', which demonstrates the importance it is seen to have. Whether it is used in a factory in the form of a robot or computer-controlled process, incorporated as a component in an electrical product, or used in a bank, a laser-scanned supermarket check-out, a travel agency or a town hall, this technology has imposed itself on the public's consciousness. In telecommunications, transport, the armed forces, teaching and medicine, at home, abroad, at work and at leisure, there is no escaping it. There is nowhere to hide except in the informal sector (the black economy) and some person-to-person services.

Microelectronics is unique in this century. The uniqueness stems from the fact that not only is it a technology that is everywhere, but that it has its main impact on the supply side of the economy. In itself it adds nothing to demand. No one will go out to buy a silicon chip or an integrated circuit, any more than people went out to the shops in the nineteenth century and announced that they had 'just popped out to buy a steam engine', returning half an hour later with the latest model. It is in these two respects that the development of microelectronics is precisely the same as that of the steam engine. This combination has not occurred at any other time in this century and the dramatic effects produced by the steam engine in the previous two centuries give us the only reliable guide to the probable consequences that microelectronics will have – socially, politically and industrially.

The supply side of the economy deals with the making and the distribution of goods and services; it does not matter, from the point of view of this analysis, whether these are in the public or the private sectors. In the nineteenth century the people who bought steam engines were the factory, mine or mill owners or the railway companies. They were used to increase productivity and efficiency, having enormous impacts on overall demand in an *indirect* manner but only a miniscule effect themselves. The same applies to microelectronics. We shall buy or rent all sorts of goods and services which incorporate microelectronics, and we shall have even more which have had a microelectronic system somewhere in the process which made, delivered or distributed them. In themselves microelectronics add little to aggregate demand, but like the steam engine they will have considerable indirect effects.

The twentieth century has had many technologies which affected the supply side of the economy (the production and distribution of goods and services), but only in limited areas – machine tools, for example. Other developments were ubiquitous, or nearly so, but had mixed demand and supply impacts. The mass-produced motor car or the television set comes into this category, as indeed do most of the consumer durables that are in use today, and the materials from which they are made.

With the advent of cabling and 'local area networks' (LANs) computers and microelectronically based machines like televisions will be linked together to form what can only be described as a new public utility. Information will flow nationally and internationally in the same way that water, electricity and gas does now. It has to be realised, however, that this major effect represents but one facet of the technological potential of the silicon chip.

Microelectronics is a very simple technology which, most unusually, has a name that explains rather than obscures, and although it is in a direct evolutionary line from the valve and transistor, it is genuinely new. The impetus which took it from the laboratory to everyday use was the space race. President Kennedy committed the USA to putting a man on the moon. This involved a light payload and required relatively small rockets which, for the Americans, meant a saving of time and money. However, it also meant that all extraneous weight and bulk had to be removed from the capsule and, as the electronic equipment accounted for much of this, a great effort was made to develop lighter and smaller control systems. The use of materials known as semi-conductors to hold the actual circuit was already established, with silicon being the most readily obtainable and the cheapest of these. On-board computers, life-support systems, the space-suits themselves and the communication systems all became miniaturised or run by miniature circuits. As the companies that manufactured this hardware were also involved in other sectors of the economy making civilian and military goods, the technology was swiftly disseminated. In hindsight this proved to be one of the great advantages of the American system of contracting out all the work.

An interesting side-effect of the space race is that the Soviet effort was oriented towards large rockets, large payloads and space-platforms, which has resulted in a large technology gap for them. They are not very far advanced in microelectronics, a fact demonstrated clearly by the concern with which they view cruise missiles. These weapons are effective because of their ultra-sensitive direction and guidance systems (resulting from microelectronic techniques) rather than their speed or destructive capability, and the Soviets cannot match this sophistication. The overseas domination at a recent computer exhibition held in Moscow was another indication of their indigenous lack of mini- or micro-computer capability. In the West, however, this technology is rampant.

We can easily see how and where this technology affects us. In the kitchen dishwashers and cookers incorporate integrated circuits; elsewhere the TV, video and hi-fi sets, some lighting systems and the odd alarm clock and intelligent bathroom-scales remind us of its presence. The bills and invoices we receive are computerised (as we realise when it proves impossible to correct one that is patently a nonsense), as are our social security benefits. When we book a holiday or reserve a theatre or plane seat, the visual display unit is there at the clerk's elbow. Intensive care is among the medical facilities that are dependent on it, our entertainment in cinemas and theatres is enhanced by it, and so are the books that we read. Our accountants and lawyers use it, schools and colleges have appropriated it as a teaching aide, push-button phones are worked by it and most traffic lights are controlled by it. Personal computers, the games we play on them, pocket calculators and digital watches only exist because of it. We see it at home, we see it at work and we see it at our leisure.

However, for each of the applications that we can see there are many others that we cannot; they may have been publicised on television or in a newspaper but our first-hand experience is limited. These are the uses which affect production and how the office, the laboratory or the supermarket actually works. There is a tendency to underestimate the possible problems inherent in the new technology because we can only see a part of its applications, but nevertheless over 60 per cent of the British public believe that it will destroy more jobs than it will create, according to a Market Opinion and Research International (MORI) survey in 1984. This percentage had doubled in twelve months. There has been a conspiracy between the users of the technology, the makers of the technology, politicians and some newspapers which has resulted in a blanket of silence being cast over technological redundancies and changes in work patterns, although some radio and TV and at least one of the allegedly quality newspapers do carry the subject in a responsible and fair manner.

One can understand the concern of the manufacturers of the equipment, the providers of the systems and the software houses; they do not wish to be held solely responsible for harmful social changes. One can even understand, although not sympathise with, politicians and civil servants who try to pretend that everything can be cured by traditional remedies and that full employment is an attainable reality in the life of this or the next parliament. One cannot, however, excuse the media, which should be informing rather than obscuring. It is not simply a question of sins of omission; we are given many misleading statements, if not downright lies, about the subject.

We have all heard, many times, that the introduction of a new system into a particular enterprise did not cause any redundancies. This is often quite true. *But it does not mean that there were as many jobs after the changes as there were before they were introduced.* There are many ways of reducing a work force, as we shall discover, but redundancy is the least used when introducing new technologies. When this statement is made it is intended to convey the impression that no jobs have been, or will be, lost. I have spoken at many seminars where spokesmen from well known companies have tried this technique and only conceded under quite strong questioning that many jobs had disappeared. Newspaper reports tend to reinforce this misconception, as do some trade or quasi-academic studies. A report on 'new technology' and its impacts in a case study for the magazine of the Department of Employment stated, quite boldly, that there had been no redundancies and implied that no jobs had been lost. Not a single piece of evidence was produced to back up this statement.

In the small business sector, however, the company that introduces the new techniques is the one that retains or increases its staff. The ones that do not keep up with technological advances go under or diminish in size once one of their competitors has started to re-equip. An example is what happened when a bed-leg manufacturer in the Midlands used a computer to plan and control his production processes and the ordering of materials. One of four small companies making the same product in the same area, it originally employed twenty people. After computerisation the company became so efficient that one of the competitors folded, one is about to fold and the other is about to computerise. Our original hero has taken on two extra people and to date forty-six jobs have been lost in the other companies. There is a lesson to be drawn from this, which is that if demand does not expand as fast as the potential supply then something has to give. With productivity increases of the order of 25 per cent and a growth in the market for beds at only around 4 per cent jobs had to be lost.

In the small business sector any survey or case study of the impact of new technology on employment must investigate the entire local market, and this includes competitors as well as the producers of complementary goods. To do otherwise is like testing for cancer using only a thermometer. A substantial report in 1984 suggested that in the companies it had investigated less than 1 out of every 500 recently unemployed people could blame their loss of jobs on a microelectronic component newly incorporated into the product. This claim received some press attention, but, although the report admitted that this figure was probably an underestimate and that it was a difficult figure to arrive at anyway, these riders were ignored. What happened to the number of jobs in the companies that manufactured the components and sub-components for the major product? It is most unlikely that the companies were all vertically integrated, and if they were small companies what happened to total employment amongst the competing firms? The major point, however, is whether these new components were replacements for older ones or completely new items. The distinction is crucial, and the motor car is a good example.

New components based on integrated circuits are being introduced into nearly all mass-produced cars. Some are replacing the tangles of wiring that skulk behind the front fascia and feed into speedometers, clocks, petrol gauges and other dials. Others are completely new. They include on-board computers, cruise-at-constant-speed controls and an airport-style disembodied voice giving instructions. These last functions are an addition to the product, have to be made somewhere and assembled so that, at the worst, the same level, and more probably an increased level, of employment results. The replacement components, however, need fewer people to make and to assemble, and this is one of the main reasons why manufacturers use them. Simple distinctions of this nature will have to be made if studies, and the subsequent propaganda resulting from them, are not to move right away from the public's ability to understand. To my knowledge this has not yet been done in Britain, or indeed anywhere else, although I may be maligning some excellent researchers. It is true that this is a new preoccupation, but the lack of intellectual rigour and simple imagination in the research undertaken up until now is dispiriting.

The use of microelectronics has four basic effects on jobs. The first is the quality. The second is who does them. The third is where they are done, and last – but certainly not least – is of course the *quantity* of jobs that will be available. The first three of these will be covered in the following chapters but it is clear that there is potential for great change on all three counts. Not all of it will be considered good, and no doubt not all of it will come to fruition. Indeed, some of the changes will create a climate among management which may militate against even further changes.

The first question that has to be asked is why we are using microelectronic technology at all. Are the public forcing manufacturers to use it in their products? Is there a groundswell of opinion which makes a retail store install an electronic stock-control system operated from its point-of-sale cash register? Most people would answer no. There are perfectly responsible and rational business reasons for using this technology and many of them have to do with adding to efficiency, productivity and cost-minimising. All three, however, can involve the loss of jobs.

Human beings are fallible, robots are not. As a rule of thumb this is a reasonable proposition – although it has to be qualified somewhat in the real world, given both the fallibility of the designers of robots and the less than 100 per cent reliability of the machines themselves. However, it means that a manufacturer should expect to get a higher standard of quality control from automated procedures than from the old-fashioned production lines or other manually based systems. New

43

electronically based testing equipment reinforces this benefit, which is an important one. Customers and clients are reassured when there is a high standard of reliability in their chosen product, and the word soon spreads if there is not. It follows that there is an incentive to use the new technologies as a selling point. British Leyland suffered from an appalling image of shoddy workmanship in the early seventies, but the introduction of robots on the Metro body-shop track at Longbridge in a blare of publicity re-established a sense of confidence in the product. People were prepared to trust the robots but not the workers, and in the event the overall standard of quality rose substantially.

This applies not only to cars but to a large range of manufactured products. TV sets and goods in the home are now made either with components that go wrong less frequently or by processes that reduce the chance of human or machine error. The fact that the last fifteen years have seen the spectacular growth of the consumer protection agencies with a back-up in the form of radio, TV and newspaper interest in the subject, has added to the manufacturers' imperative to improve quality and reliability. The 1970s were the decade of the enfranchisement of the grumbler.

The main reason, however, for using the new technology is that it gives the user a competitive edge in terms of costs, output and productivity. This is certainly true in the manufacturing sector or the mineral-extraction industries, and it affects both production lines and batch processes. The rate of technological change in this field is spectacular. Not very long ago the occasional robot was the limit of ambition for most factory managers. Computer-aided design or numerically controlled machine tools were thought of as revolutionary. We are now entering the era of the totally flexible manufacturing plant, and with it the personless factory. It is reality catching up with science fiction.

It is considerably more difficult, however, to measure the productivity benefits accruing from new systems in the clerical, administrative and managerial areas. This is because there is little in the way of a working definition of what productivity or effectiveness is, let alone how it has increased, in any but the most mechanical jobs like typing. This has not stopped the introduction of all sorts of 'new technology' gadgets, some most ill-conceived, in offices around the world. The motivation behind their introduction is similar to that found in the manufacturing sector. A series of advertisements for one particular word-processor showed a secretary looking frantically busy, while the bold type pointed out that the word-processor cost less than the secretary's salary for one year, and was ten times as productive. Cost-minimising is the game, and in offices this inevitably means people-minimising.

This is not as straightforward as it seems, however. A comprehensive report by an American consultancy, OMNI, on the uses and selection of 'information technology' gave a bundle of reasons for its adoption. These included increased speed, lower cost transactions, compatibility of equipment and expansion of services. Only 43 per cent of respondents quoted a reduction of staff as the reason.

Over 70 per cent of respondents cited the avoidance of increased staff costs as their reason for going over to 'information technology' systems. What must this mean? It could mean that the new system will prevent the people working there from putting in for salary increases – hardly likely in any circumstances. The only other way to reduce the liability to staff costs is not to employ as many, and this would seem to be what is really meant. *In other words, the intention is to reduce staff over time rather than immediately in about half of the cases where new technology is being used. The other half plan to do this sooner.* There are few instances where no staff reductions at all are contemplated. Please notice that no one has mentioned that dreaded word 'redundancy', yet the work force will diminish none the less.

If we divide the world into three sectors it will be easier to analyse where these new systems are coming into operation and what the effects on jobs may be. First, the manufacturing sector. It is here that the most spectacular advances are being made across a widening range of processes and products, and in what are sometimes the most unlikely of places. Small villages in the Thames Valley hide ultra-sophisticated processor manufacturers, whilst in the mining towns of Fife there are companies making all-electronic components for a variety of military hardware. Nowadays we all know about robots. Some of us still think that they all look like R2D2, whilst others have seen them innumerable times on TV programmes and realise that they look like reticulated giraffes. Robots are, however, becoming passé when used on their own – they are now being integrated into systems.

There is a large and growing demand for them. A survey in 1984 estimated that 64,600 were in use in Japan, 13,000 in the USA, nearly 6,000 in West Germany – and Britain was the sixth biggest user with 2,600. When they are being used as single machines or for a specific purpose they are virtually hand-crafted-Savile Row bespoke or King's Road customised, as it were. Robots are now being manufactured with artificial intelligence controls so that they have a learning capacity and are capable of registering the senses of smell, touch and sight. This tailoring is done in the UK by firms like Taylor Hitec as well as overseas by the better known companies like Unimation. Indeed, a visit to an old engineering plant next to a park in Richmond, Surrey, will reveal research into robots with camera eyes and into miniature robots for schools. The owner, John Reekie, is convinced that the way ahead in this field is through the imagination and freedom of the small company rather than the giant. But when companies as large as General Motors enter the market many preconceptions and forecasts change – as they have done recently.

The future lies not in the single-use, individual factory robot but in the General Electric or General Motors style of automated factory. These are slightly in advance of the Japanese personless plants, and the General Electric plant in Louisville is a tribute to ingenuity, technology and $38 million. Inside an ordinary-looking building are 'smart machine tools', computers, lasers and robots – all of which outnumber by far the occasional human employee. The control-room computer has authority over twenty-four other computers which monitor, check, inspect, collect and analyse the data and adjust the stock balances of the manufacturing processes. *This is akin to a nervous system*. It can even change itself to work on new products and projects, and the machine tools are capable of not only changing their own functions but also of dovetailing into the general production line changes. This means that a variety of products could be mass-produced at very nearly the same time, which ultimately will give the consumer a greater range of choice. The dishwashers that are produced in this factory should, in theory, be better made and tested than most of the competitor machines. This is a considerable advance on the automated Japanese factories which tend to produce a single product rather than a possible mix. These new concepts are called advanced manufacturing technologies (AMT), and the key aspect to this is flexibility.

General Motors plans to turn its Saginaw Steering Division in Michigan into an axle plant which will be controlled by a master computer. The plant will be based on about forty cells, each of them containing robots and advanced machine tools. Driverless carriages will take materials and components between these cells, and there will be different sizes of axle manufactured, all the machines being able to adjust to parts of different sizes. The computerisation is so intense that a machine breakdown will be dealt with by the computer re-routing production, and even the sweeping will be done robotically. Whilst there will still be the need for some humans for maintenance, technical and managerial work, General Motors acknowledge that 'far fewer production workers will be employed' as these automation techniques spread through the company. The intention is to have the plant on stream fully by 1987.

This sort of development is part of a trend. American consultants are pushing AMT hard to their clients as the only way to overcome the Japanese competition. It is a conscious attempt to reduce manufacturing costs to the level of not only Japan but Malaysia, Korea and the other NICs. Clearly the strategy will remove jobs from the manufacturing process.

There are other techniques and uses that microelectronics are put to in the manufacturing sector. Computer Integrated Manufacturing (CIM) is the total combination of Computer Aided Design (CAD) and Computer Aided Manufacturing (CAM). This system can pass directly from the design computer screen onto the computer which controls the machine tool and straight into the manufacturing process – thus bypassing all of the intermediate stages. There are also new control systems for the computer-controlled machines, tools and the networks which link them. Extremely expensive and sophisticated machine tools like the ones which operate on rotor blades at Rolls Royce in Derby or the axle hubs at Jaguar Motors are computer-controlled, monitored by TV and can do the work of several skilled engineers.

The inspection of goods is now computer- or robot-controlled, as is testing of products as diverse as rubber gloves, pharmaceuticals and jam tarts. Clever measuring devices which remember and check past and idealised measurements use vision machines in companies like Vickers or Bendix. The use of computers as a control source at companies like United Biscuits is perhaps rather 'old hat' in relative terms, but the lack of people on the production line shows their effect in dramatic fashion. Stock control, warehousing and transport – all are being automated by the more successful companies.

Competition can be a great motivator and it is this – along with its cousin, fear – that is creating this rapid chain of events. It is not only production processes that are being revolutionised. The speed at which a company can process an idea into a finished product may mean the difference between success and disaster. A new range of Philips hi-fis will have taken only twenty-one months to get through all the stages from the drawing-board into the home, a time-saving of a quarter, but even this may not be sufficient to head off the challenge of the even faster Japanese. The speeding-up of new product development depends on a combination of techniques, and one of these is the use of new electronically based systems. By using CIM and its latest derivatives, as well as computer simulation tests and analysis of market research, companies as different as IBM, Austin Rover and Procter and Gamble have all increased their pace of product development. In the electronics field, where the products are changing so regularly that new ones are appearing almost daily, the most important of all the company strategies has to be speed. Not just for its own sake but to outstrip the competition.

The next phase of shortening the production process moves up-stream. Salesmen can now call their orders directly into a production computer. Intermediaries are not needed as the computer feeds the control computer, and in the automated factory production starts as soon as the relevant machine time is available. This technique does not, however, depend on the factory being automated – Waddington's salesmen have been using this style of information-processing for some time in their non-automated factory. Goods made to individual specifications or those which are mass-produced can be handled in this manner, and the customer gets far faster deliveries. On a more revolutionary basis, experiments with a design system based on

the direct inputs of potential clients into a CAD installation
have proved to be very successful. It is a revolutionary combination of market research and practical design experience
rolled into one.

The places where clerical, administrative and managerial
work is done, for example banks and offices of all types,
constitute the second sector in which microelectronic techniques are making inroads. In this instance it is often called
'information technology'. There are more people doing these
sorts of jobs than manufacturing jobs in Britain and in almost
every other industrialised country. Because of this and the
potential spread of the new systems more jobs could be under
threat in this sector than any other. Whilst the manufacturers of
office equipment have not been slow in publicising their
achievements, the truth is that the take-up of the equipment has
been slow and haphazard. Far too many businesses have
acquired incompatible items of hardware or irrelevant bits of
software, and been promised the impossible. Nevertheless, the
growth in the word-processor and personal computer markets
is such that any data I attempted to give on this would be
virtually out of date before this paragraph was written.

Five years ago one of the most popular buzz words was
'convergence'. For the uninitiated this means the coalescing of
computer power and telecommunication networks. It was not
only assumed that all the separate functions of the office would
be linked together to form a single work station, but that we
would not have to wait very long for it to happen. While this is
still the vision put forward by manufacturers who are seeking to
sell entire systems and consultancies, especially American ones,
another school of thought is emerging. This suggests that
because the technical difficulties have proved to be greater than
was expected, and because one vital link (telecommunications)
is not as advanced as was expected, alternatives may have to be
used. Telecommunication systems are not only too expensive
for some techniques to be commercially viable, but as yet they
have neither developed the capacity nor the speed that they
once promised. Georges Anderla, once one of the high priests of
'convergence' when he was director of all information technology matters in the EEC (until 1984), now believes that for
the conceivable future individual stand-alone machines – as
opposed to integrated systems – will hold sway. They will be

small enough for people to carry them or their discs around, so files will travel *with* a person rather than down an expensive telephone line. Although this distinction may not affect the numbers of people who will be replaced by these technologies, it will mean that different groups of people will be at risk.

Within the office the 'state of the art' systems are impressive but are used mainly by the electronic companies themselves at present. Digital Equipment Corporation has a worldwide network, whilst Rank Xerox are about to move into a fully wired new purpose-built head office in which over 800 work stations will be linked together by Xerox's own local area network, Ethernet. The same types of companies are developing artificial intelligence computers which, when linked together, are starting to provide a network analogous to an organism's nervous system.

On a more mundane level the electronically based equipment coming into general use spans the widest possible spectrum of office life. Word-processors are replacing typewriters, personal computers are becoming a commonplace, and electronic switchboards and clever telephones are replacing the traditional ones. Work stations are less of a novelty, telex and facsimile machines are in common use, whilst the computer has lost some of its mystique – if not its capacity to inspire terror – as a result of its wide exposure. Some electronic filing systems and integrated office facilities have been put in place, but these are the exceptions; by and large the promise has yet to be fulfilled. It can only be a matter of time before it is, and in the UK this will be in the early years of the next decade when the all-electronic telecommunication system should have been set up.

Some of the new systems have not yet taken off, or perhaps never will. Teleconferencing is one of these, area networks are another, while cabling which, if interactive, would give a massive boost to microelectronics, is as far away as ever in the UK, though nearer to becoming a reality in France. Videotex and Teletext have yet to find their role in a business environment, although other database routines have done so. Nevertheless, some techniques have proved to be surprisingly successful, and some industries have developed specific uses for the new technologies. Satellite transmissions are making it possible to transmit clerical work or data across continents, and modular work stations are capable of being dismantled and carried from meeting to meeting. The development is for the most part unplanned, for example in the large clerical areas of government and in the ultimate of the paper-shuffling empires – the insurance companies. However, banks and financial companies around the world are enthusiastic users of electronic equipment.

The stockmarket uses the new technologies for speed, convenience and accuracy and is becoming dependent on short-wave radio and sophisticated screen-based information systems like Reuters or Topic. Although there are mutterings about buying directly using a computer screen, the big dealers will stick to current methods even when the interactive systems are in place. Research or fund management, however, which account for a goodly proportion of employment in a brokerage, will use electronic information systems in a more fundamental way. The British futures market, with its dependence on Chicago, needs a high technology background (indeed fore-ground) whilst many of the other markets, notably foreign exchange and precious metals, must use reliable worldwide communications, preferably based upon a continually updated screen. High-tech is certainly the fashion in the City and other major world financial centres. It is in the banks, however, rather than any other finance houses or institutions, that the new technologies are having their greatest impact.

There are two different and distinct ways in which the banking system is planning to use electronic technologies. Banks in countries around the world intend to improve their internal communications and efficiency, while moving into new areas (such as mortgages) or finding new ways of satisfying their customers' demands. The use of computers to provide statements and operate the automated cash dispensers is now well established, as is the electronic clearing of cheques. And cash dispensers have proved to be very popular, quadrupling in number in Britain over the past five years. Citibank of New York use electronics as their international operations basis, in addition to their highly publicised practice of having half their clerical workers linked to the bank from their homes. An additional banking system is growing up in the USA with use of the VISA system. It not only links together the automatic cash-tellers of banks but also has the advantage of having a card that can be read by electronic cash registers and supermarket scanners with the sensational results that in California *80 per cent of the cheques raised are cashed in supermarkets.* Grocery stores are now an extra arm of the banking system.

The German banks are providing electronic financial planning for clients but their main concern is to get the teletext system BTX accepted as a base for home banking (when used with a personal computer it creates a work station). It is, however, meeting with consumer resistance in the trial areas and although BTX is also behind schedule the banks are confident that, in the longer term, these new ideas will catch on. The technology is moving fast in banking areas at the moment and the emphasis on increased efficiency is running parallel with the move towards home banking and cashless shopping. One new system will enable a phone call made by operating the buttons on a telephone receiver to talk to, and receive, messages from the bank's computer; to date, Homebank claims about 5 million users of this system in six countries, including the USA. But it is in the realm of cashless shopping, where the banking and the retail systems meet, that the greatest impact is likely to be seen.

We know how quickly the credit card took off and how widely and quickly it spread; the French hope that their 'smart card' will have a similar success. The smart card has chips built into itself rather than the ordinary magnetic strip. It will store information about cash balances or which credit lines are still open, and can be used for medical records, as a security tool or as an ultra-sophisticated credit, bank and cash card. There was once an advert for a British bank which joked that when you joined the bank it was like having a bank manager in your cupboard; the smart card is like having your bank manager in your pocket. The French feel that they are on to an international winner on the same scale as radar or nylon.

The British version of this system will be known as EFTPOS unless someone comes up with a more catchy name. It is the acronym for Electronic Funds Transfer at Point of Sale. Very limited experiments have been held – by the Clydesdale Bank in garages in Scotland, by Barclaycard with railway tickets, and British Telecom have launched a similar system. The customer inserts the card into a point-of-sale machine and credit is automatically transferred to the shop's account from the customer's account. The implementation is expected to be a slow process with a great deal of resistance to be overcome, and as yet it is not certain who will bear the brunt of the costs and who will get the bulk of the benefits. The card is a debit rather than a credit card, which suggests that banks and shops rather than the consumer will benefit most, although existing credit cards will still be used.

High Street shops will soon be using these devices, as well as automated check-out and stock-control systems. Insurance brokers are starting to use self-service video systems and the next step is to put these on-line to the major insurance companies. One of these companies has its own branch offices connected to its head office in this way but the breakthrough will come when the scheme becomes all-embracing. With the possibility of cheap and efficient shopping, banking, and insurance services – all controlled from the home – there are clearly great changes afoot. There is indeed a chance that the home will become a business, commercial and leisure centre through the use of cabling and teletext systems like Prestel. All forms of networks run from the home, such as authors using word-processors, home clerical work, and selling from home, are being explored or implemented even now.

The new technologies are also having an impact on most other services and industries, covering the entire spectrum of life in a modern society. Newspapers and the electronic media are changing rapidly, with 'direct input' in journalism matched by electronic news-gathering equipment in television. Telecommunication systems worldwide are changing to all-electronic switching, and professionals like doctors and lawyers are using electronics to help them with their work – as are actors and producers. A variety of industries are increasingly dependent on electronics, such as the defence industries (for example, in their missile guidance systems and avionics), printing (computer typesetting) and mining (automatic coal-stripping machines and safety equipment). Services like tourism and hotel management, transport scheduling and control, public utility provision and fast food chains are all involved in the use of new sophisticated technologies. The list is so long that it would be boring after the 500th entry, so I shall end it here. But it is worth remembering that within the formal economy there is nowhere to hide – microelectronics is a ubiquitous technology. As a result of these changes the microelectronically based industries can scarcely be described as stagnating. For example, information technology is currently growing at 14 per cent each year worldwide, whilst most other industries are fortunate if they reach as much as 5 per cent.

These advances show no signs of slowing down. The artificial intelligence (AI) computers which can learn from their mistakes will – indeed are – starting to take decisions, and the fifth generation computers upon which the Japanese are investing billions of dollars will make even these AI machines seem primitive. The new computers will not only have better sensor systems but are designed to have a reasoning process more like that of a human being. At present computers think serially – one calculation follows upon another. People, however, take in all sorts of signals simultaneously: a person may be talking, listening to a noise outside the door, noticing how warm it has become and feeling thirsty – all at the same time. These signals are given a ranking order which then subconsciously determines our actions, but at any one time this could change; the person could stop talking and open a window to cool down, for example. The fifth-generation computers will have a design based on this approach.

It only takes a moment's thought to realise the implications of this. Whether controlling a factory or acting in an advisory capacity, these new computers will, for the first time, offer a real challenge to the indispensability – if not quite the supremacy – of human beings. The challenge will be across the board: mental, physical and creative. There are two ways in which one can analyse the effects of these technological changes on the number of available jobs. Analysing different types of jobs (for example, all medium-grade clerks in all industries) is one method, and an analysis based on different industries is the other. We shall look at both of these.

Computers – and microelectronics is merely the same principle applied in miniature – are in theory capable of being programmed to replicate any repetitive physical action or thought process of a human. In the real world, however, the theory has to be qualified by the relative costs of the new systems and of the workers who could be replaced. This has an important bearing upon which people or jobs are most at risk. Most people do repetitive jobs or jobs which have a high content of repetitious actions. Nearly all factory jobs – whether on a production line, tending a machine, cleaning or working in the stores – fall into this category, and robots could take over all these too. A televised demonstration I saw recently of a robot being programmed to paint a wooden chair, a job requiring hundreds of movements and much co-ordination, was a real eye-opener. The fact that a robot can do such a job means that unskilled, semi-skilled or skilled workers are all at risk. A very experienced machine-tool setter is in as much danger, perhaps even more so, of losing his job to a machine as an assembler on a car-track.

The incentives of better and more reliable quality reinforce the cost elements. The higher the cost of the labour, the more likely it is that a replacement system will be developed. This is of course an aggregate cost, so that thousands of low-paid workers may be as vulnerable as a smaller number of highly paid ones. It may also be easier and cheaper to develop a machine or system to replace lower paid labour, as the work is often far less complex than that done by the better paid, more highly skilled worker. However, people like lavatory attendants, road-sweepers or canteen-workers are unlikely to be replaced in great numbers as the costs for a short run of the appropriate machinery would be prohibitively expensive when compared with the low costs of employing these people. A wide range of industries – wood- and metal-works, petrochemicals, clothing and food-processing amongst others – are all facing the same challenges and problems.

In a slightly different way the generality of employees in offices and service industries have similar problems. The overwhelming majority of office workers do repetitive jobs – typing, filing, collating, post-room work, general administration, duplicating and copying – and all of these are capable of being replaced by new systems. The word-processor, used as the sharp end of a communications and information system and not as a typewriter substitute, is the key machine in this process. The problems of the staff do not stop here, however – senior staff and managers, up to the senior middle grades, are probably the most at risk of all.

Computers can think, up to a point. With artificial intelligence and the fifth-generation machines the point stretches indefinitely. Even now computers can beat very good (though not excellent) chess-players. However, if the chess pieces are upset and placed in different positions without notifying the computer, or perhaps someone cheats, the computer will lose. It can win at chess or make correct decisions only if nothing unexpected crops up, no externalities creep into the calculations. When the new generation of computers comes into more general use even these constraints may disappear, however. Most middle managers base their decisions on a limited and forecastable amount of information, and the new management information systems are based on computers parcelling out data and news on a need-to-know basis. So, as the input is known and there is an expected and restricted output (because over-zealous imagination and initiative are often considered suspect) the new computer systems should be able to do many middle management jobs perfectly adequately, and without long lunch breaks.

Given that it is becoming possible to replace middle managers and administrators, there are two reasons why senior managements will have special incentives to take this option. Managers cost their employers a lot of money and savings can be considerable if their services are dispensed with. Savings on salaries and perks like a company car and pension contributions are obvious; less so is the fact that if a manager goes then other staff like secretaries, typists, and general clerical workers who were associated with him can be released over time too (though the reverse is not true). It is a technological form of suttee. If enough managers are replaced office space can be saved, and buildings can be sold; as the joke goes, 'the company was so successful that it moved into a smaller head office'. Managers also have a tendency to be rather conservative and fearful, at least in Britain. One symptom of this is their inability or unwillingness to use a keyboard, which stems partly from the fact that British schools have never insisted on their pupils typing out essays, as they do in the States, and partly from the idea that keyboarding is 'women's work'. As eight out of ten managers are men this attitude is a great hindrance in dealing with the new technology. With the old communication systems it was a deficiency that could be shrugged aside, but with the new ones the use of a keyboard is essential in operating the system.

It will be some considerable time before voice control is

sophisticated enough, broad-based enough or cheap enough to come to the rescue of the average middle manager, and the 'mouse' (the non-keyboard entry system), though fascinating and useful – especially with the AI machines – is not precise enough for detailed communication purposes. So rudimentary keyboard skills will be increasingly needed by managers. Those without them may find themselves bypassed by the new systems, and few organisations will be able to carry such an uncomfortable and unproductive load. It is more than possible that senior secretarial staff will be able to run the new systems, and moreover take decisions, so the typically British all-purpose middle manager is very much at risk. The specialist is not in a particularly good position either. The new expert systems (which have on memory the cumulated knowledge of a particular subject) allow every office to have the best brains available at the fingertips of a computer-user on a variety of subjects from the law to personnel, and from production engineering to book-keeping. Why bother to keep batteries of your own experts when a secretarial assistant can deliver the expert view, probably more quickly and with less fuss? The day of what might be described as the managerial production line (where managers perform a limited number of specific tasks instead of coping with a variety of situations) has dawned – bringing with it the same difficulties experienced by production workers.

Computers do, however, have their limitations. They cannot be truly creative in anything other than a random sense, so artists, writers, actors and dancers should be immune from replacement, even though they might be affected in other ways. Professionals tend to use skills that are not all they appear on the surface, and although expert systems can be useful, they can't replace the intangible human skills of a doctor or a master chef. Senior managers also have to take decisions based on externalities, on hunches if you like, and computer systems cannot yet do this. So these people will be immune – as will some craftsmen, farmers, sportsmen, judges and all those in jobs which depend on judgement and intuition. The rest of us are at varying degrees of risk as far as technological replacement is concerned.

The extent of this risk is determined by the cost of employing someone relative to the cost of their replacement with some sort of microelectronic system. The balance is currently swinging in favour of replacement, as the costs of new systems continue to fall whilst employment costs continue to rise. Roughly three-quarters of the employed population is at risk, although nothing like this percentage will actually lose their jobs in this century.

The manufacturing sector will continue to shed jobs overall. In this sector the history of the introduction of robotics, computer control and computer-controlled machine tools is one of a diminishing labour force. Whether this is at General Motors or Fiat, at United Biscuits or Hitachi, the rule holds good, and with the advent of flexible manufacturing systems such as CIM we can only expect this trend to spread. Warehousing, stores and the managerial side of manufacturing industry are also affected by the new technologies. Fewer and lighter components mean less to transport, warehouse and invoice; they mean that the production process will be truncated so that there need be fewer managers and supervisors. So employment in manufacturing companies, already falling, will fall considerably further.

Another area offering great scope for reductions in overall levels of staff is that of clerical work, principally because the new technologies have not yet made a real impact on it. There has been a considerable degree of managerial resistance to change, and an equally considerable degree of managerial incompetence in the planning and ordering of hardware and software. Few systems are in operation and, where they are, too many are not being used to their full extent. There are endless possibilities which are not being fully exploited: word-processors for example being used for typing alone, whilst increases in effectiveness are being lost by imposing them on unchanged and inappropriate structures. As and when the truth dawns on senior management, jobs will be shed in massive numbers.

We are also waiting for a national electronic telephone system to reduce the costs of linking other information equipment together and to speed the transmission of messages. In Britain this will not be before the early 1990s. Some larger companies, of which ICI Mond Division is an example, have introduced their own electronic PABX systems, and saved considerable amounts of money through the resulting staff reductions and increased efficiency. The aim will be to link word-processors with mainframe, mini- and micro-computers through a tele-communication network such as cable, if it were interactive and available. This technology imparts an extra dimension to those available at present.

All messages in an electronic system are transmitted in digital form, which means that voice, text or graphics can be transmitted down the same line simultaneously. A word-processor *cum* personal computer will then act as a complete work station, telephone and facsimile machine all rolled into one. A message will be typed out on a processor, and will then go through a systems switchboard to ten other processors and the main computer. It could go anywhere on the network that you want, and you can tag the message so that it enters the screens of, say, three of the others or waits until the screen is free to do so. Other receivers might have the message tagged to enter the memory bank or be recalled after four days because the oper-ator at that number is on holiday. The machine may do that of its own accord for you, having discovered the message left on the other machine, and if you want to augment your message by voice this is easily done using the same machine.

Contrary to the expectations of many commentators, typing jobs as well as secretarial jobs will still be in demand. Secretaries often perform tasks that are not in any job description and, moreover, cannot be replicated by an electronic system, such as making excuses on behalf of their boss or ordering a good table at a restaurant. Few managers will acquiesce in the loss of such a 'treasure'. The jobs that *will* be redundant, however, are the general clerical ones of filing and switchboarding, and in the post room, administrative and information departments. This will be of little comfort to feminists, or indeed anyone who wishes to see equal opportunities in the job market, as most of these jobs at risk are done by women.

Clerical employment is found in every part of the economy: in the offices of manufacturing, trading and petrochemical companies; in state and local government departments; in insurance companies and banks – though these are beginning to streamline their clerical workforce now and clerical staff, tellers and managers are all under threat as the new technologies change the way we look after and spend our money. The larger legal and accountancy firms, the brokerages in the City, hospitals, colleges and universities all employ a considerable number of clerical workers. Millions are at risk, especially in the large commercial centres like London and Manchester, Paris and Brussels, Munich, New York and Tokyo.

The use of communication satellites has internationalised this problem, and it is now possible to import or export clerical work technologically; a document raised in New York, for example, can be typed out in Melbourne or Taiwan. The same applies to printing. Newspapers can be automatically typeset by the inputting journalist in one country and printed out via a satellite using ink-jet techniques, five thousand miles away, as practised by the *New York Herald Tribune*. Printers, sub-editors and journalists are at risk.

There are so many other industries and jobs under this technological cloud that it is difficult to know where to begin and when to stop. Draughtsmen (with the use of CAD), professional engineers (with the use of CAM), medical and laboratory technicians can all be replaced. The fourth and fifth generation computers (indeed some of the present ones too) do not need operators and will need far fewer programmers, and the use of computers in schools will diminish the need for teachers. Perhaps the largest and most important of the other areas under threat is the retail trade, which employs one in four school-leavers in the UK and which will be able to cut out hundreds of thousands of jobs in stores, warehouses and shops. Almost all of these will involve unskilled or semi-skilled people.

The informal sector is also being affected. There is a robot barman in Chicago, and the Japanese have developed a robot dog to guide the blind – so even animals have their jobs at risk. Dating and escort agencies which use computers to match people, and the pornography industry where videos are replacing live strippers, are other examples of this process.

This industrial revolution has not really begun yet, however. A report by Price Waterhouse in the United States argued that few US companies are meeting their office automation goals, while in Britain and Europe the goals are considerably lower to start with. When the TV set with an on-board computer arrives on the market in about three years' time, it will run the home. This will include the substitution of domestically based work for that which used to be done outside: shopping, banking, booking tickets of all descriptions, writing letters and even paid employment. In Germany it is estimated that by 1990 over 20 per cent of clerical work will be done at home.

The flexible engineering systems are in their infancy, even in Japan, and the electronic telecommunications system is still awaited. Managers are not yet adventurous enough to take advantage of what is on offer and too few are aware of what is possible. It's been a slow start, but we have nevertheless seen a considerable amount of unemployment caused by this new technology. Companies have increased their output (for example, car firms) and are using fewer workers than ever before to do this. Banks are increasing the number of transactions, customers and services while their labour force remains static, though five years ago these changes would have increased their work forces by a substantial number. This is *potential unemployment.*

The new technologies will potentially create a lot of unemployment. It may be in the form of redundancies, or more likely it will take the more painless forms of natural wastage or early retirement, or simply expanding output without increasing the staff. It is likely to be a combination of all these, alongside a very expanded secondary labour market (i.e. those in part-time and temporary jobs).

It is tempting to believe that traditional economic nostrums and slogans will still be relevant. The landowners thought this in the early nineteenth century, but they were wrong. It is very likely that the people today who expect things to be the same in the future as they were twenty or even thirty years ago, or those who point to the thirties and the fact that we recovered from that depression, will be wrong too. We need to look not at the last seventy years for guidance but to the last century – for the skills, the imagination and the fight that enabled the Victorians to adapt. This is the greatest challenge that has faced the concept of employment and work in the twentieth century and we cannot afford to duck it. Employment is far too serious a matter for this to happen.

4 Conventional theories
in unconventional times

In 1979 Michel Syrett, a reputable author and journalist, went to an equally reputable and very large publisher specialising in paperback books with a proposal to co-author a book on helping the unemployed. The publisher replied that unemployment would not last, so there would be no market for the book. Although he did find a publisher eventually (the book, *How to Survive Unemployment*, was published in 1981), this view was by no means unique. The conventional wisdom was that unemployment was a temporary phenomenon and that we would soon be back to normal. This was shared by both government and opposition parties, although they differed as to the policies that would bring this about. As we saw in chapter two, however, in historical terms we were already back to normal times.

The first three months of 1984 produced an even more instructive example. For each of these the long- and short-term economic indicators were looking good; growth was relatively high and the government was feeling pleased with itself. The underlying trend of unemployment rose in each of these months, however. Two government spokesmen and one minister from both the Department of Employment and the Treasury variously professed themselves to be 'astonished' and 'baffled', adding that 'this should not be happening'. Indeed, according to the most basic economic theories, it should not have been. Economic growth should lead to jobs, increased productivity should lead to jobs, wealth creation should lead to jobs, a lower inflation rate should lead to jobs. Britain was, indeed still is, shedding jobs far faster than they were being created, despite meeting three of these criteria. The same sense of failure and bewilderment applies to many of the other European countries.

Slowly but surely people are realising the existence of a new set of relationships between employment and other economic factors. Some politicians, journalists, the odd economist, the very occasional trade union leader, several industrialists and an awful lot of the public who bear the brunt of what is happening (and moreover know more of what is happening) are questioning the old slogans. The UK's 1983 general election demonstrates this inasmuch as the party that was held responsible for acquiescing in, perhaps even creating, the high levels of unemployment won handsomely, while the party that was most vigorous in its condemnation of this unemployment and promised to restore full employment lost heavily.

Every country has its own myths and legends, old wives' tales and superstitions, patent remedies and nursery rhymes. There are occasions on which the repeating of a phrase or slogan for long periods appears to convince the chanter that the slogan is correct. It is possible to see this happen at church and prayer meetings, at football matches and on political demonstrations; it is tempting to ascribe the adherence of the Establishment in the UK to some of the 'conventional wisdoms' concerning employment to this self-hypnosis. Certainly some of them seem as poorly founded in reality as the patent cures that were peddled in the Middle Ages.

One of the most frequently repeated of these slogans is 'create wealth and you will create jobs'. It sounds good, it has a ring to it, but what does it mean? First, what is this wealth that we need to create? Does this mean that we are as deficient in wealth as we are deficient in jobs? It would be very difficult to argue that in the UK, or indeed any of the Western European countries, there is a shortage of wealth. Wealth is a store – it is not income; the two are fundamentally different but are too often confused.

Think of a lavatory cistern. This is a store of water – it is wealth. Do some work, in this instance pull the chain, and a stream of water is released to flush the system. This is income. Wealth resides in the great art treasures that we hold in public and private collections; it is in the houses, factories, offices, stately homes, the farms and fields, the coal, the minerals and the oil. Wealth is our jewellery, our machines, our roads and railways and – more to the point – our savings. Europe is a treasure house of wealth, though it may be somewhat less than we imagine because much of it is not easily realisable. If you sell paintings or buildings in large numbers, their price begins to fall because it reflects their scarcity value rather than their intrinsic beauty or utility. Extract too much oil and the price drops, as OPEC knows to its cost.

When politicians talk about wealth creation they really mean profits. 'Create wealth and then jobs' really means 'create *higher profits* and the jobs will follow'. Economic theory, indeed history, identifies many imperfections in this process.

The assumption is that these profits will be invested and that the investments will create new jobs; it is also assumed that all savings (which form a large percentage of our wealth) will be invested. But this money is rarely used to create capital, buildings, plant or machinery. The savings ratio has been, in the recent years up to 1982, nearly 17 per cent – in other words £17 out of every £100 was saved (although this has fallen in the last three years). The insurance companies, the pension funds and the unit trusts together have assets of about £128 billion (almost certainly a gross underestimate) and received £11.8 billion of new investment in the first nine months of 1984 alone. Yet gross investment by all the commercial and manufacturing companies was only £9.3 billion in the same period in the UK, and less than one half of this would have been in net or productive investment. These are vast sums of money and represent vast amounts of wealth, yet where are the jobs that came from it?

The Wilson Committee enquiring into the future of financial institutions in 1980 received roughly two hundredweight of evidence. Of this all but about forty pounds made the point that the City was awash with money but that it was not wanted by industry and commerce (this information emanated from the financial institutions themselves). Where does the money go, then? The financial fund managers, who have immense power, place a considerable tranche in the gilt-edged market; this goes to fund existing government debts and the governments' borrowing requirements and to a great extent does create jobs. Some of the money goes into property (mainly existing office blocks), some into art, some goes overseas and buys stock or part of Watergate or a Brussels hotel. Most of the rest goes into the equity market – shares in companies. This is what we all call investment because, as Sir Kenneth Cork has put it, we do not have another name for it.

Real investment takes place only when there is a rights issue of shares; in recent years this has accounted for less than 10 per cent of all deals but is now considerably higher. The increase, however, is explained by the current government policy of privatisation. This involves selling state assets to the private sector and, rather than creating jobs, has been preceded by a heavy loss of jobs during the period when companies were fattened for the sale. Most dealings are on existing shares, however. Aunt Aggie dies, for example, and her estate contains a thousand ICI shares. They are sold through a broker on the stock-market, it is likely that the buyer will be a financial institution, and you get the money. Not a halfpenny goes to ICI – there has been no investment, no jobs created. This is known as the secondary market and it accounts for the overwhelming number of stockmarket equity dealings; if more people want to buy ICI shares than are selling them their price rises – if this is reversed the price falls. In either event there is no impact on jobs.

Vast wealth exists and more is being created every day. However, it is moribund. We do not need to create it so much as to resuscitate and then use it. This may mean that the short-term 'best' return will not be made, which is why large companies with vast profits like GEC prefer to loan their profits on the money markets rather than invest in physical capital.

This brings us back to the point about wealth being used as a proxy for profits. Increased profits may not lead to more jobs, and any company can do what GEC has been doing so that few if any new jobs result. Many of the largest companies are trans-national in character which makes it very difficult, at times vitually impossible, to determine what their profits or losses are in any one country. Profits can also be held in a strategic reserve or be reinvested in new plant and machinery, but the acquisition and use of the new electronic technologies from the new investment created by these profits is more likely to *decrease* the number of jobs than *create* them. Profits can also be distributed in the form of increased wages, which may create jobs by creating demand for goods and services, although many of these may be imported. Dividends to shareholders are another way in which profits may be distributed, but here we run up against a peculiarly British problem.

A large and increasing percentage of all shares are held by the financial institutions, the pension funds, the unit trusts and the insurance companies – but not the banks. These are bodies which leak out their money slowly. A pension fund is funded over forty years, so that the rate at which money reaches the economy in a mature scheme is roughly $2\frac{1}{2}$ per cent of income per year, which means that $97\frac{1}{2}$ per cent of dividends remain trapped in the fund. Insurance companies specialising in life funds are based on an even longer time frame, so even less of the dividends reach the wider economy each year. And, as unit trusts are used as capital growth devices by many people, they too are held for considerable periods, so profits do not readily get back into circulation in the UK.

Overseas, however, things are different. In Germany, Japan and France the banks convert long-term loans into equity capital, something frowned upon in the UK. Banks release their funds speedily, thereby creating capital from them, so that these countries have a distinct advantage in a modern society which needs to invest quickly and imaginatively. The UK system was designed at a time when the merchants and the early joint-stock companies held sway, but it is hopelessly inadequate today. This is less a political argument than an objection to the inefficiency of the real investment mechanisms in the UK when contrasted with the efficiency of the savings movement. When the amount of money going to building societies, which are not allowed to invest in companies or their shares, is taken into consideration, the position looks grave indeed in the UK.

There is a theory that wage increases can create jobs, and there is a counter argument that wage increases will destroy jobs. The latter is propounded by the current UK and US governments and in modified form in Germany and France. But the former is the typical Keynesian argument which suggests that if expenditure, including wages, is increased demand will rise and jobs will be created. This has been practised on and off over the past thirty years in Europe, although earnings have been controlled by a variety of regulatory mechanisms in different countries. Classical economic theory (i.e. *laissez-faire*), which predates trade unions and collective bargaining, underpins the second of the arguments. It is dependent on the theory of a 'market' wage imposed by employers. The newly industrialising countries (NICs) are the prime examples of this form of economy, where effective collective bargaining is discouraged and where there are always queues of people waiting for assembly-line or other jobs. This is very similar to the situation in the first half of the nineteenth century when the industrial revolution was consolidating.

Clearly, low wages themselves do not create jobs; if they did, then the USA would have high unemployment whilst India would have none. It is more accurate to say that a society with an ability to reduce wages and recruit or discard labour as needed will stand a good chance of creating employment, if only of a temporary nature. More is needed, however. The right social environment for risk-taking, high mobility of labour, vast natural resources, risk-capital providers, a massive demand for service and luck are all essential, at least if the USA is to be taken as a model in this respect. In essence it has to be as it is the only country in the industrialised world that has created more jobs than it has shed over the past five years. There are signs in mid-1985, however, that the momentum cannot be sustained and that unemployment is about to rise again.

In 1984 the OECD estimated that its member countries would have to generate 20,000 new jobs per day net up to 1989 if unemployment were to be reduced to the 1979 level of 19 million. Only the USA has managed to do this, while Japan, although increasing its *employment* figures, still has higher unemployment figures than in 1979, and unemployment in the European countries is still rising. The British government has repeatedly stated that wages will have to fall for jobs to be created, but has not yet had the courage to point out the full extent of the reductions that will have to take place in security benefits and the other safety nets that have been erected since 1945. Nigel Lawson has gone so far as to suggest that the future of European employment is low-wage and low-technology. This vision will no doubt appeal to budding housemaids, road-sweepers and window-cleaners, but to few others.

Most academic evidence tends to dismiss the government's view, the most recent being from the National Institute of Economic and Social Research. There is, however, an attraction in the theory in that it tends to apply to other marketable goods. If the price of one brand of soap powder falls, then, everything else being equal, one would expect more of this brand to be sold. But labour markets are not that simple, especially in the UK and Europe. Mobility and information are anything but perfect. Unions and employers' organisations distort a 'perfect' wages market, where employers and employees are free to bargain individual wages. Demand for the sort of services that would result from low wages is low, especially in the UK, and moreover there is a strong hostility to these forms of service jobs. The class-conscious British see them as menial and worth little – on both sides of the class barrier.

Several questions have to be asked, and answered. If a fall in wages will create employment, then how much do they have to fall before this policy succeeds? Will it be to starvation level? How long do you wait to find out? How low do wages have to fall before the policy is abandoned? Is the idea to compete with the NICs on their terms? Why would the formal sector employ these unfortunate people – surely the informal economy would snap them up? How would unions behave, and how would they be handled, while all of this was going on?

The theory of wage reductions is often combined with the other widely held view that increases in productivity inevitably lead to increases in jobs. This is based on the German economic miracle of the fifties and sixties, and was strongly espoused by the Treasury, the unions and the Labour governments in the sixties and seventies. The increases in productivity were relatively modest, not like the huge increases that are possible today with the use of the new technologies. The most important factor, however, is that productivity itself means nothing – *it is the relationship between productivity (output per capita) increases and output growth that has the crucial effect on the number of jobs that are needed.* This is just starting to become a respectable argument.

The Times can be fairly described as a supporter of the present UK government, especially its approach to economic policy. In late 1984 the following words were used in the course of a discussion on unemployment. 'The heart of the matter is not excessive real wages, but that productivity growth has been above output growth.' The same sentiments and arguments can be found in both the *Guardian* and *The Financial Times*. The message is clear. If productivity increases outstrip output increases fewer people will be needed to produce the goods. This is an inevitable arithmetical deduction given the definition of productivity as the amount of output per employee.

The new technologies are guaranteed to increase productivity substantially. The increase has been described as a 'quantum leap' by academic commentators not usually given to hyperbole. Output growth, however, has been at or around 4 to 5 per cent in the more successful countries and 3 per cent at best in countries like the UK. On nationally based data this must mean increasing unemployment. In reality the situation is even more critical.

Productivity increases are not spread uniformly across the economy or geographically across the country; in some industries and areas they have been particularly high. The telecommunications divisions of electronics companies or the motor manufacturers are good examples of this higher-than-average rate, while town halls and insurance companies demonstrate the reverse. In addition to this patchy technological implementation some areas are also running down the older industries like shipbuilding or textile manufacturing, with inevitable loss of jobs. The replacements, if there are any, for these lost jobs tend to be in new factories using modern equipment and a smaller and different labour force to that used before. Both of these factors reinforce the regional employment imbalances that cannot be explained by reference to national statistics.

As the application of microelectronics spreads at a faster rate, so each area of the country will have most of its employing institutions increasing productivity at the same time. Inevitably this will lead to increases in unemployment until such time as the effects of the resulting savings in costs seep through the economy. In the past such changes would have been in a localised area only and there would have been the luxury of time to allow these 'economic multipliers' to work. On a regional scale this breathing space is not available.

We continually refer to productivity in terms of people rather than machines, so that it is possible to arrive at productivity increases by reducing the number of workers more than the level of output. In the UK this form of decline, which has been happening over the past five years, has been hailed as a victory! It has resulted in Britain having to be a net importer of manufactured goods for the first time since the industrial revolution began, as industries, companies and products have disappeared from the British scene along with the jobs. Increases in productivity as currently measured may be a very bad thing indeed.

Economic growth has clearly accounted for both the increase in the number of available jobs and in living standards over the past century. However, the periods when high productivity techniques were instituted were also those of high employment. In the same way that the productivity/output ratio is the important factor in unemployment terms the productivity/growth ratio plays the same role.

The new technology has been displacing people in the medium and medium-low salary ranges; the low and high paid have been retaining and will continue to keep their jobs. Most of the displaced people will be receiving less money than before and will buy less; they will have fixed commitments and will often literally have to eat into savings and redundancy payments (if they exist). Many of the people still at work and those in jobs created by the new technologies will be in the better paid knowledge-intensive posts. They will not spend all their money, but will save a considerable percentage. As we have seen earlier, however, these savings tend not to create jobs in the UK. For aggregate demand to rise, the amount that the people in work spend has to increase more than the reduction in spending caused by those now unemployed (the amount of savings that will have to be spent must be deducted), and there will need to be increases in wages that will gladden the heart of any militant trade unionist before this can happen. Whilst increased demand cannot guarantee increased jobs, because productivity may have increased or imports have risen even more, the converse appears to hold true. If demand falls then the number of available jobs falls with it.

To add to this dilemma, the more people that are unemployed the more the government has to spend on them. If it does not do this, and their benefits are cut in real terms, demand falls again, but if the benefits keep their value some governments may compensate by cutting spending in other areas. This becomes a vicious circle with each round of cuts adding to unemployment. It is becoming intensified because there is now a greater incentive for government itself to cut costs by introducing the new technologies into its own services – thus adding to unemployment. This is the scenario which is being played out all over Europe at present. For the unemployed or for the young it is a question of 'heads you win, tails I lose'.

*

Increased investment may not lead to more jobs. There are two main forms of investment: capital widening and capital deepening. Capital widening is where new plant and machinery add to the existing stock, often being used in new ventures, and to make new products. This may well add to the total number of jobs available, but when the product or service that stems from this investment competes with and overcomes an existing one, the overall number of jobs may fall. There will be a time lag, however, and the resulting job losses may not show up for years. An example of this was the advent of the cinema in the UK, which replaced the music halls. Most of the jobs created by the cinema were overseas, whilst those in the labour-intensive music halls were lost in the UK. The same result can occur when a transnational company makes an overseas investment combined with a predatory pricing policy. The company *may* force indigenous competing companies into bankruptcy; it is then able, faced with a complete lack of competition, either to reduce its output, import its own goods from the parent country, or raise its prices and use the profits to invest overseas. Whichever happens, the overall number of jobs diminishes greatly because of an original capital-widening investment. The zip industry in the UK followed this pattern.

Capital deepening is worrying the OECD. Some eight years ago the Organisation commissioned a report by Professor McCracken which pointed to a surfeit of capital deepening investment in Europe. This is where companies replace existing plant and machinery in order to provide the existing ranges of goods and services more efficiently and often at a lower cost. This may not mean a lower price, however. This position has not changed, and at the beginning of 1985 the OECD were warning that capital deepening rather than capital widening was still the major investment pattern in Europe. As most of this investment is being used to apply electronic, computer and robotic technology, it is little wonder that unemployment is continuing to grow apace. Increased productivity is the aim, but demand and output are lagging behind – in short we can produce far more than we can use. It is like the 1880s all over again.

This is not the case in the USA, Japan or many of the NICs. Capital deepening, although prevalent, has been compensated for by the emphasis on investment in brand new products –

including many of the new capital goods that we are using in Europe.

Another familiar argument is that the new products that will be spawned by electronic technologies will create new jobs. Here one has to distinguish between the product that is replacing an existing one and one that is for a new market. A new product for an old market may actually diminish the number of jobs available. The digital watch is a good example. It replaced the old clockwork watch, which was labour intensive to make and was produced in Switzerland, France, Germany and the USA. The digital watch was demonstrably new, it was cheap, and more of them were sold than of the older type. Employment in Europe and the USA fell dramatically (it has recovered somewhat since) but the jobs created in South-East Asia, where the new watches were assembled, did not compensate for this. The watches were easy to assemble and the small number of components were mass-produced; in fact packaging became the largest slice of overall employment.

Several things happened here: the total number of jobs decreased, the jobs migrated across continents from the old industrial to the new industrial countries, the new jobs contained far less skill content, and an increased number of the new goods were sold.

The electronic pocket calculator is a similar but different type of example. Pocket calculators simply did not exist ten years ago, and their uses as promotional presents or gimmicks make them a new product for a new market. The desk calculator, however, is not produced today, but ten years ago it was made by a very labour intensive process. The pocket calculator, which replaced the desk and business machines, is thus both a new product for a new market and a new product for an old market. Exactly the same thing has happened to employment as happened in the case of the watch. Overall, fewer people now manufacture and assemble calculators; employment in Germany, France, Switzerland, the USA and Dundee in the UK has been lost, but gained in South-East Asia and Central and South America, whilst many more of the products are being sold. A new product for a new market, however, *must* lead to increased employment overall.

There are and probably will be more new products for new markets stemming from microelectronics. It is very difficult to identify many of these, however, despite the considerable number of professionally optimistic commentators and forecasters trying to do so. Within the electronics industry itself there is the production of silicon chips and the machinery that is used in the processes. Personal computers, video recorders and tapes, software, databases, credit cards, telephone information services – none of these could exist without microelectronics and there were no previous markets for them. The same applies to several pieces of health equipment like scanners, and some medical and surgical techniques, whilst there is a massive scope for using new technology for the alleviating of hardship amongst the disabled and the elderly. Part-time and temporary jobs in the ancillary industries, shops, marketing, deliveries and administration will also increase.

There are limits to these, however, especially in the foreseeable future, and the numbers involved will not be that great. Products will tend not to be completely replaced, but amended with the use of microelectronically based components; these will both replace older electromechanical and electronic devices and add to the functions of the product. Amended products, however, tend not to add to demand or jobs. Even if a new car model has three extra microelectronic gadgets, both fleet owners and individuals will wait until the depreciation time is ripe before they replace the old one. Only those who need to buy things that others don't have, the 'positional goods' addicts, will buy the car as an addition to their normal purchases – by definition these must be a tiny percentage of people. Washing machines and cookers, electric blankets and bathroom scales – these are among the amended products which have neither added much to demand nor to employment. Indeed, employment has fallen overall because, as General Electric in the USA and the Japanese manufacturers have shown, these are products that can be made in automated surroundings, and the replacement of miles of wiring with a single integrated circuit has enabled new techniques to be used.

The amendments to some of these goods may be so overwhelming that they really represent a new product for an old market, like the digital watch. In theory the price of these goods should fall as their manufacturing costs fall too, but this, all too often, is not the case. Amended products rarely fall in price, other than marginally. A car with five electronic functions increases its price at the same rate as one with none at all. It is more often true that prices rise in order to establish the gimmick, though some products may not increase in price as much as they might have done had there been no change in components. However, given the haphazard nature of European and especially British pricing policy this is very difficult to substantiate. Certainly, factors like energy prices or the exchange rate have a greater impact on prices than the addition of new microelectronically based components.

New goods, especially those for new markets, generally fall in price after an initial high-price period. The ballpoint pen is one example, the calculator another, and home computers, video equipment, colour television sets and microwave ovens have all dropped their prices since they were first developed. Clearly this adds to demand and hopefully to jobs. There are two reasons, however, why this optimism must be tempered.

The number of jobs created in the industrialised countries making these or similar goods are few. Many of the new products are manufactured in the NICs (South Korea or Taiwan, for example) and if the complete article is not made there the microelectronic components almost certainly are. The jobs that do remain in the industrialised nations divide into two distinct groups: those in the retail, some light assembly and service sectors, and those in the highly knowledge-intensive sectors which deal with design, engineering and systems. The first of these groups employs a significant percentage of women and part-time workers. The second group is made up of very skilled programmers, designers, electronics engineers, analysts and computer scientists. This particular group of people not only have little difficulty in getting jobs at present, most of them are in short supply across Europe. However, this may not last for all that long in some instances, of which programmers are an example.

The change in the trading patterns of the world brought about by the ascendancy of Japanese manufacturing industries and the ascent of the NICs may force a re-evaluation of the free-trade principle in the coming years. Free trade, one of the economic holy of holies, is based on the principles of competition between equals and comparative advantage. The different cultural ethics of the West and East, together with the new technologies, give Confucianism a decided edge over the relatively libertarian West. The conventional wisdom is already under threat: the EEC imposes external tariffs, the Americans have had an arrangement with Japan to restrict car imports into the USA, and the French use all sorts of non-tariff barriers. This 'wisdom' is honoured as much in the breach as in the observance, and the equalisation of national potentials brought about by microelectronics may prove to be the spur to new conventions in world trading arrangements. The comparative advantage has moved away from its traditional epicentre in the northern mature industrialised countries.

Most governments believe that a reduction in working time is irrelevant, at best, to the numbers of people employed. Only the Dutch, Belgian, Swedish and French governments appear to have taken a more adventurous view. The unions, however, along with some of the European Socialist parties, believe that reductions in working time will increase employment, and the European Trades Union Confederation has a very firm commitment to reduce the working week to 35 hours – or by 10 per cent. The EEC Social Committee has had a draft policy to force a reduction of hours worked across its member nations, but the UK government refuses to ratify it. Whilst the grounds for this refusal are more to do with high emotions and the maintenance of profits than doubts about the effectiveness of the policy, the evidence supporting the shorter working week as an employment generator is distinctly underwhelming.

When, in 1973–4, the Conservative government under Edward Heath imposed a three-day working week in response to disputes in the energy industry and rocketing oil prices, one would have expected a reduction in output of about 40 per cent. But after two years, when all the statistical adjustments had been made, it was discovered that output had fallen by less than 20 per cent and productivity had actually risen. At the time it is probably true to say that there was a degree of overmanning in British industry so that some slack could be taken up. Today, however, matters are different. In much of the production industry sector the hours worked by people are becoming less relevant to output, as systems rather than employees are increasingly the major factor.

In recent years there have been reductions in working time across European countries, with the most limited of success in terms of the creation of employment. In Britain cuts in hours have often been negotiated with the proviso that unit costs of products and services remain static or are even reduced. As a result there has been a considerable reduction in the number of jobs as a result of agreements designed to protect or increase the number of jobs. Despite this the policy is continuing unchanged. In Holland and Belgium the governments have cut working weeks in the state sector, while in France 'solidarity contracts' have attempted to give employers fiscal incentives to create jobs. These initiatives, along with the newly reduced hours of work in the German engineering industry after a lengthy and bitter dispute, have done little to stem the tide of job losses in these areas, however. Indeed, they may have proved to be an extra incentive for the employers to introduce new equipment and new shift systems instead. Over the past two years the basic hours of work for manual workers have been reduced from 40 to 39 or 38 in most European countries, yet unemployment has climbed in the relevant sectors in each of the countries.

Several factors are at work. The new technologically based systems automatically improve productivity, and compensation for decreased working time (especially if it is as little as twelve minutes per day or one hour on a Friday, as it was in the UK after a much vaunted 'breakthrough' by the Amalgamated Union of Engineering Workers) can be arranged through system changes. It is only when large sections of labour are withdrawn, as when an extra week's holiday is gained or a four-day week is negotiated, that a real impact on manning levels is noticeable.

Overtime working is the other bugbear. All European countries with the exception of Ireland and the UK have statutory limits on the amount of overtime that can be worked, although these are flouted in many instances. In the UK, overtime is used to raise weekly earnings to acceptable levels. Management and unions have often colluded in this, resulting in low basic rates so that the chance of getting a breakthrough on overtime restrictions is negligible – neither side wishing to do so. Without such a limit, the slim chances of a cut in working hours leading to increased employment virtually disappear.

The re-evaluation of working lifetimes will be dealt with later in this book, but there is clearly a good case for spending less time at a job. This concept, however, requires a much more radical approach than that taken by the European unions. The question of *pro rata* earnings and state payments and subsidies will have to be considered, as will differential retirement dates and the age at which young people enter the work force, amongst a host of other factors. As we shall see later (in chapter seven) the work force itself is changing in a way that enables employers to cope with normal workloads with a smaller full-time labour force. This too makes the drive for the shorter working week little more than a well-intentioned but all too often counterproductive exercise.

There is a consensus building up around the proposition that the service industries will take up the employment slack created by the loss of jobs in the manufacturing sector. America is cited as the shining example. There is, however, a world of difference between the demand for service found in the United States and the almost complete lack of demand in the UK. How many times does anyone come to your car in a self-service garage and offer to check the oil, water and tyres and then clean the windscreen? More to the point, how many Britons complain when this does not happen? American people expect to have fast-food restaurants spotless, the iced water poured and changed and the floors swept. Do they in Britain? In America there are food deliveries, in Britain we have take-aways. In America bus boys carry the supermarket goods to the car, in Britain we are lucky to be able to park anywhere near the supermarket. The Americans get what they demand, we don't get what we do not demand. It is not easy to persuade the British to make a scene or a fuss – our upbringing and education militate against this – but the American system encourages assertiveness. These sort of services will not be available for Britain until both the education and social systems change.

There are two other service areas which are generally cited as good employment growth prospects: entertainment, sport and leisure industries and the large financial sector. The first of these areas will be explored in detail later in the book. It should be the engine of some limited employment growth, although there is a pretty low limit to the number of performers and technicians that a country can sustain without fundamental structural changes within the industry, such as changing Equity limitations on membership and encouraging semi-professional work at a local level. As the trend towards making the home the entertainment base shows no sign of diminishing, this acts as another in-built limit to this area's employment prospects.

The annual growth of employment in UK banks, insurance companies and building societies was 2 per cent in the 1970s and has since decelerated markedly. A paper from the Institute of Manpower Studies in 1984 suggested that these industries are about to enter the decline stage of a four-stage employment process that is controlled by technology. First there is employment growth, then a period of steady state (the present stage), then a rapid decline followed by a steady low-employment state. This lasts until the next phase of technological development. The paper concludes that there is no chance of the financial sector providing a net addition to jobs in the future, and goes even further in claiming that no service industry amenable to microelectronic technology will be a creator of jobs. On the contrary, some will shed jobs. The bank unions agree with this prognosis, as does a government report in France (Nora-Minc), a report from Siemens in Germany and some senior retail trade consultants.

Other services, especially in the person-to-person fields like the health, social and educational services, are capable of being expanded in order to meet existing needs and demands. Most of these services, however, rely upon government funding, so that if the number of jobs is to expand the current attitudes to government spending will have to be reversed. Whilst this Keynesian approach may have a beneficial impact in the shorter term, the inevitable UK longer term economic and social constraints need to be overcome before it can be considered as a long-term solution. Employment in the small business service sector – hairdressers, shopkeepers etc. – should remain roughly as it is.

Overall, however, it does not look as though sufficient jobs will come from this quarter to compensate for the loss of jobs in the rest of the economy. Indeed, there may well be an aggregate loss of employment in services if the policies restricting local and central government spending remain in force for any length of time. This will be a severe blow to those who are pinning their hopes on the service sector as a provider of jobs; regrettably, they will not find out they have been wrong until it is far too late and millions of people will have suffered.

The rules have changed, but those in positions of authority refuse to acknowledge this fact. The chosen methods of reducing or alleviating unemployment are as ineffective as was the carrying of an indulgence against the ravages of the plague. It is a matter of concern that few estates in any of the European realms are doing anything other than despair, and the conventional remedies still hold sway to a considerable extent on both sides of the political divide. It may well be that the populations of the industrialised nations, especially the younger elements, will not allow their leaders to take refuge in them for much longer.

5 The political dimension

What have babies, Mother Teresa, freedom, democracy, and the Queen Mother in common? They are all what the public relations trade calls 'halo' words or concepts. Everyone agrees that they are a good thing and no one will argue against them, at least in public. Every group of people have their own 'halo' words; politicians have more than most.

The phrases 'right to work' and 'full employment' come into this category. No politician can be seen to be against them – they are both universally approved. From time to time a government will argue that there is no such thing as a right to work – the current Tory one has flirted with this – but is most unlikely to carry the argument on beyond the preliminary stage. However, in the Western capitalist (or free) world there is no right to work, nor has there ever been.

All political parties feel obliged to offer the prospect of full employment. This may be one of the main planks in the party's programme, or it may be slightly muted and put in the form of criticising the alternative – unemployment. Most of the left-wing and left-of-centre parties rely on support from 'the workers' and are explicitly in favour of work and the right of everyone to have and do it. The more right-wing parties tend to make less noise about work; the last Conservative party manifesto promised increased employment, but rather quietly. If challenged, however, no Conservative politician would have conceded that the intention was anything other than to provide jobs for everyone who wanted them, although by an unspecified date.

Politicians tend to be at their most confused and confusing on the subject of work. Of course, they do not mean work at all – they mean employment. Most politicians transpose the two, thus helping to maintain the delusion that a work ethic rather than the employment ethic still exists. Because there are insufficient jobs to go around, and employment is considered to be so important by the public, it might be thought that the UK government would consider that it had failed. This is definitely not the case. Ministers have been on the offensive and have been suggesting that the unemployed consist mainly of the work-shy and job-avoiders, in the full knowledge that most of the people without a job would love to have one. Whether or not Norman Tebbit did say that the unemployed 'should get on their bikes' is irrelevant. Most people believe that he would have said it, even though he did not, as it is well within the philosophy of the government.

As the government's 'scrounger' argument was commonly disbelieved, other reasons for the continuingly high unemployment had to be found. The world slump was one of the first of these, but it was soon apparent that other countries did not have problems of quite the same magnitude – after Belgium the UK has the highest percentage of unemployment in the industrialised world. High wages became the next scapegoat, along with strikes (despite the fact that there were so few of them). These arguments were backed up by citing the miners' dispute, unions in general, low productivity, low profits, restrictive practices by workers, the high degree of government spending, local rates being too high, too much bureaucracy and red tape, taxes too high, not enough incentives and sheer laziness, especially amongst the young. Many of these arguments are unique to the UK, especially those which put the blame on unions and their activities. In March 1985 the government finally managed the archetypal British excuse – it blamed the weather.

The excuses and rationalisations are incidental; most of them have been demolished by the more serious newspapers, reputable academics or the better TV analysis programmes. Public feeling about unemployment is so keen and deep that politicians cannot shrug it off. It is not good enough to say 'we are trying to do something about it' if success is proving elusive; scapegoats have to be found, and policies to attack them put into operation.

The right of trade unions to take effective industrial action has been constrained, enterprise zones to reduce rates and the red tape involved in running a business have been tried, tax changes theoretically adding to incentives have been made, employers' financial and statutory employment obligations have been lightened, and it is probable that the government will make 'quasi-jobs' for the young compulsory in all but name. But none of these measures have stemmed the steady haemorrhage of jobs. Where different treatments have been prescribed in other parts of Europe the bleeding has been less severe, although it has not been staunched altogether.

If the problem is as deep-seated, as fundamental and as long-term as I believe it to be, then the attitudes of politicians and the actions of governments are of paramount importance. I am not the only person who believes that unemployment simply will not go away. Various papers have been produced by the Institute of Manpower Studies, surveying both individual industries such as metal working or textiles and the entire national industrial scene, which point to a continuing high level of unemployment and a drastic change in employment patterns. The Science Policy Research Unit has taken a similar line based on technological developments, and the Hudson Institute has also produced plausible scenarios of this type. Research institutes and think-tanks in Scandinavia, Australia, France, Canada, New Zealand, Holland and Belgium amongst others, have come to similar conclusions too. In Japan the trade union Sohyo are suggesting that robotics will reduce the total number of available jobs, whilst independent research is suggesting that the job market for women there is drying up.

Other forecasting agencies which are taking medium- and short-term views are predicting an increased level of unemployment. In its 1985 White Paper on Public Expenditure the UK government itself assumed a continuingly high level of unemployment, indeed a marginal growth in jobless figures, over the next five years. This runs counter to other public pronouncements that they have made on the subject; indeed, it directly contradicts the Leader of the House of Commons, John Biffen, who in 1985 anticipated falling unemployment by 1988. The government is predicting that in 1987–8 over 31 per cent of its expenditure will be on social security, as against 25 per cent when it took office in 1979–80. Much of this will be related to unemployment.

City of London economists envisage continuing economic growth alongside increasing unemployment. Simon and Coates expect growth of over 3 per cent with unemployment rising by another 100,000, while Grieveson Grant anticipate a level of unemployment of around 5 million by 1987. The Society of

Business Economists conducted a poll among over 100 of its members in banking, finance and manufacturing industries. Two-thirds believed that growth would be between 2 and 3 per cent, while at the same time more than nine out of ten forecast a rise in unemployment of between 50,000 and 250,000. The chairman of the forecasting group described the unemployment outlook as 'depressing'. The OECD has estimated that unemployment in its member countries will rise by 2 million over the two years to 1987. As it is also predicting, somewhat optimistically, that the unemployment rate in the UK will remain stable, it may be that its overall forecast is over-optimistic too.

Setting aside the very real feeling of concern that many politicians have regarding the unemployed, the matter of election and re-election looms large on their horizons. Fear seeps in. In Europe two out of five unemployed workers have had no job for over twelve months and governments have started to sense instability. Rather than attempt to treat the causes, however, repressive measures are being taken against people who are demonstrating against the symptoms. The increased funding for the forces of law and order, the harsher juvenile prison regimes and the attempt in some countries to force young people to undertake 'quasi-work' against their better judgement are three of the tactics. Alongside this runs an austere thread of conservative banking principles which contract rather than expand the economies. Both are old remedies, but this is a new situation.

In its journal *Employment Outlook* the OECD argues that better and more flexible markets, including the labour market, and the ability to respond to structural change are the keys to success. It suggests that member governments should direct their policies to these ends. As structural change in social and economic institutions is being driven by the new technologies and is affecting international trade with the NICs at least as much as intra-OECD trade, these keys would seem to be for the wrong cupboard. The OECD believes it will find employment inside, but many forecasters, including myself, disagree. We believe that lasting employment will not be created for another twenty years, at the best. Finding the right key is not the answer, we have to fill the cupboard first, otherwise it will be as bare as Mother Hubbard's.

In the USA the economic miracle has been taking care of

unemployment. It has been falling by 2 per cent over the past year without any need for the government to manipulate the statistics as they have in Britain. Much of this expansion has been in the service and high-tech areas, and the enormous budget deficit – a strangely Keynesian tool for a very monetarist government – is fuelling the growth. However, not unexpectedly this is now starting to fail.

If the American government has been coping, and it is hard to stifle the thought that they are doing so by accident, then they are alone. Governments of all industrial countries have interventionist economic policies to some extent, but the US government tends to put up the money for a given project and then allow companies a free reign in its development. For example, the space programme, military expenditure and research on 'Star Wars' projects speedily inject billions of dollars into the economy, whilst at the same time widening the capital base. The Japanese central government on the other hand (through its central ministry MITI) has considerable power over its companies; it can cajole and threaten, it can instigate research and it can insist on inter-company co-operation. The MITI has powers undreamt-of in Western Europe. Despite this, however, and despite staggeringly high growth rates of output in some industries, unemployment in Japan is rising slowly. Because their productivity rates are increasing so rapidly, growth will have to be even higher if they are not to face rapid increases in unemployment.

The problem for the Japanese government is fourfold. Firstly, it must continue to find new markets for its goods and, secondly, it must maintain the existing ones, which is more difficult than it sounds. Many European countries and the USA are concerned by the Japanese penetration of their domestic markets and have arranged voluntary limits on import quotas or, as in France and Italy, virtually banned Japanese cars (whilst the Americans would like to keep Japan 'free' and successful as a Pacific bulwark against Asian communism, there must be limits to their generosity). China is the biggest new market the Japanese need to secure, and history makes one hesitate to predict that they will make permanent inroads there. Thirdly, Japan will come under pressure to buy more Western goods and relax its protectionism. Japanese companies are opening more and more plants on foreign soil to overcome these problems. They assemble many of their own imported components, but the pressure is mounting for more components and materials to be made locally. In other words, the Japanese are starting to export their own jobs.

The fourth problem facing the government in Tokyo is that the social system depends on success. Paternalism, what passes for social security systems, and the fact that redundant workers are never actually laid off all need to be supported by vibrant and expanding companies. If growth starts to falter, or if too many jobs are exported, the stresses will soon become obvious. The financial system with its very close ties between financiers, banks and industrial concerns is highly effective in growth periods, but the very factors which contributed to success will become the accelerators of failure in the event of the economy slowing down. The Japanese government is walking a tightrope, with some skill at present, but sooner or later the performer will have an off day and disaster will strike.

European governments are still attempting to make do with minor alterations to their economic and industrial policies, and without exception they are continuing to preside over rising unemployment. The German government is promoting earlier retirement (subsidised from the age of fifty-eight) if a new worker is recruited in the retiree's place, and it is also starting to weaken workers' rights by making unfair dismissal more difficult to prove. Part-time work is easier to get and more profitable for the employer to introduce, and arrangements like job-sharing are being encouraged. But despite these actions (perhaps because of them) the rate of unemployment is increasing. In Holland there is also a two-pronged attack; it is now easier to dismiss workers, whilst unemployment benefits were cut in July 1985. On the positive side, the existing voluntary reductions in working time may be supplemented by legal action in the late eighties.

In France, employers are campaigning strongly for a relaxation of the hiring-and-firing regulations and have succeeded in getting the government to reduce unemployment benefits. 'Solidarity contracts', which give government aid to companies that cut working time and promote early retirement in order to provide jobs for the younger unemployed, are said to have created upwards of 100,000 jobs, although many believe this to be an overestimate. Italy has a similar scheme operating with the trade unions. Both France and Belgium have enhanced training schemes for unemployed youngsters, and in Belgium there is a plan to cut working hours by 5 per cent and salaries by 3 per cent in an attempt to create jobs. The UK government also has tried many of these measures; employment legislation has been amended, making dismissals easier and easing other obligations of employers, like maternity-leave provisions.

In the UK various more or less cosmetic attempts have been made to deal with unemployment, and training and 'quasi-jobs' are provided by the Youth Training Scheme (YTS), which is available to all unemployed school-leavers. Over 200,000 youngsters prefer to leave it before their year has been completed, however, or fail to join it at all; the government has been stopping benefit for a five-week period for some of these young people and is proposing to stop it indefinitely in the near future. An attempt has been made to get people to retire early and have younger people taken on instead, and another scheme has tried to promote 'job-splitting' as opposed to job-sharing. Both have been outstanding failures, due mainly to the financial penalties incurred by all who took part. Other projects like Community Enterprise, various skill centres and training courses, some government-inspired enterprise boards and schemes to provide small businesses with advice have proved to be less than dynamic for the most part, and no more than peripheral in their effects. As with the rest of Europe, the UK government is fighting shy of the major problem and is having a singular lack of success.

A good example of this approach came with the political response to the riots in Toxteth in 1981. Because the riots came at the end of a period of unrest around the country, and because it was patently clear that both the conditions and prospects of the residents were very poor, a task force was set up. High-flying civil servants and the then Secretary of State for the Environment, Michael Heseltine, commuted to and from Liverpool 8 for a time. The chief result of their labourings was a 'Garden Festival' which regrettably brought little permanent employment to the people of Liverpool 8 – unemployment is still around 30 per cent. When visitors to the Festival arrive they go directly to it and then leave, so the economic spin-off for ordinary Liverpudlians is far less than that which follows a long Cup run for the Everton or Liverpool football teams.

It may be pretty, it may be the late twentieth-century equivalent of one of the major urban 'greenings' of the mid-Victorian era, but it has failed Liverpool 8 on two important counts. It has done little or nothing to arrest one of the major European examples of inner-city decay, and the project was not initiated by the inhabitants themselves; it was imposed upon them. I shall argue at length later in the book that this is precisely how to guarantee failure. People need to have a stake in their own communities – indeed they have a democratic right to such a stake.

Democracy, in most of Western Europe and in the UK in particular, is more about the mechanics of voting in elections than political philosophy. The concept of a democratic system is to allow an individual the right to express his or her view in the political process. This implies a vote. It also implies that voters will be listened to, but this is not always the case. At both national and local levels some elected bodies behave as though they have dictatorial rights during the period of their office, and they listen to no one. This can be a threat to the very concept of democracy at a time when so many crucial decisions need to be taken about vital issues like unemployment.

The deeds of politicians and governments control the lives of the whole population. Legislation on taxes, defence, legal procedures, town planning, driving a car, drunkenness, divorce, pornography or education affect us all in ethical or personal ways. But most of our lives are lived, and our time is spent, on another plane – with family, friends and acquaintances, in our homes or nearby, and the joys and problems that spring from our personal lives preoccupy us far more than do the concerns of national politics. The local area, the community, is generally unaffected by national party politics, apart from the rare occasion when an external threat such as a proposal for a motorway, oil refinery or an airport intrudes. This isolation is as much a reality in the huge cities as it is in the more rural areas, and accounts in part for the intense hostility that was provoked when non-local police moved into Brixton's communities when difficulties arose there.

Computers and the electronic media are revolutionising politics, however. The computer has refined the art of sampling public opinion, which nowadays can be analysed with such uncanny accuracy (with some notable exceptions like the

87

Brecon and Radnor bye-election of 1985) that it virtually determines policy formation in the USA and, to some extent, in the UK. Television has brought politicians closer to the electorate than ever before. People can see and hear a president or a prime minister in their own homes more intimately and regularly than they can see their own elected national or local representative. Together, these factors have tempted less scrupulous politicians to manipulate popular sentiment and exploit people's fears. The morality of such a policy comes a bad second to its expediency.

This has led inexorably into the politics of 'the week'. The time scale of political decision-making becomes shorter year by year, and when Harold Wilson coined his famous phrase 'a week is a long time in politics' he was to be more prescient than he could ever have realised. Highly dramatised 'emergency' decisions fill the airwaves from the moment they are leaked on the Monday to the moment the subject is becoming cold on the Thursday. Unemployment is presented by the local media in terms of the opening of a new factory or the closure of an old one without any examination of the wider implications. The fact that there is a long-term trend or even a longer term problem is not relevant – human stories take precedence over analysis.

Politicians live and work in this short-term world, and in the UK the furthest most of them look ahead is thirty months. A government spends its first year trying to implement the major campaign promises that resulted in its election. The second and third years are spent coping with the damage that the policies of year one created, and much of the last two years or eighteen months are used to start the next election campaign. Even if one takes a less cynical view, a five-year parliament inevitably imposes a five-year maximum time limit. Long-term problems are incapable of resolution in a system such as this.

Long-term trends in unemployment can be identified by statistical analysis, although it is generally the academic rather than the political world that does the research. In the short-term world of politics few solutions, especially those of a long-term nature, have any hope of identification or implementation, let alone success.

There are occasions when politicians try to look into the future, however. Enoch Powell, for example, has always taken a longer view than most other politicians, however abhorrent his views on immigration may be to some people. James Callaghan, the quintessential 'short time-horizon' prime minister, saw the BBC programme 'When the Chips are Down', on technological unemployment, in 1978 and immediately recognised some of the fundamental truths it contained. He was arranging a Church House Conference on the subject when his short-term instincts failed him and he lost a delayed general election. Many of his senior ministers and civil servants, however, shared neither his insight nor his enthusiasm.

The main element of continuity in British politics is provided by the permanent civil service. It continues throughout changes of government, and acts as the repository of all wisdom – or at least custom and practice. Given this role, the task of senior civil servants should be to identify long-term trends and advise ministers accordingly. But by and large they do not do so; instead they have become even more adept at the short-run control of government than the ministers themselves. This is certainly not a result of individual intellectual deficiencies, it is more a result of an overwhelming ambition to protect the basic *status quo*.

The role, status and competence of the civil service differs markedly between countries. In the USA the Cabinet tends to be appointed, as are most heads of the civil service departments, on a political-favour basis which results in a very short time-horizon prevailing. The Senate, however, with its far-reaching powers, its committee structures and the large armies of researchers and lawyers maintained by senators, can act as a countervailing force bringing longer term issues to the fore-front. France has the most technologically literate civil servants in the world, and as a result they are capable of offering their ministers political advice which is based on their own perception of scientific possibilities, rather than having to paraphrase second-hand scientific reports.

Scientific and technological changes have always created special difficulties for politicians and governments, one of the reasons being that so few scientists enter politics themselves. Scientists are like other people in that they are unlikely to make recommendations or give advice that will reflect badly upon their own work, whilst they will stress the positive and ignore the negative sides of their projects. Civil servants who can both understand this and interpret technological developments for politicians are probably the most valuable of commodities in government today. Governance has never been easy; rapid change and an ever-increasing number of experts dominating smaller and more specialist fields have made it nigh on impossible.

We are in the midst of many new technological advances which are posing terrible legal, moral and political dilemmas. Advances in medicine have made death, hitherto the only great certainty, a debatable occurrence. We now have to decide whether to switch off machines that keep people 'alive' – transplant surgery and another person's life may depend on the decision. The ability to fertilise or even develop offspring outside the natural mother's womb strikes at the heart of nature (as traditionally defined) and surrogacy has become a hotly debated issue. Quite how the law will come to terms with cloning in the coming years is anyone's guess. Legislators are finding it difficult to cope with the uses and abuses of video recorders, tape recorders and photocopiers in the area of copyright, whilst laws constraining abuses of data storage and transmission have, as yet, passed Britain by. As a result the UK is probably the most notorious 'data haven' in the industrialised world. The new communication technologies allow security services to operate without their political masters ever knowing, whilst spying has ceased to be the romantic labour-intensive profession of past years.

Politicians should be leading the public in enlightened debate on these difficult topics and be preparing appropriate legislation. But in very few instances is this happening, the topics themselves being technically beyond the competence of the average politician who prefers the cut-and-thrust of traditional political concerns. Compounding these omissions are the rapid changes that are taking place in the social attitudes of people across the industrialised world.

Governments and ordinary people alike have been left uncertain and bewildered by these changes. Attitudes to divorce, sex, homosexuality, pornography, soft-drugtaking and alcohol abuse have been liberalised over the past years with confusing consequences. Long-held 'truths and certainties' have disappeared, with few new ones to take their place. Widespread unemployment has come on top of these changes and as a result is seen as part and parcel of a difficult period –

merely another symptom to be tackled. The reaction of politicians is to retreat into ever more traditionally entrenched positions. The right becomes more hawkish, the left more convinced of the approaching demise of capitalism. Both take refuge in stronger jargon: the right talk of personal responsibility, self-advancement and law and order, whilst the left preach the class war. Neither approach seems to be relevant to the changing circumstances of today's world, if for no other reason than that they are not sufficiently flexible to cope with the current fundamental changes concerning employment, production and investment.

The nineteenth century, during and after the first industrial revolution, was an unsettled period, and the political system had to change several times in Britain to avoid the revolutions that were taking place across the Channel. The social structure had changed faster than the Establishment institutions but, fortunately for the future of the parliamentary system, true statesmen like Peel and Disraeli were in power at crucial periods. They took the longer view rather than the short-term political expedient, and forced through electoral reforms that they knew would damage the immediate prospects of their own parties. Such statesmen may be needed here before too long to pre-empt social unrest, perhaps all over Europe.

There are growing signs of concern amongst the governments of the EEC countries. They have realised that the type of young person who is likely to remain jobless will be the educational under- or non-achiever; employers are appointing the most suitably overqualified young person for the most menial jobs. So those who found the least use for school have the least chance of finding a job. In Britain this is a very class- and race-based distinction. With the free movement of EEC nationals across Europe applying as much to the young unemployed as it does to the Samsonite-grasping businessman, we can envisage the possibility of a marauding mobile destabilisation squad which would make the average Chelsea football supporters' rampage seem like a choirmasters' convention. This prospect does not fill the EEC Commission staff with joy, but they have been unable to make the member states take the basic remedial actions necessary to head off possible confrontations of this nature (other than police means).

Politicians the world over are in the business of encouraging rising expectations. No political system has dared to go before its electorate without promising more of most things. It may be goods in the shops, it may be education or health services or it may be victory over the enemy, followed by peace and then more goods to buy, but 'more' it has to be. In a situation of high unemployment, the expectations of those without work are bound to be frustrated; the higher the expectations are pitched the greater the disappointment of those who are missing out.

We are continually being exhorted, by politicians, industrialists and trade unions alike, to increase productivity. The fact that most of these increases will come from the applications of machinery or systems, which depends on clued-up management rather than the ordinary worker, appears to have escaped notice. Productivity is in danger of becoming a 'halo' word in itself. If productivity increases are leading to fewer jobs in the short run and the fruits of the productivity increases are not being allocated properly in the long run (a situation suffered by the UK), then the cause of full employment would in theory be best served by *decreasing* productivity. Despite the evidence, despite the increasing number of economic articles on the matter, politicians are moving along the same tramlines they were using fifty years ago. Only the Green party in Germany, echoed by the Ecology party in the UK, has had the far-sightedness to question the shibboleth of high-productivity politics.

Politicians, and indeed most economic commentators, tend to ignore many salient facts about productivity. The all-party Employment Institute, launched in April 1985 in the UK and heavily biased towards the Alliance in its personnel, appears to be falling into this trap at its very inception. It is a hybrid body which will undertake research and campaign on jobs; its precise role is vague, but it seems from its membership that it will be committed to the shorter term, consensus, Treasury/ NEDO/TUC approach. In an introductory *Guardian* article it suggested that although productivity has been low, output has been lower – thus leading to unemployment. It follows, according to the Institute, that if output is raised unemployment will fall. However, as they also wish to raise productivity to increase international competitiveness, output will have to be raised by a greater amount in order to maintain employment. They do not quantify this – indeed they do not even mention it.

Productivity is not the homogeneous commodity that most politicians and journalists say it is. Some industries or services may have high rates of increase of productivity whilst others may have low, or even negative, rates at precisely the same time. Other areas of the economy may have no easily measurable output on which to base any notion of productivity; the public sector, health services, education, and many office and clerical workplaces come into this last category. As these employ a majority of the work force the concept of a national measure of productivity is tenuous in the extreme. This is compounded by the fact that the areas of high productivity growth may be shedding a good deal of their labour force, whilst those of low productivity growth will be shedding none. Overall, productivity will thus appear to be low whilst in reality it is high in the areas that matter; these are the circumstances in the UK today. As the office sector is one where output and productivity is rarely measured – and this sector will soon be shedding jobs in vast numbers – the argument of the new Employment Institute, like that of many politicians, is disingenuous in the extreme.

Traditionally, intervention or letting the free market work are the two separate and distinct political approaches that can be made to try to increase the number of jobs. The government has argued that it is taking a long-term approach to economic policy overall and is looking ultimately for structural changes to create jobs. The March 1985 Department of Employment paper entitled 'Employment, the Challenge for the Nation' states: 'The biggest single cause of our high unemployment is the failure of our job market, the weak link in our economy.' This is rather like blaming a motorway for road accidents rather than the car drivers. Their policy is thus to remove imperfections from the market: to weaken unions, remove the rights of employees, lower wages and encourage mobility.

The alternative view is taken by the Labour party, which believes that direct government intervenion can create jobs. In their paper, 'Labour Working Together for Britain', recently updated, thirty-six separate employment areas are listed, including energy conservation, rail electrification, care of the elderly and canals. Direct intervention is backed up by the Keynesian policies of expanding consumption and demand in the economy, especially in the public sector, through government expenditure. There is no doubt that jobs can be created in this way but, as we don't have an economic climate comparable to the immediate post-war period, questions as to how many jobs, for how long and by when, must be answered. Certainly these methods, along with the more brutal market-oriented methods, have not been conspicuously successful in the recent past.

In 1964 Harold Wilson, the then leader of the Labour party, raised the standard of 'the white heat of technology' and won the general election. Despite instituting a Ministry of Technology and a new Department of Economic Affairs, the policy foundered on the rock of conservatism in all the main Establishment areas, especially the civil service. This has been the only concerted attempt by a political party in the UK to make technological change the pivot upon which its other policies would depend. Its failure has made it more difficult for the tactic to be repeated, yet today such a recognition of the power of the new technologies is more necessary than ever it was in the sixties.

The formation of the new Employment Institute is a recognition that the government's policies are seen to be failing and that the Labour party alternatives leave something to be desired. It is unlikely – given its structure, its potential political schisms and its uncertain role – to make much of a contribution, however, and its greatest handicap is probably that because it is mainly directed by politicians it will neither take the long-term view nor espouse radical alternatives. It too will travel along the well-worn tramlines.

Politicians and governments remain committed to the traditional short-term reactions to long-term unemployment, and tend to stay wedded to a centralist approach. Their attitudes to leisure, however, are more rudimentary still. Other than the French, no government has taken the issue seriously enough to give it a departmental status. In Britain we have had Ministers for the Arts for the past twenty years, but we define 'Arts' in a traditional manner; we have had Ministers for Sport for roughly the same period, but these have often had to double up with other jobs (Dennis Howell was also responsible for drought, floods and cadmium). The French, however, developed a Department of Free Time after recognising that there was going to be more of it, one way or another, in the coming years. It has certainly had an impact on vacation investment and almost certainly raised the consciousness of the French people about the activities that their country has to offer them.

Leisure, or free time, is generally thought of as a residue after the time spent at employment. Governments tax and constrain it to some extent, though leave it to the forces of the market more than any other type of activity, but laws controlling what you can do and where are legion. Signs saying 'keep off the grass', 'no ball games' or 'no smoking' are one area of controls, and another is control over the use of drugs or alcohol or the activities that are forbidden in the name of public decency.

Free time means increased leisure time, and it is of vital economic importance. There would have been much less economic growth and employment if the world had devoted itself merely to the making of capital and essential goods. It is during our time off that we buy most of the things we need, and we spend most of our money when not at work. So we need leisure to survive economically. Given this, the lack of direction or intervention by politicians is surprising in the extreme. But there is still a feeling, especially amongst the more puritanical elements of society, that leisure is the same as enjoying oneself – and by definition this is a bad thing.

Politicians may feel that leisure is a frivolous subject and not a suitable topic for earnest deliberations, or that it carries less weight with the electorate than the more traditional political preoccupations. Whatever the reason, however, politicians tend to ignore the issue almost totally – except when airing a prejudice. The political lip-service to leisure is seen only in the obligatory sprinkling of entertainers and sportsmen in the Honours Lists. The MBEs given to the Beatles were a landmark in this respect, in that popular culture was recognised for the first time, rather than the more elitist sector which up to that point had monopolised this type of award. Later in the book I shall be looking at the differences between the way various groups of people choose to spend their free time, but one thing is quite clear: the unemployed neither feel free nor feel that they have unlimited leisure at their disposal.

Local politicians realise this. Unemployed people spend more of their time in the area in which they live, because not only do they not have to travel to a job but they also have little money to get away. The brunt of caring for the unemployed thus falls on the local councils and other groups. This may take the form of providing facilities for sport, recreation, shelter from the weather or educational, cultural and group activities. It may involve the subsidy of these activities or the transport to and from them. But, whatever the service provided, it falls to local politicians to decide what should be done, how much it should cost and who gets it – central government has little or no role in this matter. For the councillor or other elected member, leisure is an important priority area. Whilst city councils as far apart as London and Wellington, New Zealand have shown considerable imagination in providing all sorts of leisure facilities, their efforts have often been denigrated by their respective governments. Having created much of the demand for leisure activities, central governments then wash their hands of it. It is not a pretty political sight.

Both extreme left- and right-wingers have romantic views about employment. They agree on its medicinal and social properties and both believe that not to work is a sin. However, a member of the Monday Club might feel that not to work in the Soviet Union would be to exercise one's undoubted right of choice, while a member of the Far Left might feel that work in a country like Britain is really a condition of wage slavery and should not be undertaken either. Everyone makes their own exceptions to their own rules.

Politicians all over the world will have to come to terms with the changing circumstances that surround employment, and they will have to shake off the habit of using inappropriate and patronising analogies when talking about economics. Comparing the national economy to running a household, or international trade to the local vegetable market, conceals more truths than it reveals and makes the understanding of economic difficulties that much more remote. Politicians will have to tell the truth in terms that people understand, without talking down to them. The idea that 'real jobs' lie at the disposal of the private sector alone, and that most public sector jobs are somehow artificially created and of no real value, is another non-truth that will have to be dropped from the (Tory) political vocabulary. This is perceived as nonsense by most people who have needed health care, boarded a train, drawn a pension or picked up their child from the local school. It is, however, a nonsense that forms the basis of current UK economic policy.

There may well also have to be changes in the ways that politicians and governments think about costs and benefits. It is clear from the period 1980–5 that a government committed to the reduction of inflation at any cost will reduce employment. In doing so the concept of economic costs has been paramount, and that of social costs has been forgotten. In the short term a reversal of the current government policies in the UK as well as in other European countries could well reduce unemployment. To what extent, for how long and what other economic and political costs would be incurred are all matters that we shall follow through in the course of this book.

Other political points arise. Can political systems cope with the stresses that will arise from the conjunction of free markets and the new technologies? This will inevitably lead to a regressive distribution of incomes and wealth because the owners of capital are made more efficient at the expense of non-owners. Can permanent high unemployment be socially acceptable over the long term and under what conditions? Can a state committed to total employment cope with a technology that can deliver the goods and services but needs fewer people to do so? If a technology exists which gives the option of very high efficiency and productivity gains can a state command that it should not be used for these purposes – or indeed not be used at all? Is there a way of using the technologies to increase the welfare of most people but not to increase productivity? These are questions which will have to answered in practice, not in the abstract, before this century is out.

In democratic states we give our political representatives remarkable power for the duration of their period in office. We allow them to control the flow of information; we allow them virtually unlimited freedom until they have to face the electorate again. In a fast-changing situation there needs to be a check on this authority. Their power implies responsibility, and this must mean telling the truth, no matter how painful, and putting proper choices to the electorate. In turn this means a change in the attitudes of politicians in both government and the opposition parties.

If the existing politicians do not lead this re-evaluation then new ones will. We could see the upheavals of the nineteenth century all over again – and for precisely the same reasons.

6 Who does and who will do what

Small numbers are easy to comprehend. We can understand a mining disaster when four men have been killed or a fire which makes a family with three children homeless, and because of this our compassion is easily aroused. When confronted with disasters on the scale of the famine in Ethiopia or the gas leak in Bhopal the numbers are so great that after an initial spurt of guilt, anger and charity the numbers of maimed, dying and dead often tend to numb our reactions. The same is true of unemployment.

We can get angry when a son or daughter cannot get a job. We can despair when a spouse is made redundant or is retired early and cast into a personal and economic limbo. We can tut our tuts in the local pub about the closure of yet another small firm or worry about the new pressing machine in another, but the numbers involved in national statistics are too large. We cannot grasp either the sheer scale or the human misfortunes that underpin the figures. They lose their meaning.

There is another sense in which we cannot cope with size and that is when we look at society as a whole and ask what it does and how it goes about doing it. Even a single medium-sized town can create problems of scale. Society has become so complex in its interrelations that the simple question of what it is there for cannot be answered easily. The concept of employment, of a job, is one of the few that strikes a common chord. However, if you ask people why some jobs are done, whether they are useful, whether we need them or who thought them up, you will not be overburdened by perceptive answers.

We tend to create jobs to make others, and yet others to check that the original jobs are still being done – for example, the second secretary to make the tea and do the filing, or the personnel manager whose job is to look after other workers. There are people who are doing jobs, have done jobs, are training to do jobs or are looking for jobs. In short it is like an ant heap, though a very dignified one. The regimentation is nothing like as fierce, the demarcations nothing like as rigid, but the motive force is provided by employment – in fact the entire reason for the existence of society, or bits of it like towns, cities and suburbs is employment. This of course stands the original reason for work on its head; work was originally done to survive, and now we live to be employed. Remove work and the structure does not collapse, it deflates. The numbers involved in this are huge, even when looked at only in the context of the UK. In March 1984 there was a working population of 27,106,000 of whom 23,986,000 were employed.

Human ingenuity shows itself in all its forms when it is put to the task of defining and naming jobs. Some have a beauty of their own – 'sagger maker bottom knockers' have an advantage over 'clerk, grade 3' every time. There is a continual evolution of jobs, partly as a response to technological changes and partly because the needs and demands of people are not static. The acceptable level at which we feel people should live changes. When Josiah Wedgwood made his two famous studies in the late eighteenth and early nineteenth centuries of poverty in York, with a twenty-year interval between each, he knew that he was not comparing like with like. The definition of poverty had changed. Standards had risen, and what was tolerated initially was considered to be poverty the second time around. The TV set is today's touchstone: twenty years ago it was a luxury but today access to a set is considered an essential.

There is a constant ebb and flow of new jobs to meet new needs, and old jobs disappearing because they are outdated. The job of social worker is one which has been stimulated by the concern that society has shown towards people who find that they need assistance to cope with today's society. It did not really exist forty years ago, and films like *Cathy Come Home* and real-life tragedies like that of Maria Colwell (or, more recently, Heidi Koseda) have hastened the development. This sort of change, where people's attitudes are evolving, runs alongside the change in consumption patterns resulting from new products or services. New treatments and techniques of health care bequeath us with scanner-operators, for example, or video-cassette salesmen or indeed bingo-callers. Other jobs like quillpen-making, accumulator-charging or taking in washing have disappeared, while new forms of jobs spring up within existing organisations. The information engineer, the knowledge engineer and the telecommunications manager are examples.

Some trends can be discerned in this process, and two of them are of great significance. Firstly, there is the shift of jobs away from the manufacturing sector into the service sector. Many of the new positions are what can be defined as communication or information jobs and are performed by a totally different set of people from those who were working in the manufacturing sector; this shift is not confined to the UK but runs the length and breadth of the industrialised world. Secondly, there is a large increase in the number of women participating in the labour force, mainly as part-time and temporary workers, and again this is a worldwide movement.

In 1961 37.5 per cent of the labour force worked in non-manual jobs in the UK; by 1984 this had risen to 52 per cent, an absolute majority. These are estimates, however, as it is not easy to define a manual or non-manual job. In which category would you place a shop assistant who may have to move heavy loads, or a train driver whose skills nowadays are more like those of an airline pilot? The definitions must be regarded as arbitrary and subjective. The self-employed, a significantly increasing proportion of the population, are not included in these statistics; if they were the percentage of non-manual workers would be even higher. However, the service sector absorbs a greater proportion of workers in the UK – 64.5 per cent in March 1984 as opposed to 55 per cent a decade earlier. By the middle of 1983 the average in the EEC was 53.5 per cent and Holland, Belgium and Denmark all topped the 60 per cent mark; Sweden has an even higher percentage, and in America a staggering 68 per cent of workers are in the service sector. In all industrialised countries these increases have been stimulated by corresponding decreases in employment in the manufacturing sector. In the USA only 22 per cent of workers are in what they term the 'smokestack' sector; in the UK it is 26 per cent.

These similar figures conceal very dissimilar scenarios. In the US industry has moved, has changed, has invested, has innovated and pioneered and overall has competed; fewer people work in it because it is more efficient. In the UK industry has fewer people working in it because it is less efficient, has not invested, has not innovated and has seen its share of the world trade decline. 1984 was the year when the UK imported more manufactured goods than it exported for the first time in its history. It is supposed to be a 'leaner and fitter' sector – and it is certainly leaner. As Margaret Thatcher put it, 'Who could have foretold in 1970 that today [1984] in Scotland there would be more jobs in the new electronics than there are in steel and shipbuilding?'

The rate of women's participation in the labour force has been rising sharply all over the world, but while it would be nice to be able to attribute this to anti-discriminatory social forces the opposite tends to be the truth. Women are a cheap option for most employers. In 1982 58 per cent of women in the UK, 75 per cent in Sweden, 61 per cent in the USA and 50 per cent in West Germany were available for work. In the UK over 43 per cent of the working labour force was made up by women in June 1984, nearly half of them working on a part-time basis. Many of the jobs are in the service sector, especially in the retail trade, but an increasing number are in the newer manufacturing industries. Light assembly is replacing heavy manufacturing industry, and women are providing much of the labour – both skilled and unskilled.

It is impossible to overemphasise the importance of this shift. The traditional solutions to many problems will simply not work in the future. The assumptions that our fathers and grandfathers made about their right to decide the disposition of family resources are no longer practicable. As this applies to the mobility of family units the effect on the job market and/or the institution of marriage will be immense.

These changes come about in the context of an overall decline in the demand for labour as expressed in the conventional labour markets. This does not mean that all the needs and demands of any one population are being met or that there is nothing left to do in the world. Equally it does not mean that each person doing a job is meeting a need or demand or adding one iota to the welfare of others. The International Labour Organisation (ILO) has estimated that one billion new jobs will have to be created by the year 2000 if there is to be full employment. The director-general, a realist, added, 'It has to be fully understood that there will be no situation of full employment if we are speaking of conventional employment.'

People work to meet the demands and the needs of others, and this work is usually done in the context of employment. The demand for goods and services and the needs of people (not at all the same thing, as I shall argue later) should thus determine the amount and the type of work that is to be done. In fact they do do this, but only in part. Income and wealth distribution, geographical location, educational patterns, age and health distribution, peace or war, and variables like the policies of governments and the level of technological sophistication have a greater impact overall. Total employment depends on these and a multitude of other factors, some of them incapable of being quantified.

Unemployment depends on a different set of factors, however: the number of people in the work force and whether it is increasing or decreasing, the age of retirement and the age of entry into the labour force are all influential. The number of hours worked per year and the years worked in the average working lifetime affect unemployment too. The social environment (especially concerning the role of women), the definitions of employment and unemployment and the methods of collecting the data referring to them also have an effect on the statistics. Finally there is the vexed question of how a labour force is defined overall. It is not as straightforward a concept as it appears at first sight; only recently (February 1985) the government acknowledged that their figure for the number of people in the work force was wrong and that employment overall had been increasing more rapidly than they had thought. One reason was that most of these extra jobs had been filled by people not registered as unemployed. In other words they were tacitly admitting that the unemployment figures were wrong too.

In this chapter we are not interested in the number of people who will be *unemployed* so much as those who will be *employed*. To gauge this we will have to make estimates and judgements about other matters, such as the number of people in the work force, the number of hours worked, the political attitudes over a lengthy period and the take-up and progress of technological change.

Chapter three contained a profile of the types of people who may well be surplus to requirements in the labour force in the future and chapter four outlined the macro-economic background. These need amplification and refining. Output per head is rising; it fell from 1978 to 1980 but by the end of the first quarter of 1984 it had risen by almost 20 per cent – an increase overall in excess of 6 per cent per year. Output per person per hour worked has risen almost as swiftly, which means that for a given amount of goods and services, fewer people will be needed to deliver them – or fewer people hours will be needed. The amount of goods and services delivered over the same period rose by less than half as much. Over the past decade one can trace the parts of the economy that have shed the most labour, and most are in the manufacturing sectors. In March 1984 there were 7 per cent fewer people working than in 1974 – an overall loss of about 1.5 million jobs. Within this total, agriculture lost 17 per cent of its work force, metal manufacturing lost 42 per cent, mechanical engineering lost 27 per cent, the motor-vehicles sector lost 40 per cent, the textiles, clothing and leather sector lost 44 per cent, and even transport operated with 15 per cent fewer people. Other sectors like finance, education and medical services all increased their manpower.

There is a similar trend at work today. Productivity increases are accelerating in some industries more than in others, but still accelerating overall, while growth of output and gross domestic product is far less. Given the projections for the flatness of world trade and the low levels of growth in other industrialised countries (but the high level in the newly industrialising countries), the productivity/output ratio will probably remain broadly the same over the next five years, though if anything this errs on the side of optimism about output in mature manufacturing countries like Britain. Beyond the five-year period one is in the realms of prophecy rather than prediction. *The acceleration in productivity is, however, starting to come through in a totally different set of sectors. It is this more than anything else that will result in fewer people being needed to produce and deliver an increased number of goods and services.*

The new technologies are introduced to increase productivity or efficiency; this need not be the sole reason, but at present it is. There are some parts of the economy, notably in the public sector, where these are difficult if not impossible to measure. How do the armed forces measure their productivity? What is the measure of the Home Office's efficiency or the effectiveness of the Department of the Environment? In all cases it has to come down to cost – the lower the cost, the better or more efficient the service is thought to be. The same principle applies to local government and health services. The fact that efficiency may be gravely impaired does not matter in this scheme of things drawn up by accountants and endorsed by cost-cutting governments. The easiest way to minimise cost is to reduce the number of workers, preferably replacing them with new systems.

The sectors which have increased their productivity so markedly in the decade since 1974 are those which have started, *merely started*, to introduce the new microelectronically based techniques. Nearly every example in chapter three was from an overseas country, and most were from the USA or Japan. There is a long way to go in Britain before the flexible manufacturing systems are in place (there is only one small experimental one in operation at the time of writing), but no doubt there will be a gradual introduction of these techniques into the UK and Europe. The most intensive wave of new system changes, however, will be in the white-collar working areas and the service sector.

A UK factory worker has equipment valued at around £12,000 at his or her elbow; the average office worker has only £1200 worth of machinery at his or her fingertips. As the percentage of the labour force working in offices increases, so the incentive to make this part of an operation more cost-effective becomes stronger. The same constraints that apply to the private sector apply to the public sector in this respect. In neither case can productivity be measured with accuracy other than for typists or telephonists, whilst managerial effectiveness is not only unquantifiable, it may actually be counterproductive to make an inefficient manager more effective (inasmuch as his or her inefficiency would be given a wider reign). Nevertheless, this is the area where the largest amount of new technological penetration is about to take place. This applies particularly to 'information workers'. In the USA a recent survey estimated that over 60 per cent of workers can be defined as working with information in jobs as various as teaching, librarianship and telecommunications engineering. This analysis was used to determine the jobs most at risk from the implementation of microelectronic techniques in the workplace.

The motives and disciplines of private sector managers are

different from their counterparts in the public sector, however. The private-enterprise manager works under the constraint of the profit motive, or at the least the avoidance of loss; this is what the company is about. A manager makes his or her reputation by increasing profits or sales or market share or whatever. A public sector manager, on the other hand, has no similar yardstick by which his or her status can be easily determined; the one that is generally accepted is the number of people under the direct and indirect control of the manager. As a result the public sector management is less likely to accept a technology that reduces the head count, and thus damages the basis of their own power and esteem, than their counterparts in the private sector. This will create a considerable differential between the two sectors in the rate of adoption of the new technologies, despite considerable government pressure.

There have been several attempts to estimate the numbers and types of jobs at risk. In 1978 the Science Policy Research Unit (SPRU) at the University of Sussex took broad occupational groupings, such as information-handlers and industrial or agricultural workers, and graded them at high, medium or zero risk of replacement by technological means. Over a fifteen-year period the estimate was for a 16 per cent job loss – or 4 million fewer jobs. The maximum-risk jobs identified by SPRU included library assistants, draughtsmen, billing clerks, telephone repairers, book-keepers, warehousemen, materials-handlers and typists. These are all information-related jobs. If they were repeating the analysis today they would almost certainly add some others; retail trade employees, transport workers and middle-range managers would be on the high-risk list, along with some jobs in the financial sector.

Where are the jobs of the future going to be? Who will do them? To answer these questions we must make some basic assumptions. I shall assume that for at least ten years the shortening of working time will have little appreciable effect on the supply of jobs, although it may well do so subsequently. I shall assume relatively unchanged government policies with regard to the new technology itself, continued parsimony in public spending and a general capitalist rather than socialist philosophy (but I am not including the detail of everyday government in this). I will also assume that there will be an imperfect take-up and/or exploitation of the technology because of social factors, as well as self-interest and incompetency, and that this will result in a less than 75 per cent return on efficiency from the new systems overall.

Using a combination of the SPRU and the American risk analysis (based on research by the US Department of Commerce office of telecommunications in 1976) and medium- and long-term forecasts of the growth of various industries, the composition of the labour force in these industries and the application of newer technological systems and machines to them, the following estimates emerge. These are neither predictions nor forecasts – they are merely signposts along the way to the future; over the lengthy time periods involved predictions are a nonsense. In *The Collapse of Work* we used a similar system with, in the short term, very creditable results and, as with that analysis, I have attempted here to take into account all the compensating factors such as increased profits and incomes of those in work, and the multiplier effects that they will have on the economy. The new jobs, and indeed new industries, that have emerged since then will also be taken into account, as will the current high unemployment levels. It is interesting that this is greater than Clive Jenkins and I suggested would be the case in *The Collapse of Work*, yet at the time we were accused of scaremongering and undue pessimism.

I will take June 1984 as a starting point. The base statistics are from the Department of Employment *Gazette*, and the industrial categories are aggregates of the indexed industries; the data refer only to people in employment. There were 20,917,000 of them in June 1984, of which 11,759,000 were men. In addition to this there were 2,440,000 self-employed, some 300,000 in the armed forces and 3,200,000 registered as unemployed. This gives a total labour force of nearly 27,000,000. Three projected time periods will be used: a short term up to around 1990, a medium term up to 1995 and a long term up to the year 2010. The data are in thousands.

There are three distinct bands of change. The first, in and around the 1990 period, is of an increase in the present level of technological change at about the same rate as at present but over a wider range of industries. The second, from the end of that period to the mid-1990s, sees the information and, more especially, telecommunications revolutions. All electronic telecommunication systems like Systems X in the UK and the cabling of homes and businesses, especially with interactive fibre cables, will coincide to give an explosion in the quality and quantity of communications whilst reducing their price; satellite technology should be aiding in this as far as the Europeans are concerned. The changes brought about in this band will affect information workers and clerical and administrative staffs. The third band, around the turn of the century and into its first decade, will bring the proper use of expert systems and artificial intelligence machines through the 'fifth generation' technology. This will not only reduce the numbers of managers and administrators, it will increase the efficiency of all control and information systems and create new robotic and sensor forms. This third band will have as great an impact as the silicon chip has had – it will be a watershed in itself.

Agriculture, Forestry and Fishing

Present	Short	Medium	Long
330.4 (men 246.9 women 83.5)	300	290	260

There are some technological improvements and increases of unit size savings possible in these industries, especially in large-scale agriculture. The limited job losses will affect men and women equally.

Energy and Water supply

Present	Short	Medium	Long
627.3 (men 545.5 women 81.8)	600	500	400

Whilst the numbers in the coal-mining and oil-extraction industries will decline and the nuclear industry is capital intensive, some new energy forms such as solar, wave, hydrogen and the use of barrages should employ additional people in the long term. The female clerical areas will be reduced substantially.

Metal manufacture and extraction

Present	Short	Medium	Long
254.3 (men 232.3 women 21.0)	240	220	200

Steel tube and alloy formation are processes which will be affected by control technology improvements and more efficient stockholding. Women are employed mainly in the clerical areas and will lose jobs accordingly. The newly industrialising countries (NICs) may be *the* strong competitors.

Chemicals, artificial fibres and non-metallic products

Present	Short	Medium	Long
541.6 (men 409.8 women 131.8)	540	550	580

This is a sector where the indigenous technology is at least as buoyant as microelectronics. The new cryo and microbiological products will be made in this sector, as will those genetically engineered. The increases in jobs from these will be more than sufficient to replace the jobs lost in the clerical, administrative and managerial areas. Many of the new jobs will be in research, however, and highly knowledge intensive.

Metal goods

Present	Short	Medium	Long
383.7 (men 296.8 women 86.9)	310	290	270

This entire area, from the foundries themselves to the manufacture of metal doors and windows, will be under increasingly heavy pressure from the NICs. Imports will rise if a construction boom takes place, as so much capacity has been lost and this will exacerbate the employment problem. The new technology will affect indirect employment (storage, transport, clerical, etc.) more than the actual production areas.

Mechanical engineering

Present	Short	Medium	Long
782.3 (men 660.9 women 121.4)	650	550	450

Shortages of some skilled personnel notwithstanding, this is an area where the new technology in machine tools and robotics plus the flexible manufacturing systems will replace skilled labour. Women generally do the clerical/administrative jobs and will lose their jobs in the medium term – before the men.

Electrical, electronic, office and DP engineering

Present	Short	Medium	Long
729.6 (men 499.0 women 230.6)	750	650	500

Demand for all these products will remain high. Much of it will be met from overseas suppliers, however. The light assembly jobs that will not be automated will be done by women until the longer term, when even those jobs will start to disappear under pressure from fifth-generation robots. This industry is the one which will use the highest element of the new sophisticated equipment as the managers will be familiar with it and there will be less of a culture barrier.

Motor vehicles and transport equipment

Present	*Short*	*Medium*	*Long*
590.1 (men 525.2 women 64.9)	550	500	350

The pattern of world vehicle manufacture should ensure a presence in the UK for strategic purposes, if little else, by the mass-market producers. The medium-term job losses will be information-related. The longer term losses will be due to the introduction of new systems and materials in the manufacturing process. Flexible manufacturing and the use of robots in almost all processes will be the main changes.

Instrument engineering

Present	*Short*	*Medium*	*Long*
110 (men 75 women 35)	100	80	60

The new electronically based instruments need far fewer people with less skills to manufacture them. Pressure from overseas will diminish the industry even further and it may follow the UK motorcycle industry into oblivion. If not, women will probably make up the majority of the work force in the long term.

Food, drink and tobacco

Present	*Short*	*Medium*	*Long*
617.3 (men 364.8 women 252.5)	550	450	400

The use of computer-controlled processes will continue to make inroads into employment in this industry, as will changes in social habits. The growth of home shopping and ever larger hypermarkets will mean the standardisation of products (labels apart) and the need for less labour. Men and women will be affected equally.

Textiles

Present	*Short*	*Medium*	*Long*
233.7 (men 120.2 women 113.5)	200	200	160

This is an industry in decline in the UK, but it is also a low-paid industry. This factor, along with a high degree of existing technological change and a growth in specialist areas, should maintain employment. The major job losses will be due to communications improvements.

Leather, footwear, clothing

Present	*Short*	*Medium*	*Long*
297.2 (men 84.3 women 212.9)	270	250	230

Another industry in decline in the UK with the classic symptoms of a low-paid labour force. The introduction of laser-cutting and computer-designing, plus competition from overseas, have reduced the labour force considerably in the formal sector, though the fashion and designer sector should expand. In the informal or black economy the entire industry is flourishing. Few men will be employed in the industry in the long term.

Timber, wooden furniture

Present	Short	Medium	Long
204.7 (men 164.8 women 39.9)	170	140	120

Yet another declining industry in the UK with a very reduced labour force. Overseas competition plus the use of high-technology machinery in the large companies and the increasing use of other, mainly plastic-based, materials will reduce the work force even further. Reproductions will be the growth area – but some will be in the informal sector. Some women clerical workers will lose their jobs in the medium term.

Paper, printing, publications

Present	Short	Medium	Long
487.6 (men 326 women 161.6)	440	380	300

The technologies of printing are proceeding apace, but have as yet merely scratched the surface of possibilities. Both men and women have their jobs at risk. Satellite-driven printing and changes in the way in which we receive information (i.e., by going electronic) may make my long-term figure very optimistic, however.

Rubber, plastics and other manufacturing

Present	Short	Medium	Long
249.2 (men 163.1 women 86.1)	220	200	200

Much of this industry is conducted in small units and these should retain employment, although the rubber industry is ailing in the UK. There will be losses in clerical functions and in some sectors like toys, but other small product lines associated with tourism should fill the gap, providing imports are resisted.

Construction

Present	Short	Medium	Long
974.8 (men 856.1 women 118.7)	850	1100	970

This is an industry with many under-used resources, not the least of which is the unemployed labour force. Whilst current policies and high interest rates will depress the industry even further, so much needs to be done that employment should start to recover in the medium term, before new communication technology and the smaller buildings that will stem from it arrive in the longer term.

Wholesale distribution and agents

Present	Short	Medium	Long
957.8 (men 661.1 women 296.7)	800	700	500

The current moves towards automatic stocktaking and warehousing, and the newly found ability for sales reps to input directly into the productive process, are bypassing the wholesaler. The information technologies will affect the direct mail-order houses and women's jobs, whilst shopping from home will reduce the work force even more.

Retail distribution

Present	Short	Medium	Long
2114.7 (men 793.5 women 1321.2)	2000	1700	1150

This industry employs more women and more young people than any other. The growth of the supermarket, automated checkouts, and automatic stocktaking and replacement have decreased the labour force over the past five years. The newer technologies, leading to shop/bank credit and deficit cards and shopping from home via teletex, combined with a British hesitancy about demanding service, will decimate this work force in the longer term. I do not expect to see the Japanese-style robots as shelf-stackers etc, except as a gimmick in one or two stores.

Hotels and catering

Present	Short	Medium	Long
1008 (men 349.6 women 658.4)	1050	950	900

Basically this has to be a labour-intensive industry, though there are opportunities to reduce staffing in the reservation side of hotels and the fast-food side of catering. Tourism, however, should always be solid in the UK – given favourable exchange rates and a relatively stable society – and it is tourism that keeps this industry going. This is not an industry in which the British care to work, and vacancies tend to be filled by foreigners on work permits.

Repairs of goods and vehicles

Present	Short	Medium	Long
208.8 (men 161.3 women 47.5)	220	200	200

As more microelectronics find their way into goods, so the number of parts that can go wrong decrease and, at the same time, products are supposed to be more reliable. However, service people will continue to be needed as both the number of gadgets increase and the microelectronics themselves are not conducive to home repair.

Transport and communications

Present	Short	Medium	Long
1301.6 (men 1039 women 262.6)	1200	1100	700

On the transport side railways are declining, while the other services are getting more capital intensive. Optimal scheduling and planning are removing jobs, as is the increase in the number of cars. On the communications side the electronic telecommunication systems decrease employment in exchanges, post offices, switchboards, and among service engineers, postmen etc. New types of communication systems will develop, however, and along with motorised messenger services will compensate somewhat up to the longer term.

Banking, insurance and finance

Present	Short	Medium	Long
745.8 (men 352.6 women 393.2)	740	600	400

An industry at a point in its development ripe for technological transformation. Home and shop banking, home and store stockbroking, home and shop direct insurance-buying, plus a probable all-purpose finance house premised on the building societies, promise to cut employment in this sector. As the entire industry exists to transfer information – the fifth-generation machines will reinforce this pattern.

Business services, rentals, real estate

Present	Short	Medium	Long
1129.4 (men 617.8 women 511.6)	1200	1100	700

The new communication technologies will make some inroads into an otherwise expanding area, especially in the small business sector. The fifth-generation systems, however, will remove the need for many of the employees, but may also inspire them to open some new businesses of their own.

Public administration and defence

Present	Short	Medium	Long
1543.7 (men 839.2 women 704.5)	1400	1200	1000

Current government policies will be followed by the wave of communication technology breakthroughs. This sector is *par excellence* the 'shuffler' of information and is very vulnerable to job loss, especially amongst women.

The fifth-generation systems will have less of an effect than they could because of the hostility shown by the senior management to their implementation.

Sanitary services
Present	Short	Medium	Long
295.1 (men 114.6 women 180.5)	300	300	250

There will always be a need for some people in this sector. Over 90 per cent of the women involved work part time and are low paid, and many more work unrecorded in the informal sector. The smaller office sizes and more efficiently controlled disposal systems will see some reduction of employment in the longer term. The low wages will probably hold back the development of robotic replacements.

Education and public research and development
Present	Short	Medium	Long
1673.1 (men 603.8 women 1069.3)	1550	1550	1250

The current cutbacks in education and staffing have not yet finished; when they have, only the administrative staffs will be under threat from the new information systems. Primary school rolls will be starting to rise at this time too. In the longer term artificial intelligence and home learning will reduce the numbers of teachers. Given the present predominance of women in the primary sector, it will be men who bear the brunt of the job losses. Research and development jobs will remain roughly static; there will be more R and D, but cleverer systems will mean human job losses.

Medical, health and social services
Present	Short	Medium	Long
1814.2 (men 359.2 women 1455)	1800	1500	1200

Women dominate in this sector, with over half of them working part time. There will be new systems in place in the medium term, and new appointment and recall systems, which will cost some clerical jobs. The longer term will see medical expert systems and new equipment so that ancillary professions will be at some risk of job loss. Much will depend on expectations and policy, especially in the social welfare and the other caring services fields. There is a possibility that many of these jobs will be done outside the formal employment sector.

Recreational, cultural and tourist
Present	Short	Medium	Long
465.6 (men 218.6 women 247)	500	600	700

This is a growth area. The natural inclination to prophesy even more people working within it has to be tempered by the realities of the new technologies. Many of the performing arts are becoming capital intensive, e.g. computer lighting. The electronic media will also employ fewer people than one would suspect as leisure remains home-centred.

Personal services

Present	Short	Medium	Long
176.4 (men 42.7 women 133.7)	200	250	400

This is another growth area. Many of the services are of a person-to-person nature – such as hairdressing, window-cleaning and legal services – and are unlikely to be replaced by technological advances, and many jobs now being done in the informal sector will be in the formal sector in the longer term. Small businesses will dominate, as will cooperatives etc.

In the short term there will be 19,700,000 in employment, a decrease of 1,217,000 or 5.8 per cent. In the medium term there will be 18,100,000 in jobs, a decrease of 2,817,000 or 13.5 per cent and in the longer term there will be an estimated 14,800,000 in jobs, a decrease of 6,117,000 or 29 per cent. These figures concern decreases in *jobs*; the increase in *unemployment* will almost certainly be much greater. *It cannot be emphasised enough that these estimates are not inevitable*. My assumptions preclude any halfway radical policy changes. They rule out changes to the way we allocate employment amongst ourselves, changes in the way we control the economy, changes in the structure of employment and changes in the ways in which we control and develop the new technologies. All four of these assumptions should be challenged; this will be done in the second half of this book.

The labour force will, however, be increasing by the end of the century. An extra 1.4 million people wanting jobs will confront the UK over the coming decade, as the 1960s baby boom comes to maturity. However, the self-employed sector will also have been increasing rapidly. At present it stands at roughly 2.5 million people and, whilst many of these businesses are precarious in the extreme and will probably go into bankruptcy, there is an ethos abroad which suggests that such failures will neither deter others from trying nor the same people from having another go. The personal service sector and the tourist market will provide many of the outlets for this, and by the year 2000 the number of self-employed may well be approaching 4 million. It is by no means impossible for this to 'soak up' the increase in those seeking jobs.

Some people believe that one of the more attractive properties of a breakthrough in technology is that the direction it will take and the offspring it will spawn are largely unknown. These optimists see it as a challenge, but there are many pessimists who view this as frightening. Some new industries, categories of employment and jobs are certain to emerge, however.

Knowledge engineers, for example, will be part of a new industry. There will be knowledge and information brokers, knowledge handlers and knowledge consultancies. The transfer of information will transcend indiscriminate database preparation, and experts will be needed to prepare and update the databases and retrieve the information that clients will want. The sheer volume of information that will be available will be confusing and counterproductive unless discrimination and judgement regarding its selection and dissemination is exercised by these new employees. It is most likely that the international nature of this flow of knowledge will dictate that a single country takes the lion's share of the total work market. For many reasons, amongst them the use of English as an international language, the lack of constraining legislation and a large pool of skilled workers in this area, the UK must be a firm favourite to succeed.

In the long term this would provide about 500,000 jobs by early in the next century, although the majority will be knowledge-intensive themselves. Information and knowledge are, and will be increasingly, the power bases of the future. For the UK a pre-eminent position in this field would confer economic advantages similar to those provided by international banking and insurance in the nineteenth century. As well as leading to job increases within the industry itself, these developments could also generate as many as 1 million jobs in other industries over the coming twenty years.

New advances in telecommunications with videophones and teleconferencing facilities are possible, although to date the latter has been a grave disappointment. The systems and equipment have to be developed and manufactured and these should create extra work in communications engineering. Indeed this whole field is ripe for expansion, but there is a grave danger that most of the products will be manufactured in the

NICs – as are many of the clever phones today. The space programme could also be the stimulus to a substantial job creation if the European effort, based on the rocket *Ariane*, achieves a proper lift-off.

Although the category of 'business services' includes computer services (only 57,000 people are estimated to work in this sector at present), this industry will undoubtedly expand. This will be greatest in the software houses; there will be a far greater number of both tailor-made and customised programs for the home, the television controller and businesses. This will mean jobs for a new breed of systems analysts, and new types of programmers. Analysts will have to know about a variety of subjects from sociology to TV repairs or accountancy, and there is a likelihood of far more specialisation in this area. The day of the conventional programmer in the large installation has already passed its peak, except in the security-sensitive areas of defence establishments and systems. The new programmers will have to be far more creative and be prepared to work either unsocial hours or on shifts. There will probably be 'program shops', where we will be able to buy packaged programs on any subject, or have one written for us, rather like the scribe system of earlier ages; computer literacy is not going to spread fast or deep enough to obviate the need for this in the next twenty-five years or so. These developments and the suppporting industry will create at least 250,000 jobs in the longer term.

Communications in a broader sense will form the basis of another industrial grouping. People will describe themselves as communicators or communications consultants, and their jobs will be to chart a path through the increasingly complex communication systems and find an optimum way for an organisation or an individual to get the message across internally or externally. Another 100,000 jobs could emerge here and merge with those in the new software industry. At the other end of the scale, the growth of the home as a centre for entertainment, business and leisure will probably stimulate the transport and delivery services. There is a chance, however, that these will be part of the informal economy – one which will have been growing rapidly up to the turn of the century.

The imposition of VAT has probably been a far greater stimulus to this unofficial economy than high personal taxation or even stark necessity. No one knows how many people are working in this economy in the UK, or indeed in other countries, although most commentators agree that this form of trading is on the increase all over the world. We do have some figures about children working, however. In Cumbria a survey of schools revealed that about 7000 children had paid jobs, yet only 325 permits had been issued! This illustrates the scale of the informal part of this sector. One disincentive to employing people in the formal sector is the cost of social security, health and safety provisions for workers which employers incur, and these are likely to be even higher in the coming years. This applies also to pension funds, which are already starting to look unhealthy in the face of continuing high unemployment, and consequent lower aggregate contributions.

Part-time employment now accounts for over one in five of all jobs in Britain, and about 45 per cent of women's jobs come into this category. It is likely that these will increase greatly in both the short and longer terms. Men will start to take part-time work seriously, especially when sub-contracting, and this will mean an increase in the numbers of people at work – although neither on a permanent nor a full-time basis. Consequently national employment statistics will be even more deficient if they continue to concentrate, as they do now, on the full-time employed or the full-time unemployed. This trend has already started, as we shall see in the following chapter, and about another million people – maybe more – will be brought into the employment net in this way.

Training schemes are supposed to give people the skills with which they can then get a job; they also have the useful function (from the point of view of the government) of keeping those without a job off the unemployment register. As they do not form part of the employment figure either, they appear to be in some sort of statistical 'Bermuda triangle'. In 1985 nearly 700,000 people have been excluded from the figures because they are involved in 'special employment and training measures', and this is despite a shortfall in the YTS placement take-up. With a diminution in the number of school-leavers in the medium term, but with the expansion in the labour force overall, an estimate of about 1.2 million in this category by the start of the next century may prove to be not too far off the mark. This assumes that little or no extra provision will be made or legislation enacted.

Permanent unemployment resulting from a combination of high productivity combined with medium to low growth, as has been outlined, is one future possibility. Another is not to compete internationally, close off the borders to all trade and make the currency non-convertible. This single-state 'Comecon' arrangement could only be undertaken by some sort of dictatorship, however, so great would be the fall in living standards. A third alternative is to muddle along on a low-growth, low-productivity path, as the UK was doing in the fifteen years prior to 1980, but the general consensus of economic opinion is that this would lead to at least another 4 million unemployed on the assumption that competing countries would be growing faster, and that we would still be open to trade and currency movements.

There is little choice in conventional terms. If we remain on our current political and economic path we shall have between 5 and 6 million unemployed people by the early twenty-first century. If we revert to the traditional Keynesian post-war policies then the resultant low growth and balance of payments problems will lead to the same level of unemployment. Only a new approach can come to terms with difficulties of such magnitude.

Of the 6 million or so jobs identified as unnecessary in the longer term to deliver the goods and services demanded (given a modest growth rate of 2 per cent but a high rate of increased productivity of around 8 per cent), we have now discussed 2.8 million. This would give an overall unemployment figure for the turn of the century, or the early years of the next, of 6.3 million. Those in work will be a different cross-section of people. There will be fewer of the jobs traditionally done by women in offices and light assembly, but greater numbers of skilled women will be in the knowledge-intensive jobs as technicians and managers in the new industries. There will be far more part-time working. Manual work, both skilled and unskilled, will be decreasing despite an increase in the construction sector; this implies that men too will be required to do more technical and knowledge-oriented jobs. Unemployment will decline in the under-25 age-range as the bulge passes through. The long-term unemployed, as now, will be drawn from those with the least skills.

The trend in employment is clearly towards what have traditionally been thought of as the 'nicer' parts of Britain. The

Thames Valley and the corridor from London to Bristol have seen a considerable amount of company immigration, and the main job loss areas have been in the older industrial areas of the north, Scotland and the Midlands. There are signs that this may be changing, however. If the cost of setting up or expanding in the south becomes prohibitive, then there will be a stimulus to settle in the cheaper areas, and there is some evidence to suggest that this is happening as the pressure on property prices in the south grows. The cheaper areas are those where demand for buildings is low, and these are the areas where unemployment is now high. Communications will prove to be a less important feature in this decision unless transportation of heavy loads and equipment is needed, as electronic communication will replace much travel. The availability of appropriate skills or qualifications to meet the needs of the moment will be an important factor and these will be spread all over the country, not just in the cities. The 'nicer' parts of the north and Midlands may be in for a revival, especially those areas with ease of access to airports or docks. However, it is easy to be too optimistic in this respect – the herd instinct is very strong amongst companies and economic rationality may fail.

One of the ways to approach the problem of high unemployment is to change the way we think about work. Whilst this is not happening at present, we are certainly changing the patterns of employment in a major way. These changes in turn are having an impact on social relationships. Together, these are revolutionising the way that millions of us in the UK and in other countries approach our jobs and the way we do them. They are also changing leisure time and what we do with it.

There may be less work available in the industrialised countries, but what there is is being done in novel ways. The current slump has acted as a catalyst for two things: new labour-saving systems have been 'smuggled in' past the trade union sentinels, and they have then been used in ways which unions have not always seen as being in their best interests. This set of changes will be of immense importance in the next twenty-five years, although as yet it has received little publicity in comparison with the immense media coverage given to some of the minor changes. In the following chapter I shall examine the new working arrangements.

7 The changing faces of work

Once upon a time, and not very long ago at that, a person would consider their job, their trade or their profession to be one of the most stable features of life. Indeed, the early decision about what job to do was intended to carry them through life; once a plumber always a plumber, once a clerk always a clerk – that was the rule. This was thought to be the scheme of things and most people approved. Despite some exceptions – notably among the self-employed, the few workers who escaped into the managerial levels and the few who just changed jobs – the majority of employed people had a job that defined their position in society almost as rigidly and as permanently as the Indian caste system. This was true through the post-war years up until the early 1970s, when quite suddenly all the certainties evaporated. What our forebears, indeed our fathers, took for granted was no longer true. A quiet revolution has been taking place.

The concepts of a job for life, a skill for life, a full-time job or a permanent job have come under extreme pressure. There has been virtually no planning, no co-ordination, no government legislation and no philosophical or political underpinning for this. These changes were initially dictated by economic circumstances and subsequently fuelled by a combination of technological change and the weaknesses in UK, US and European trade unions.

The changes have been sweeping. The balance of men and women in the labour force has changed and continues to change, paralleled by the drift away from employment in the production industries. Unemployment – particularly long-term unemployment – is increasing, whilst competition from Japan and the NICs is putting pressure on long-established European techniques and habits. This acts as a back-cloth to the changes that are happening in the way that we organise employment. It is an extremely muted series of changes; there is a high degree of fear within the Establishment that the public is not yet ready to acknowledge the existence of these new patterns. Job-splitting – which was introduced by the government – and the job-sharing idea on which it was based, have had some degree of publicity, but twilight shift-working and the growth in short-term contract jobs have escaped press or even TV comment except in specialist outlets. Their image with the public is that they are a second-best measure, associated with problems and unpleasantness, rather than that they are new structures designed to enhance personal freedom and choice, which is the preferred Establishment view.

It *is* theoretically possible for this sort of working pattern to fulfil both of these aspirations, but this is not the case at present. The changes have been introduced by the employers and the employees have, for the most part, no option but to go along with them. The only developments that have been instigated by employees are those which have resulted in the shortening of working time. That this is happening all over Europe and in the UK is beyond dispute; the hours worked per day and per week are less, the number of weeks' holiday per year has risen, whilst the retirement age has effectively crept downwards. The entire working lifetime has been truncated, but it is by no means the first time that this has happened.

Workers in the first industrial revolution had to go to their job for six days a week, and each working day lasted for a minimum of ten hours (often as much as fourteen) for fifty-one weeks of the year. Holy days like Christmas and Good Friday were precious holidays. There was no retirement age and no minimum starting age – it is difficult to envisage slavery as being more arduous. And it is a mistake to believe that these hours were reduced easily or willingly. The ten-hour day was conceded only after a very bitter strike by engineers, and the minimum working age and the prohibition on women and children doing hard or dangerous jobs like underground mining came only after vigorous campaigning and was accompanied by dire warnings by the employers of the potential collapse of industry.

The process of reducing working time has been extremely slow. The eight-hour day arrived only after the Second World War, Saturday-morning shifts were usual up until the 1950s, and paid holidays were not widespread until the 1950s. The next step was raising the school-leaving age to sixteen in 1972.

Each movement along this path has been resisted, often bitterly; the shorter working lifetime is not something that managements have, until recently, countenanced. Even the reduction in weekly working hours from 40 to 39 in the UK was conceded only after an extremely expensive series of industrial actions by the engineering workers' union (AUEW) with the German metal-working unions having to go along the same road in 1984. In recent years, however, there has been a movement which has resulted in total working hours being reduced at a much faster rate. The most interesting factor is that for virtually the first time the employers and their federations have initiated discussions with unions about some of the mechanisms involved. This is not only true of holiday entitlements; the more far-sighted employers have seen what the enterprises which were initially forced to concede shorter working weeks have managed to squeeze out in increased productivity subsequently. There are good reasons, some associated with the new technologies, why this should be so.

The obvious point is that reduced working hours can be in the employers' interests, altruistic employers being thin on the ground in the UK. New systems often need new methods of working and this may mean new shift patterns. Because fewer workers are required overall, an incentive for the acceptance of, say, a five-shift continental system (which involves unsocial hours being worked) will be a reduction in weekly hours averaged over a two- or four-week period. From the employers' point of view this will still allow an overall reduction in the real wage bill, while increasing productivity considerably. The fact that this coincides with a trade union campaign to reduce working hours is a bonus for the employers in that it defuses most of the possible opposition.

The number of hours spent at work has fallen for a second reason. Overtime is the great British epidemic; adequate wages are often earned only by a combination of low base rates and a lot of overtime. In the recent slump, however, overtime working has been reduced. It has always been subject to cyclical variations, although until recently has always been relatively high even at a time of depression. A third reason is that there has been an increase in part-time working, especially amongst women, and this reduces the average number of hours worked in the national statistics. The average tells us little overall except how inadvertently misleading some UK statistics can be. Figures for the weekly hours of those working full-time cease to be an important statistic if those working part-time or for part of a year only are starting to become a significant proportion of the entire employed workforce. When this sector represents the only growth area of employment the statistics become increasingly misleading.

Estimates of the averages of hours actually worked vary quite alarmingly from survey to survey. The EEC statistics simply do not correspond with the UK statistics on the same subject. For example, the EEC believes that for the year 1982 the average working week in the UK was 39.6 hours, yet the UK Department of Employment estimated it at 41.6 hours. Their statistics show that in 1977 a manual male employee worked an average of 45.6 hours in a working week; by 1983 this had fallen to 43.7 hours – a reduction of about 4 per cent. Women, however, worked almost precisely the same hours in both years. In total, weekly working hours fell by 80 minutes to 41.4 hours, a reduction of about 3 per cent. The decrease in nominal basic hours, however, was far greater. There are few areas in the UK where a full-time working week is defined in terms of anything greater than 39 hours; for many non-manual workers the basic working week is as low as 34 hours, while technicians at Westland Helicopters now work a 32.5-hour week as a result of white collar union (TASS) negotiations. It is an interesting breakthrough for unions and the management. New CAD systems had been *in situ* for up to five years but had never been used efficiently. A new double-shift system will enable the company to use their new CAD equipment for 86.25 hours per week, rather than for just over 37 in the pre-agreement period. The benefits (there are financial adjustments too) clearly accrue to both sides, but it is doubtful whether any new jobs will arise from this reduction in working hours – which of course is what the European Trade Unions Confederation and TUC policy is supposed to achieve.

It is overtime working which accounts for the differences between nominal hours of work and the hours actually worked. The UK devotion to overtime is exemplified by the fact that it is almost the only West European country which refuses to impose a legal maximum amount of hours that can be worked. Employers have always favoured it as a method of giving them flexibility without having to take on new staff; union members want it because of the extra money it brings in. In some areas – transport, the post office or local government are examples – overtime is systematic. It is worked week in, week out and the workers' standard of living becomes dependent upon what is seen as a right. Union officials and leaders preach the virtues of low overtime and more jobs, but the sermons fall on deaf ears and fuller pockets.

In 1983 over half the male manual workers in the UK worked overtime, and as a group they averaged over 9 hours per week; far fewer women work overtime and when they do it tends to be in the 2 to 3 hours per week range. Considerably less emphasis is placed on this type of work in other countries. In Germany, for example, a male worker in manufacturing industry worked an average of only 1.7 hours' overtime per week in 1983, whilst in the USA the average hovers at around 3 or 4 hours per week.

What is happening in the UK is that the reductions in the working week are neither affecting the hours of the workers nor creating jobs – they simply add to overtime. In chapter four we looked at this problem and suggested that it was a misunderstanding of the way that the employment system works to suggest that reductions in working hours would create more jobs in an economy. This is borne out by the lack of success in countries where this is a deliberate part of government policy. Countries which restrict the amount of overtime that can be worked – like France, which has a maximum 10-hour day and 48-hour week, or Greece with a yearly maximum of 2500 hours per year – have to ensure that their laws are obeyed. There is some evidence to suggest that there is a great deal of slippage in this respect, but in any event unemployment is rising in both France and Greece irrespective of these laws and despite the fact that both have socialist governments committed to job creation, albeit in very conventional ways.

The hours of work per week are falling but so are the number of weeks in the year that people go to work. Holidays are on the increase. The word has a nice ring to it – redolent of enjoyment, relaxation, amusement parks and sand between the toes. Holiday rain is thought to be of a better quality than work-time rain and is tolerated more readily. People look forward to their holidays in the same way as they do to the approach of the weekend, although whether the participation matches the anticipation is another matter which is discussed later. As a general rule, increases in holiday time are considered to be a good thing and more 'goodies' in the shape of long holidays have been distributed to the British population over the last few years than at any time since paid holidays first emerged after the Second World War.

Two in every three manual workers in the UK in 1972 had holidays of less than 3 weeks per year; by 1974 this had fallen to one in three, whilst this type of deprived full-time worker is now virtually non-existent. In 1972 only four workers out of every hundred had between 4 and 5 weeks' holiday; nowadays 77 per cent have this and a further 18 per cent have more than 5 weeks. This is a veritable holiday explosion. In addition there have been small increases in the number of statutory days available for holidays, though the UK is still somewhat behind the average for the rest of Western Europe. West German workers get nearly 30 days' holiday a year whilst many other Europeans get 25 and over. The USA and Japan, however, have a far lower entitlement of 21 and 15 days respectively, and indeed a survey by the Japanese Ministry of Labour found that, on average, only 9 days of this entitlement were actually used.

Not all of these newly acquired holiday times can be taken whenever the employees wish. As with the nineteenth-century 'wakes weeks', employers close factories, offices or shops for a fixed period. This is particularly true of the period around Christmas and the New Year, but as the weather is not conducive to domestic holidaying in the UK – even if the money were available – this new lengthy holiday often attracts complaints that it is too long and even boring. The closures, however, may well suit the employer – running costs are reduced and essential maintenance can be done without disturbing production.

New features are emerging in the holiday field. Holiday banks are becoming more common, holiday time not taken can be stored and taken at a later date, unpaid holiday time is on the increase, and so is the practice of giving extra days for long service or as a bonus for good performance. Study leave and sabbaticals are a form of non-workplace work which can be treated as a holiday; academics and some journalists and doctors have had this form of leave for a considerable time, and it is slowly on the increase elsewhere – for example among senior management, trade unionists and civil servants.

The longest holiday of all is retirement. As the hours worked per week diminish and holidays increase, so the number of years in a working lifetime is decreasing. This is happening at both ends. Young people are increasingly staying on at school or college or going into quasi-work schemes like YTS, which delays entry into the labour market. At the other end more people than ever, mainly men, are retiring before the statutory retirement age of 65. Many organisations now have earlier retirement dates built into their contracts of employment: miners retire at 63, many insurance companies have retirement from 62 onwards as an option, executives at some companies – for example Shell – retire at 55. In addition to these formal arrangements, informal or emergency schemes to enable an organisation to shed labour have been built around voluntary early retirement schemes. Few people are allowed to work on past normal retirement age (though there are of course some exceptions – notably judges and politicians), so that retirement overall is coming at an earlier age.

This movement is not always so clear cut in other countries, however. In Japan there is a twin move towards setting a formal and immutable retirement age – 60 is the favourite at present – and reducing retirement benefits. The overall ageing of the population is generating this concern, as indeed it is in Europe; in Scandinavia more than one person in five is now over 60, and this is expected to be the norm in other countries by the end of the century. At least two countries are thinking of extending their retirement age and in Denmark it is set at 70; on the other hand in France it is about to be reduced to 60. In the Soviet Union retirees are being encouraged to return to work in great numbers, and over one in four do so, yet in the USA the number of early retirees is rising. This is despite legislation that allows workers to stay at work until the age of 70 without jeopardising their pension entitlements. Incentives to retire early probably account for the findings of a retirement consultancy organisation in Chicago that 80 per cent of employees retire before they are 65; those who stay on past this age leave before they are 67.

So the working lifetime is shortening. A typical manual worker in the manufacturing sector will be working from the age of 17 (after YTS) to 62, for 47 weeks each year and for 42 hours in that week (inclusive of overtime); this is a working life of 88,800 hours. An office worker tends to work less, at about 72,400 hours, because the working week is shorter. These figures apply to men. When pensions were first introduced, it was assumed that all men and women were married and that men would be five years older than women on average in this partnership, so women were forced to retire at 60. For them the average hours worked as above are 75,000 and 67,000 respectively, with the different patterns in overtime working taken into account and assuming no maternity leave. As Charles Handy has pointed out, in his book *The Future of Work*, it was not very long ago that the 100,000 hour working lifetime was the norm, and at the height of the industrial revolution it was nearer to 175,000 – if the worker managed to live until 62. Despite these recent reductions in working hours, however, unemployment has continued to increase.

Employers would welcome shorter working weeks if earnings were reduced on a *pro rata* basis, but not unnaturally both the unions and individual workers wish to reduce the amount of time spent at a job with no decrease in remuneration. The union position is perfectly tenable given that no other income maintenance mechanism exists. However, the resulting increase in the number of people employed (and thus an increased salary bill) could not be matched by productivity increases unless the number of workers were reduced again or demand and thus output was increased substantially. In the former case the whole point of reducing working hours to create jobs would be lost (this tends to be the current position in the UK), whilst the latter requires a complete change in both domestic economic strategy *and* a resurgence, indeed a new direction, in world trade. The amount by which output would have to rise and the length of time it would have to remain at its new height has no precedent in industrial times; it is in the realms of 4 to 5 per cent per year for twenty years.

Shortening working lifetimes will not have enough of an impact on unemployment to make a serious dent in the figures for two other structural reasons. These are, firstly, the growth of the informal economies and, secondly, the new basis of employment – i.e. the growth of flexibility which is being superimposed on the current changes to the working lifetime. This is the 'quiet revolution'.

We have all heard of the 'black economy'. It has been dramatised, indeed glorified, on stage and screen and embraces a wide range of activities from working for cash in a domestic or 'sweat shop' environment, running a small business on the side or having an undeclared second job, to prostitution and activities bordering on the criminal. In all these areas the black economy exercises its influence. How many people work in it or live by it is, by definition, unknown, though estimates do exist. The Inland Revenue put it at 7.5 per cent of expenditure in 1980, a very high estimate, and others have put it as low as 1 per cent – much depends on the definition chosen. Some areas of Britain have survived only because of the informal economy. The East End of London is one of these, as is Liverpool, whilst some of the smaller 'fiddles' have acquired a legitimacy over the years – petty pilfering from employers, managerial/professional manipulating of expenses or the use of an employer's telephone, stationery, photocopier etc. These all take money from the formal economy, reduce demand and so reduce recordable employment. The consequent loss of taxation revenue reduces formal employment even further.

Charles Handy in *The Future of Work* defines two other informal economies, the mauve and the grey. The mauve is built around the self-employed and those running small businesses, many of whom are not profitable enough to be caught in the VAT net. In chapter six I suggested that this sector will grow in relation to the labour force as a whole, and this will be covered in depth in future chapters. (There is an overlap, however, in that some of the small businesses employ people on black economy terms.) The grey economy will be dealt with in the next and subsequent chapters; it is exemplified by the growth of the do-it-yourself sector, the new labour-saving devices in the home, gardening, unpaid baby-minding or knitting – the 'self-service' economy. Both of these other informal economies, legal though they are, reduce the amount of employment within what we consider to be the 'regular' economy, and therein lies their importance.

Flexibility at work is completely different. It applies to the employed rather than self-employed, although this need not be the case – especially as some people have a foot in both camps. The reasoning behind a flexible workforce is the realisation, amongst managements the world over, that it is possible to staff an organisation according to the levels that are needed at any one time, rather than to maintain it at a high enough level to meet peak demand. This is especially true of the UK, where the recent shake-outs have revealed a substantial degree of over-manning. It is unlikely that managers will allow this to happen again, and the new technologically based systems will impose another constraint and at the same time provide the means to keep this flexibility going – it is here to stay.

A type of flexibility which is not truly part of this new system is flexitime. This is a method by which the rigid nine-to-five working discipline can be ameliorated; employees can vary their hours on a day-by-day, week-by-week or year-by-year basis. Each employee has a 'core' time which must be worked; if this is four hours per day then the remaining hours can be arranged to fit the personal circumstances of the individual. This will give a working parent the chance to pick up children from school, a person who wants to go to the theatre a chance to work late and so on. Hours can be banked in the same way as holidays, and an 'overdraft' facility generally exists. One interesting feature is that a form of clocking-on machine is needed to establish the hours worked. Most of the establishments operating flexitime are in the clerical/administrative domain and this type of machine has been kept out of these areas up until now but, where introduced, it has been a success in terms of morale and the maintenance of a contented work force. However, the difference is that flexitime is operated by the employee, and flexible working by the employer.

John Atkinson of the Institute of Manpower Studies has identified three types of flexibility that employers want: *numerical*, to increase or reduce speedily the number of people actually in employment; *functional*, to enable employees to tackle more than one job or skill as and when required; and *financial*, to fit the total salary bill into the external labour market requirements. The new methods of working can all be aligned under these headings.

In order to achieve maximum efficiency under this new regime the internal labour market of the firm is fragmented, which makes it possible for different groups of workers to be treated in very different ways. These new divisions are based on completely different lines from those that have existed previously, and the traditional schism between white-collar and manual workers, while still applying outside a flexi-firm, is less relevant within it. The new division is between the core and the peripheral worker, or the primary and the secondary employee.

Core or primary workers do what our parents believed were real jobs. They are the people who are doing the jobs which are specific to the firm, they are employed on a full-time and permanent basis and they are on a promotion ladder, no matter that it may have very few rungs. The change that has taken place, and that our parents perhaps would not recognise, is the flexibility between jobs. Craftsmen are becoming multi-disciplinary so that the job title of 'maintenance engineer', for example, will now include electrical and electronic engineering skills. As a result of this, many of the older demarcations in industry are vanishing. Intensive and more frequent training and retraining are another consequence of the changes, as is the accelerated move towards 'single status' workers. For the uninitiated, this is the term given to equalising the conditions of service between staff and shop-floor workers and will involve equalising pensions, holidays, sick-pay arrangements and fringe benefits, as well as canteen and car-parking facilities, amongst a host of other in-work class-related differences.

Primary workers tend to be transferred on to incentive pay systems, be subject to frequent assessments and be consulted about their opinions either formally or informally – in 'quality circles', for example. (These began in Japan, where workers and managers meet to discuss production methods, efficiency etc; they are being introduced in this country with mixed success.) As a group their jobs weld them into the fabric of the enterprise; they may have skills which notionally could be purchased in the labour market outside, but in practice they are doing jobs specific to the enterprise. Managers are a prime example of this type of worker, as are designers, systems analysts or production engineers. They may have specific policy duties in an insurance company or administrative duties in a government department, but what they all have in common is that their skills could probably not be replicated instantly by a person recruited from the ranks of the secondary workers. Most of the jobs in this sector are highly skilled.

There are several types of secondary workers. Full-time employees who do less skilled work than the core employees, and jobs which are not specific to the enterprise, make up one of these groups. They are not on a promotion ladder and within the framework of employment law have little job security. The training given to them is minimal, and their tasks are often repetitive in the extreme – clerical, assembly, packaging or sales jobs come into this category. Recruitment is aimed at the high turnover groups, young married women for example, to allow for the flexibility needed. It is this factor plus the dead-end boredom of the jobs which, even in times of high unemployment, guarantees the employer the rapid and constant turnover that is desired. With legislation making it easier to dismiss a person fairly in the UK and other European countries, numerical flexibility is increasingly dependent on these employees. These types of workers existed previously but on an *ad hoc* basis. The difference is that they are now a structured part of corporate personnel policy.

One of the major changes of recent times has been this growth of the secondary employee group who have neither full-time nor permanent jobs. Ken Davidson of Manpower has called these people 'flexiworkers', and from the point of view of the enterprise concerned they meet the needs of all three categories mentioned above. Often they have enterprise-specific skills, but those that are needed only at particular points in time; the jobs may range from assembly to secretarial and from computing to maintenance. Canteen and retail trade staffs form another large chunk of part-timers, and banks and the other finance houses are increasingly using them. Although the Department of Employment is behind the times in that it is concerned almost exclusively with full-time permanent jobs when collecting work-force data, it has estimated that roughly 20 per cent of all jobs are now part-time. Nearly 50 per cent of the jobs done by women are on a part-time basis, while only 7 per cent of men work in this way – although this figure is increasing. Given that for very short periods of work per week, under sixteen hours, National Insurance contributions do not have to be paid, there is a financial incentive for an employer to use part-time employees if possible.

Part-time work is often associated with other changes. Twilight shifts, extra shift patterns and the use of auxiliary production rooms are used to cope with peaks in demand. Job-sharing is another way in which part-time working has been overlaid by another technique. Job-sharing is where two people divide a job between themselves, often applying for it jointly in the first instance. The salary is shared too and, given the hand-over period, an employer generally gets about 115 per cent of normal time for the same outlay. Job-sharing is found in both the public and private sectors, most often among women, and the jobs can involve considerable skills and responsibilities – librarians, editors, senior administrators and doctors, for example. It has received press attention which has been disproportionately large compared with the small number of people involved. The job-splitting scheme, on the other hand, which was the brainchild of the government, launched in 1982 and intended to take a person off the dole to pair with someone already working, has been a flop by any standards. The jobs involved tend to be at the lowest levels, with little financial advantage, and it is more than likely that this scheme will be abandoned to die an early death.

Working for parts of a day or week can fit well into the lifestyle of employees, as well as suiting the employer. Married women, especially those with the responsibility of looking after young children, or those who are single parents, can find this the only way they can get back to work. GEC in Coventry has a very large job-sharing scheme in operation which is staffed predominantly by such workers. Of course other groups can benefit too; for some, circumstances may dictate that they can only work for part of the time, whilst others may actively choose to do so. The main problem, however, lies in the low income and marginal security, and this acts as a limitation on the numbers of people who will take advantage of this type of work arrangement under present circumstances.

Employment for a short period is another method of achieving work-force flexibility. The 'temp', well established in office folklore, is one old-established example of this type of work; the 'casual' dock labour scheme, now ended, was another. In Fleet Street the permanent casual and the temporary casual are well-known characters, and the most enduring of examples is of course seasonal work. Employment at holiday resorts or in children's camps provides staple jobs for students or the unemployed, as does the need for extra shop staff at Christmas. Farmers have always used temporary labour to get the harvest in, ski-instructors tend to be unemployed during the summer months and the ultimate short-term job of the lot is the professional Father Christmas. Some imporant changes have been taking place in this pattern, however.

Whilst actors and performers have always lived with the uncertainty of the short-term contract, as indeed have junior hospital doctors and research people in universities, the people concerned knew the rules of the game before they started to play. This is changing now. Short-term or fixed-term contracts enable an employer to meet surges in demand, planned or sudden, and the skills involved run the gamut of industrial and commercial life. Clerical, managerial and computer personnel, nurses, doctors, dentists and pharmacists are just some examples of this wide range. At the top end of the scale we read about the managing director with the service contract who is asked to leave and does so with a platinum handshake, whilst at the other is a chambermaid taken on for the season at a small seaside hotel. This area of the job market is the one that is showing the most spectacular new growth and is being fuelled by the companies and agencies which sell the services of these staff to the traditional employers. From the point of view of the ordinary employer, this minimises the commitment to the employee in the most dramatic way while at the same time adding precious flexibility. The traditional or seasonal element has been submerged under the weight of this new awareness.

Staffing for the duration of one contract or research project is now becoming a normal method of appointment for these types of jobs. The advantage for the employer is that there are savings on pension and sick-pay requirements, and on holiday entitlements, but the employee may have advantages too. There is variety, which is not available to a person staying with one company or in one job, and there is often a premium on the salary to compensate for the insecurity and lack of other benefits. For an unattached person who does not wish to 'settle down' this can be an attractive lifestyle, especially as some of the jobs involve work overseas. The government of China, for example, has realised the value of part-time and temporary work, and has reached an outline agreement with Manpower, the largest temporary-help agency in the world, to provide and train staff for foreign companies operating in Peking. This is just the most recent evidence of a worldwide shift to temporary labour. Germany and France are both amending legislation to make this type of employment more attractive and viable for both employers and employees.

There are three ways in which a potential temporary worker can get a job. The first is to apply directly to the organisation which needs the labour. The second is to go to an agency which acts as an intermediary and covers a wide range of jobs, mainly temporary, from clerical, computing, managerial and catering to medical and nursing – you name it and they will supply it. The third way is to go to a company which employs the workers and then subcontracts them out to the enterprise which needs the staff.

This is the most interesting from the point of view of future developments. These 'labour only' subcontracting companies are starting to fill the vacuum left by the traditional employer in that they are providing paid holidays, sick pay and some pension entitlements as well as (in one instance) trade union membership. Admittedly, these benefits are well below average at present, but the point is that the subcontractors are starting to act as a surrogate for the responsible employer and are providing commitment to the employees. The most important change, however, is that some of these companies provide training for their workers. In some clerical areas the technology is moving so fast that individual enterprises feel they cannot keep up, (word-processing and information handling are examples), but the labour-only employers keep their staff well trained and up to date. The market is burgeoning for all sorts of staff, and so short of suitably qualified staff are these companies that large incentives are being offered to employees who introduce others to the system.

Companies have taken yet another step towards flexibility by copying the Japanese and buying in some products and services which were previously supplied in-house. Some of this may be done through agencies and temporary-help companies, while a great deal is arranged through subcontractors. It may be using a tea-vending machine instead of a tea-trolley, or using an external specialist agency in software, design or even personnel – the principle is the same. Several small companies supplying components give a sense of security of supply that internal sourcing did not, and in all these cases there is a chance that the new, small companies are staffed by previous employees of the original enterprise.

The 'outsourcing', as it is known, is starting to take different and well-defined paths. Large companies are letting senior executives go and encouraging them to set up their own business – often providing finance, finding premises and other clients or customers. Many of the workers then follow these executives into the new business. The same thing can happen when a department is about to be closed and a limited form of 'management buy-out' takes place; we are witnessing some companies exploding into several semi-autonomous profit centres. Linked subcontracting is a feature of this type of company. Several people in a department might be made redundant by the original employer, and receive their redundancy pay; the employer then employs the services of these people as independent contractors or consultants as and when they are needed. In the public sector there have been the much vaunted 'privatisations' of various services. Building and construction, along with refuse services and gardening in the local government sector have all been hived off to private companies; cleaning and laundry services have met the same fate in some of the health authorities.

There have been complaints about bad service and the poor treatment of workers in the 'privatised' public sector. In one instance the cleaners at Barking Hospital went on strike for over a year as a result of the cuts in earnings that followed privatisation. In some cases the employees in the department under threat combined to put in a bid for the service, while in nearly all cases the existing workers went on to the new employer – except those who accepted redundancy terms. In most of these instances the number of people working in the department concerned has been reduced. The new smaller private firms are often at the mercy of the larger parent firm which acts as a monopoly buyer for their services, and in turn this puts pressure on the companies, who put pressure on their employees. Many hard-won rights and conditions of service of the work force are being lost in this process.

A variation on the management buy-out is the Xanadu scheme developed by Phil Judkins at Rank Xerox in the UK. Managers who were identified as high-fliers but likely to leave were offered a new type of deal; providing that they were the sort of person likely to cope with working from home, they were set up as a free-standing separate company. They were provided with sophisticated computers and processors which linked them to Xerox, and their contract stipulated that a certain amount of work had to be delivered to Xerox per year for five years. The rest of the time was theirs to use as they pleased – they could expand their company or they could spend their time playing golf. Most have expanded, recruited extra staff (their former secretaries act as their link at Xerox) and are burgeoning. These 'networkers' cover a wide range of disciplines – lawyers, accountants, salesmen and computer analysts are all represented – and the scheme has been particularly popular among expectant and nursing mothers.

They had to be given a substantial amoung of training, however, as skills such as bargaining or marketing are not well developed except as specialities within UK enterprises. The next move is for some of the networkers to band together and move into a new Xerox 'office shop'. From the company standpoint the benefits have come from managers who might have been lost to competitors but who are still providing Xerox with their expertise, and there has also been a reshuffle of offices in which a building was sold for clear profit. While it might not suit all companies and definitely not all employees, this is clearly an imaginative and workable method of retaining – indeed remotivating – key staff.

This form of home-working has been called 'telecommuting' and is bound to grow over time, especially as telecommunications costs fall or local area networks expand. Companies like Citibank in New York, which has roughly half of its clerical work performed by staff from their homes, or F. International, which employs women programmers at home, or the brokers around New York, who work from home rather than commute into the city, are well established in this new area. Previously a manager might have worked at home but then had to come into the office to make sure that the practical and routine tasks were done, whilst anyone under this exalted grade had to go into the office every day. The complete range of work, other than business lunches, can now be performed from home rather than the office; only the eyeball-to-eyeball confrontations are missing.

Working from home involves the loss of one of the most important aspects of modern employment, however – the ability to meet and talk to people. The 'office shop' is one method of getting around this, and there will be two types. The first will be run by British Telecom or Mercury, and this network carrier will bring together different types of equipment or work station. The other type will be when one company, like Xerox or ICL or Wang provides the hardware and software, with either a local area network or a telecommunications link. Companies will pay a rental on behalf of their staff, who will be doing their work and communicating with their head offices from the district or suburb where they live. They will be planned with the employees in mind, and will include kitchens, rest-rooms and crêche facilities as well as the normal office services; this should mitigate considerably the loss of the traditional socialisation element. Employers will buy space and time for their employees at one of the centres, which will be cheaper than paying a big city premium on a salary. If conducted properly, the city office space released by the tele-commuters could be reallocated and/or be sold. The employee does not have to cope with the trauma of the rush hour nor spend increasing amounts of wages on travel costs. It could be a welcome move for both sides.

This is very much the probable future employment pattern for many types of staff, although undoubtedly it will be modified as we learn from both successes and errors. It also has social implications, as we shall see later, that far transcend the changes in work practices; it may well change the demographic map as completely as did the first industrial revolution, in addition to putting pressure on personal relationships. At present there appears to be little resistance to the concept, although these are early days yet; the unions have yet to acknowledge that an entirely new set of problems exists, let alone confront them.

Exciting and fundamental as these changes are, there are many other examples of new ground being broken. The flexi-year is one of these. After a discussion with the employer, the employee decides how many hours to work in the coming year; this can be revised at a later date. If too many people want to work (or not work) at any particular time after the quarterly schedules have been discussed, a form of brokerage is conducted between departments. This is conducted through an 'hours bank' where hours can be bought, sold and loaned. With this system a person can choose a working pattern that suits his or her personal circumstances. Children can be cared for by the employee having the school holidays off and finishing early in the light summer evenings, or an employee may be a skiing fanatic and want to spend most of the winter on the slopes – that too can be arranged. The company can thus meet variable work loads more easily. It is a revolutionary and surprisingly easy method of arranging for flows of work. At least ten German companies are experimenting with it and six have applied it to the entire work force.

Maternity leave is now a standard provision throughout Europe, though not in the USA, and paternity leave is being taken in a limited number of cases in the UK and Scandinavia. Three-quarter-time working, by either partner, is a Scandinavian feature which allows parents to spend more time with their children when they are growing up, though apparently employers are not too keen on the idea. The arranging of employment to fit the circumstances of the family, rather than the family having to adjust to the job – as has been the case in the past – is a radical and far-reaching move which will undoubtedly find favour amongst many social groups.

As the retirement age decreases, so the number of people who are perfectly capable of working effectively but have little or nothing in the way of formal employment is increasing. The use of these people on a part-time basis within a company is growing, and they are paid on a part-pension and part-salary basis. One method of operating it is to start five years prior to the normal retirement date; the employee works one day less per week every year until he or she is totally retired.

A variation on this theme comes from Japan and is called 'constructive demotion'. The Toho Mutual Life Insurance Company has a mandatory retirement age of 60 for men, but at the age of 53 section chiefs are obliged to take a lower position and department heads have to step down at 57. Another Japanese insurance company expects its employees to become 'exclusive duty section chief' or 'exclusive duty department head' at the ages of 50 and 52 respectively, but they no longer have any employees under their control. These stratagems are being used to shorten an increasingly lengthy promotion ladder. As older employees feel more pressure than younger ones, these moves are also being seen as a method of preserving the life of the older men for a longer period. And because of their loyalty to the company, it is possibly not resented as much as it would be in the Western world.

Companies are loth to let good staff go even when they leave of their own accord or are made redundant, and many companies maintain lists of such employees. When demand rises – it may be seasonal, as with Christmas-pudding packers – they contact the people on the list to find out if they want a temporary job. The point here is that many of these people are not registered as unemployed (especially married women and men who have retired), so that jobs are filled but the official level of unemployment remains unchanged. This is an integral part of flexible work-force arrangements.

The internal demarcations between different grades within a firm are coming under pressure too. While this used to apply to the factory floor, with distinctions between different crafts as well as between skilled and non-skilled workers being eradicated, the office is now becoming susceptible to these new pressures. The development of work stations rather than separate offices, and the fact that different grades of employee use them for different ends, is upsetting well-established hierarchies. Not only do managers have to wait in line behind the clerical assistant on some occasions, but fundamental conflicts are stimulated. The tyranny of the job title is becoming less appropriate to conditions where skills are becoming blurred – where managers have to use keyboards, where secretaries take instant managerial-style decisions and where well over half the office workers will need a modicum of computer literacy, at the least.

Where does this leave the traditional job evaluation system with its rigid definitions? How do we define a computer worker or a specific type of clerical worker? Should managers have to learn keyboard skills or is this a waste of their time? What sort of promotion pattern changes will occur because of rapidly changing skill needs, and how will training needs be met? What sort of organisational changes are we going to need both to accept the advantages and minimise the disadvantages of the new technologies? These are but some of the questions that need to be asked today, and which we must try to answer. The tragedy is that precious few people in positions of influence or authority are doing either.

The traditional relationships of employees with one another

are changing. The typist/manager relationship is very different from the word-processor-operator/manager combination. The office manager or foreman has become more of a systems manager in a modern factory or office, whilst ironically people-management is being undertaken and monitored by electronic machines and systems. Different types of employees are being thrown into closer proximity than ever before as they use common factory or office facilities. Yet despite these changes there is a hankering to cling on to the job titles and the attitudes of yesteryear.

Oliver Tynan of the Work Research Unit is thinking about the future. He believes that organisations will have to become fluid internally to cope with new information technology; indeed he describes them as 'shaking, quaking moving bags of worms'. He cites the operator who overrides production plans by changing programs when a tool breaks, or the salesman who controls tomorrow's production schedule from his hotel bedroom, as representatives of this new flexible hierarchy. A is *not* over B, who is *not* over C, in this new system; they are each 'over' the other for some of the time – a very difficult situation to manage. Again, this makes remuneration, promotion and job evaluation policy very difficult if we stick to the existing tools. British managers are notoriously poor at initiating and then accepting change, especially when it affects themselves, but the changes in the way we work are happening now, not in the far-distant future. We cannot afford the luxury of being able to sit back and admire our prescience when adjusting our in-work systems to the technological changes. There is an imperative to act quickly if the avoidable costs are not to outweigh the possible benefits. The Oliver Tynan model is clearly one for the future, but there will need to be an awful lot of persuasion before the consequences will be accepted widely.

Flexibility will ultimately have to benefit both the employee and the employer, and this will entail a shift in the present balance towards the employee. In the long term, the only way the technology can be used to enhance flexibility is if all the schemes are voluntary and the benefits more equitably shared. The alternative is to keep the existing attitudes and systems or risk both in-work and external disruption of an increasing intensity.

In the UK we are drifting into yet another of our 'two

nations'. We have had Disraeli's version; we still have the north and the south and the employed and the unemployed, and now we are getting the primary and the secondary employees. Of those who work, some will have careers, security and relative prosperity; but the secondary employees will have lower wages, no future and no security. Even if unemployment could be mopped up in this manner, and this is highly unlikely, we would end up with a singularly divided society.

This is not inevitable. Changes are needed and if made could change all the options radically; secondary work could be part of the mainstream employment sector, and private and public benefits could certainly outweigh social and public costs. There are imperatives for this change, but one thing must be made clear at the outset. They are not costless themselves, they go far beyond mere tinkering with the existing system, they will not please everyone and they require statesmen and stateswomen of firm purpose and wide vision. These people emerged in the nineteenth century when they were needed, and it is to be hoped that their successors can repeat the trick this century.

8 The need for change

Today's society is based on yesterday's needs. This has ever been the case. The time-lags between the changes in what society does, how it does it and who does it, and the way that society adapts itself to cope with these changes have always existed. Minor changes may have caused some inconvenience at the time they occurred, but the adjustment process was able to work slowly and, if not well, then tolerably. Major changes, such as the invention of gunpowder or the steam engine, created years of chaos as adjustments in the way that societies adapted to them trailed well behind the advances themselves. Throughout history the rate of change has been slow; a techno-logical, philosophical or political breakthrough every sixty years or so was the rule up until this century.

Time is no longer on our side in this respect, however. Changes come upon us ever faster; no sooner have we absorbed one than another wonder has taken its place and we are always well informed about these developments. The electronic media bring us news of events as they happen, almost before they happen; we not only know about our own community or country but about events all around the world. Information crowds in upon us, making instant analysis and hasty judge-ments only too regular occurrences. This speed of change gives us little time to reflect, to sit back and observe what the sum of the changes have meant to society and the people and institu-tions within it. Even academics, who ought to be able to provide this relaxed, detached analysis, have been subverted by the media's need for immediacy whilst trapping themselves in increasingly narrow specialisations. The short term, already built into our political and information systems, is reinforced by this effect. We really cannot see the wood for the trees.

It is very difficult to recognise that one is living in fundamen-tally historic or pivotal times. The first industrial revolution was an example of this; the people living through it, mill-owners, workers, clergymen or farmers, had no conception of a revolution. It is only with the benefit of hindsight that we have realised what was happening and the effects that it had; there was no fixed point in time when it was possible to say: 'This is the industrial revolution.' It started with the steam engine and the joint-stock company and continued in waves for 120 years – with new inventions, products and techniques regularly coming to the fore. The changes were immense but few of them were capable individually of disturbing society to any great extent, and none of them happened overnight. Their cumulative effect, however, meant that the Britain of 1900 bore almost no resemblance politically, demographically, environmentally, socially or industrially to that of 1780.

The technological changes had elicited social and political responses. Some were made freely, others coerced; some came out of fear, others from altruism. It was an unplanned, piecemeal process in the course of which millions of people across Europe were sacrificed to the secular god of profit by 'the market'. Far from being a golden age for the majority of people, the changes created misery on the grand scale. This is often forgotten by the people who continually hark back to and romanticise the certainties of the past. Living standards did rise in this 120-year period, as did expectations. By 1900 more people were living longer and, for want of a better description, nicer lives than they had before the industrial revolution started. The costs associated with this, however, were incurred by the generations of people who had had to work in the intervening period.

The need to change institutions and attitudes is greater today than it was in the nineteenth century. The potential for technological changes is at least as great, more people know about and are affected by these changes, and expectations are incomparably higher. To these must be added the speed of the new changes; whereas the first industrial revolution took over one hundred years to work its way through, the current one will be complete in twenty years and at that point it is highly possible that another equally major breakthrough in technology will be emerging.

If there are high standards of living, high expectations of both a material and political nature and if people have more vested interests than ever before, then they have more to lose and thus an extra incentive to hold on to what they have. People in the developed world today have all these in abundance, especially when compared with those that lived through the first industrial revolution. The hardships that our ancestors endured and the sacrifices they were forced to make in the workplace, as well as in ordinary life, would not be tolerated today. If the same burdens, even of a considerably lesser degree, were to be placed on modern employees in the industrialised world, they would not acquiesce in them – history would not repeat itself.

The first spur to change is thus the fear that will be generated by the possibility of change of a more violent character if voluntary adjustments are not made. This will stem from two distinct sectors of the population. The working class and the unemployed are, and will continue to be, the most adversely affected group for the next five to ten years. From that point onwards, when the second and third bands of change overlap, the lives of the middle classes and the prospects for their children will alter for the worse, and this will stimulate a second potential area of destablisation. The two may well not reinforce each other, indeed they could prove to be mutually antagonistic, as any unscrupulous and aware political party may recognise and exploit for its own ends. The instability will stem from a large, articulate and hitherto economically powerful group of people whose expectations will be unfulfilled and, what is worse, who see no chance of them ever being met.

In addition to these two groups, politicians (believing that destabilisation would destroy government and their own careers) and those concerned with the making of profits (fearing that the goose that lays the golden egg might be killed in the turmoil) would also be powerful proponents of peaceful change.

Society is by no means static, however. It has been altering its public and private face in reaction to events, at times itself stimulating further change. We have noted the marked liberalisation in attitudes to social matters like sex, marriage and discrimination, each of which has been the subject of recent legislation which either reacted to public opinion or attempted to lead it. There are still huge areas of society, however, where the formal or theoretical position no longer corresponds with reality and where yesterday's views still rule.

Despite the fact that almost half of the labour force is made up of women, the fiction is maintained that men are the breadwinners in families. This myth forms the basis of income tax law, the basis of pension fund rules (though not trust law), the structure and composition of promotion ladders and the facilities that are available for people at the workplace. The family itself is not the sacrosanct institution that it was a mere twenty years ago; divorce is high and on the increase, whilst an increasing number of couples ignore marriage completely. Variations in sexuality are better tolerated than in the past, and a homosexual parternership is almost as widely accepted as a heterosexual. Less than one in three households now consist of a husband, wife and child(ren), so 'the average family' is no longer a meaningful concept. The availability and reliability of birth control has enabled women to have more control over their lives, and this in itself contributes greatly to the changes in employment patterns.

There are considerable knock-on effects from these changes. The mobility of men and women has changed in complex ways. Men need to consider the earning capacity of their partner when contemplating an employment change, whilst a smaller but increasing number of women are having to make the same calculations. The number of unattached (in a legal or formal sense) women prepared to pursue careers and travel to where these might take them is increasing at the same rate as men are finding that they are dependent on a second wage and discover that their own mobility is restricted. The number of single-parent families is increasing dramatically, generally with a woman at the head, creating both a new work force through necessity while making conventional full-time employment that much more difficult for those concerned. Some employers have realised the opportunities that have opened up for them with this change but many others, and most trade unions, are ignoring this new reality. Masculine attitudes still rule in a world where power is starting to be diffused. This will have to change as the penetration of women into employment deepens, and the potential loss of valuable expertise in not employing them becomes ever more apparent.

The Sex Discrimination Act, not a conspicuous success in itself, is having some effect in that it is raising the consciousness and expectations of young women in terms of the choices that are (or should be) open to them. This is happening through the school system and the plethora of magazines aimed at young and ambitious women, although the institutions which control much of the world of commerce, trade and politics are still heavily male-dominated. Changes will have to be made here too, if the representative nature of UK institutions is to survive.

Institutions are all about power. The men (mainly) who work in and for them are skilled in the exercise and manipulation of this power and are loth to relinquish it; when this attitude is compounded by a threat to their masculinity, resistance is sure to be bitter. Institutions are under attack from other directions too, however. Most depend on the tolerance and respect of their members or the public for their existence. When it is widely felt that the institution is no longer necessary, no longer doing a good job or no longer representative of the wider interests, survival is threatened. Nothing destroys the faith of a population in its institutions more than a manifest inability to do the jobs that they were designed to do. This applies to many of them. Politics, the legal processes, the machinery of government, the trade unions, the taxation systems and the forces of law and order are all coming under pressure to do better and to reform themselves.

The growing percentage of Asian and Afro-Caribbean people, amongst other minority racial groups, is not at all well represented in the Establishment at any level. The unemployed, young people doing quasi-jobs, the disabled and the poor have few, if any, organisations taking up cudgels on their behalf with any real hope of achieving a change in their circumstances. The uneven distribution of work, which has created areas of very high unemployment alongside those with relatively full employment, has made people in the former group bitter. They too feel disenfranchised, although the way they express their resentments and frustrations may not be expressed quite as elegantly. The rate at which changes occur adds yet another stress to a system that is already showing signs of strain.

Flexibility, that quintessential eighties concept, will have to form the basis of the new institutional structures in industrialised countries if they are to cope with frequent change. The ability to respond to new circumstances will be one of the most valuable assets of the future. European countries and the USA and Canada are faced with similar changes in their work forces and in social attitudes, and they too will have to adapt to the new circumstances.

Politicians are widely held to be incapable of coming to terms with some of today's more intractable issues – such as unemployment, Northern Ireland or hunger in the third world – but the main problem is their inability to keep up with volatile public opinion. The stimulus for these changes may be a high-profile scandal, perhaps the neglect of a child or a violent murder; it may change as a result of a concerted media campaign or because one minority section of the population feels itself to be threatened. Whatever the reason, the swings in opinion and changes in attitudes are coming at more frequent intervals and are being felt more widely. Most politicians use their tried-and-tested rhetoric rather than address themselves to the newer moods and ideas in ways that strike a chord, and television – acting as an instant newsbringer, forecaster, pundit and opinion-former – exacerbates this mismatch as well as exposing politicians to the closest of scrutinies.

The machinery of government in most democracies was designed to meet the demands of a more leisurely age, moreover, one where the majority of the electorate had little interest in, and less opportunity to find out about, what was happening at the governmental level. An election every five years is adequate if there are few changes in that period, but if changes come thick and fast then it is an overlong hiccough in the sampling of public opinion. Opinion polls and attitude surveys, valuable as they may be, are no real substitutes for elections, and democracy may not be as representative as we would care to believe in such circumstances. The openness of government in this age of instant comment and all-embracing information flows will also have to be improved. Slow decision-making, or an inability of the system to take a new problem on board at all (except after a considerable time-lag), is a function of the durability but also senescence of these systems. This in itself may prove to be one of the strongest stimuli for change. The civil services around the world, and the representative bodies at the local and community levels, will also come under pressure as the new technologies both create new opportunities and expose existing inadequacies.

The legal system affects most people for most of the time, albeit in indirect ways. It is tolerated because there is public confidence in it, but this is now being shaken. New technologies are creating the opportunities for new offences – such as fraud, copyright abuse and industrial espionage – while at the same time the law is failing to cope with the growing threat to personal privacy and security of information. This is happening in a period when the waiting time for court appearances is increasing all over Europe as the incidence of crime, especially petty crime, rises. Many authorities believe that this is caused by the increase in unemployment, although the UK government does not, citing the 1930s as a vandal-free example. This minority view overlooks the rise in expectations over the past half century and, moreover, underestimates the amount of crime and vandalism in the thirties which was not the subject of prosecution – it was treated by a clip around the ear! Cracks are starting to appear in the system. The police no longer have the full automatic confidence of all the public and have virtually none among some large minority groups. Many people not normally associated with radical opposition are showing disquiet at some legal decisions and at the failure of the law to come to any decisions at all on matters which stem from the newly found, technologically based abilities of human beings to alter their circumstances. Surrogate births, genetic experimentation, abortion, damage from pharmaceutical products, pirate and community broadcasting are all among this growing number of controversial issues.

Trade union membership accounts for roughly half the employed labour force in the UK and the greater proportion in some other countries. The increase in the number of women workers, the drift in public attitudes against collective actions, the growth of home and other property ownership and high unemployment have taken their toll, however. Membership is falling, battles are being lost or avoided and laws inimical to their development are being passed. Unions themselves, however, are changing but little. If they lose the propaganda battle they blame the media rather than trying to circumvent them or use them for their own ends. If they fail to mobilise their members, too many union leaders believe it is because the members are at fault. Technology is fragmenting work forces, creating unemployment, removing the power of the stewards and conveners and has shifted the balance of power firmly towards the employers. The new jobs in the secondary labour market are seen as an aberration and somehow not real, partly because they are mainly for women. But unions, if they are to represent their members properly, will have to change at least as much as politicians; in short, they will have to represent the new working classes and what André Gorz has called the class of the non-class (the long-term unemployed), rather than the working classes as they were before unemployment and technology intervened. Yet again fear will be the spur to change, the fear of unions becoming irrelevant.

Taxes are one of the most universally unpopular facets of life, though most people would agree that they are essential. All nations have a wide variety of taxes, the most common being those on incomes and on sales of goods and services, and the effects of the new technologies are even now being felt in these areas. Fewer people in employment means a smaller income tax yield, or a higher tax rate; it may also affect sales taxes as consumption will be lower than it might otherwise have been. As high unemployment appears to run hand in hand with a larger informal economy, tax yields fall even further. From a government perspective this argues for a complete re-evaluation of the taxation system (as indeed does the increased number of women in employment and as heads of families).

The need to adapt in response to technological changes and their immediate repercussions is not confined to the government or other institutions. More time spent at home or in the vicinity of home will have a large impact on social and family relationships. It is likely that the number of divorces will increase, along with the breakdown of other relationships. Many marriages have had their success based firmly on the fact that the partners did not spend that much time together, distance or absence lending enchantment; whether because of unemployment or less employment, or perhaps employment at home or very near to home, the chances are that families will spend more time with each other. This will put a very heavy strain on some of them, children included. The attitudes that we display to the people involved and the facilities that are made available to them will need careful thought. If the present level of consciousness in these matters continues, we shall find it difficult to contain the scale of the disaster.

Whilst men are still thought of as the primary breadwinners, and women as family-makers first and jam-makers second, the relationship between them will become increasingly strained. The new technologies, coupled with the decline of the traditional manufacturing industries, are elevating women into a central position in the work force. For men who have been brought up and educated to believe that their main function is to provide for the family, this realisation can come as a great blow to pride, to ego and to their masculinity. It is brought home in a dramatic way in towns like Glenrothes in Fife where the new jobs are for women and girls in the new 'Silicon Glen' (as employers prefer them for this work), while the men do the shopping, housework and look after the children. This is traditionally a mining region and the new town was built for miners and their non-working wives; it has just opened its second branch of Alcoholics Anonymous. Role re-evaluation of this type is painful, yet will be vital. The clock is unlikely to be turned back.

Many of our leisure provisions are built around the notion that people will be working during weekdays. It is difficult to get to theatres, get a drink, go to the cinema, or even play bowls or other games in the mornings – and sometimes afternoons. In the provinces, places of entertainment tend to close after about 9.00 in the evenings. For a night-shift or split-shift worker this can amount to a virtual embargo on organised leisure-time activities. The importance of this lies in the fact that the new technologies are making it easier and cheaper to arrange such shift systems, and an increasing number of people will be working what have been described accurately as unsocial hours. The facilities that are available in the hours usually thought of as working hours tend to be targeted at women, on the principle that they are at home and the men at their jobs; this applies to activities provided by both the private and the local authority sectors. So in this area too the technologically-driven changes are demanding a second-round change of considerable magnitude.

The difficulties in expanding the economy for long enough to create sufficient employment to make a serious dent in unemployment should also act as a stimulus to change. The UK problem has been demonstrated over the years. Expansion of the economy after a slump runs up against bottlenecks initially, and in present circumstances this is exacerbated by the reduced capacity in much of manufacturing industry, especially amongst component manufacturers, and the loss of skilled labour and the closure of steel and fibre-manufacturing plants. An economic recovery would therefore have to bring in more imports than ever before. In turn this acts adversely on the balance of payments which, despite oil revenues, can easily go into massive deficit. While this is bad enough, our competitors have stolen a march on us in the international marketplace in terms of new products, distribution etc. More imports and falling sterling will increase inflation and most probably interest rates, which in turn will stimulate higher wage demands.

It is possible to break into this circle at two points. Imports can be reduced in some way, which will mean either a slowing of growth as essential goods are barred or extra inflation (or both), as well as an outcry against the consequent reduction in choice by both Tory and Alliance politicians and consumer organisa-tions; it will be a difficult policy to maintain in operation for any length of time. Secondly, it must go hand in hand with a restriction on wages, quaintly but erroneously known in the UK as an 'incomes policy'. No incomes policy in the UK has lasted longer than four years and, given traditional manage-ment/union relationships and class divisions, it is unlikely that one can be devised to do so. Even without import controls, an incomes policy would be needed to damp down inflation in the event of a dash for growth.

Two other factors come into play. The first is that import controls would only be instituted by a Labour government, but they would have the greatest difficulty in making an incomes policy last for more than three or four years. Union leaders would probably agree to this; union members, especially middle-class ones, would not. On the other hand, a Conserva-tive or Alliance government would weaken trade unions to the extent that little or no opposition would be forthcoming, but would neither expand the economy as much nor control imports. The second factor is that every industrialised or industrialising country will be trying to do the same as the UK: move into high technology, expand exports and grow. Given sluggish world trade, it is impossible for this strategy to succeed in all countries. One country's surplus must be another's deficit. Only when the existence of these obstacles in the way of growth is accepted by politicians will alternative paths begin to be explored.

It is easy to construct a theoretical model where the economy continues to grow, thus creating additional jobs. The blockages, however, are in the real world and involve the mass psyche of different and competing groups. These are factors which are difficult to model in quantitative terms, so are generally left out of the model, an omission which makes it less than reliable. It is this repeated error which leads UK governments into attempting to run incomes policies long after they have outlived their usefulness, and accounts for their surprise when the policy collapses in ruins, as in 1974 and 1979. The real world is not forgiving, will not trade off distant long-term gains against immediate and medium-term costs, and will not allow governments the time to get anywhere near to full employment using conventional policies – even supposing that this was a feasible proposition in any case.

The UK is one of the more backward countries of the industrialised world when it comes to training (as opposed to education). These, particularly education, will be discussed in chapter nine, but the problems are so profound that they should act as a stimulus to change, preferably sooner than later. Training should be given on a continuous basis to employees so that they can keep abreast of the latest technological changes, but the opposite seems to occur in the UK. Training is given only after it has been decided to change equipment or systems, often after they have been purchased or installed. This cannot be good enough if there is to be a genuine attempt to maintain contact with other technologically sophisticated countries; pre-emptive training is necessary. The attitude that training is an avoidable cost runs right across the board. It affects office and shop-floor staff, high-tech employees and traditional trade apprentices, union officials and managers. In recent years the abolition of some of the training boards, coupled with a pathetic and unrealistic reliance on the secondary school system to provide them with fully-fledged mini-workers, has cost UK employers dear in competitive terms, and will continue to do so unless a radically different approach is taken. For those who have never been employed (young people), training is all too often perfunctory and based on dying crafts and skills; for them the system offers little hope.

Other in-work changes are happening which will need amendments in structures and attitudes if we are to come to terms with them. The new technologies have made many old skills redundant or less valuable to an employer, whilst other skills – generally new ones – command a premium. As these changes take place, wage differentials and relativities are distorted, job evaluation schemes become outdated and promotion patterns are turned on their heads. The tensions at the workplace while this is happening will be palpable and, when combined with a declining work force, the resulting insecurities may boil over into a series of haphazard and, on the face of it, improbable disputes – such as an outcry over management plans to cut a minute from the tea break. In a limited way this happened in the 1960s when the financial institutions (particularly insurance companies) installed their mainframe computers and created new information systems. The stampede to join TUC-affiliated unions was led by those who were most affected; young to middle-aged career staff who could see younger employees taking the promotions that they thought were theirs by right.

These incentives to change will only be recognised, let alone acted upon, if there is a change in the way that we analyse events. In this respect we tend to fall into three traps, any one of which could prove to be a serious handicap. Firstly, we compare ourselves and our condition with the recent past, as though there has been a smooth continuum rather than the discontinuity that new technology and social and world economic affairs has imposed. We should more realistically compare our situation today with a time of similar hiatus, either the first industrial revolution or its second phase at the end of the nineteenth century when the electric motor came into use. The remedies for our problems, especially unemployment, lie in learning from the mistakes of these periods. At present we are actually repeating the errors.

Secondly, we are guilty of analysing events in terms of comparative statics (two snapshots, for example) rather than dynamically (using a videotape, as it were). We need a dynamic analysis more than ever before to chart today's changes as they happen. It is not the start and end point that will give us clues on how to achieve success, but an in-depth examination of how we reached that end point – be it a disaster or a victory. The more enlightened businessmen and academic accountants like Anthony Hopwood at the London Business School are attempting to trace through the possible costs of changing back to the original position and starting again in a new direction. These studies will have to be built upon, widened and made more 'popular', to form the basis for a new form of accounting.

The third fault in our analytical procedures is that they are short term in the extreme. We deal in yearly accounts, half-yearly results, bye-election swings and yesterday's strikes. A longer perspective is needed, but the long term is not merely the aggregate of all the short terms. Room will have to be made for the strategic thinker, the scenario-writer who will offer possibilities and probabilities to employers, unions, politicians and the people alike. Of all the changes in method, this will be the most difficult to implement, as it will attack the short-term philosophy of the existing structures.

Increases in leisure time, changes in the composition of the employed work force, the location of jobs and the lasting effects of unemployment on a substantial number of people are all stimuli for change, and these changes themselves are stemming from technological changes. As the nineteenth century unfolded, so the physical environment, the institutions and people's relationships with each other changed too. Our forebears adapted over time; they accepted wages, cities, parks, consumer goods and employment in lieu of 'work'. We shall have to make changes of the same magnitude but over a very much shorter time-span.

The structure of our society is at risk, because it is based firmly on employment. Identities, status, hierarchies, respect and self-respect are all dependent upon what sort of employment people are in and how much they earn doing whatever it is that they do. We have an employment-based society where money determines value, and for most people this money has to be obtained from their employment. If everyone is in employment this poses little difficulty, but if there are a substantial number of people who are jobless the value system starts to look lopsided and less than universally applicable. If one believes that high levels of unemployment will be with us for some considerable time, then it is permissible to look for changes that will take us back to a universally acceptable value system.

Like most of the other changes that could be (should be) on the cards, this is difficult. In industrialised states we have been brought up to accept certain truths, one of which is that the more goods and services a person can command, the better they are doing and the more worthy they are. Our beliefs about employment and work, about money and ownership, about what is right and proper and what is not, are conditioned by our parents and our schools. Education can imprint a young person for life – as the Jesuits, the most eminent of teachers, know full well. We charge our education system with looking after the future and in uncertain times this charge must be examined carefully. Quite what we require of the system and whether it is fulfilling its role adequately are questions whose answers are vital to the future of everyone who lives in the UK, and indeed throughout the industrialised world.

9 Learning to live

I make no apologies for marking out education as the single most important element in coping with society. It equips us for today, tomorrow and the day after that; it shapes attitudes and responses as well as imparting technical knowledge. Education is another example of a 'halo concept' – few people will be prepared to argue against it and the more of it that there is the better off people are supposed to be. This has not always been the case, however; indeed ideas of what education should do for people have changed markedly over the centuries.

The monasteries of the Renaissance educated their novices in the belief that knowledge itself was a good thing. Learning was for learning's sake, although the craftsmen needed within the community were trained under a separate arrangement. Reading and writing remained the prerogative of the minority for hundreds of years up until the industrial revolution, and the people who were literate were content to maintain this state of affairs. The clergy, landowners, employers and government could maintain their sway over the people as they interpreted as well as wrote the laws and other regulations. Training, however, *was* available. The guilds relied upon apprenticeships; clerks and scribes were trained; doctors, apothecaries, thatchers, specialised farmworkers and weavers all had to have the backing of a formidable training system. The wider view of education was lost in this welter of vocational instruction.

The need for literacy and numeracy was highlighted as the industrial revolution gathered momentum. Workers who could read simple instructions or warnings proved to be more efficient than those who could not, while those with the most schooling were able to learn their tasks faster and became the foremen and overlookers. Schools sprang up, literacy and numeracy became increasingly widespread. With this came the danger that the establishment had feared; political pamphleteering fomented thought, prompted questions and inspired unrest. When an education bill was being discussed in the Commons, a Tory MP coined the couplet, 'Better a brutal starving nation than men with thoughts above their station.' He lost, the industrialists won and education became available to all.

It was, however, employment-oriented from the very outset. Whilst Oxford and Cambridge continued to perpetuate the Renaissance view of education and the Grand Tour was an indispensable part of a wealthy young man's education, the new schools for working-class youngsters concentrated on imparting the skills that their prospective employers would be requiring. The same was happening all over Europe. The middle classes soon realised the value of education for their children, and private schools, a few new universities and a respectable professional class emerged. Paradoxically, the only people who received an education even remotely like the early clerical one were middle class women. They were taught accomplishments, but the reasoning behind this was to please their families rather than fulfil themselves, and in a very real sense this was their 'job' and therefore a type of vocational teaching.

Very little has changed in the basic premises underpinning the education system in the UK and most industrialised countries over the last 120 years. Free education is universally available, the school-leaving age has been raised gradually to sixteen, there are considerably more universities and other places of tertiary education, more young people continue in their education systems for longer than ever before, and there is a growing awareness that girls should have precisely the same educational opportunities as boys. However, the Renaissance spirit has disappeared almost totally, and education is now almost entirely vocational. There may have been trends and fashions in subjects and the methods of teaching them, there may have been changes in the structure of schools, but the basic principle has perpetuated itself. *We still use the system as a preparation for employment and any other outcome is either accidental or peripheral.* The unchanged nature of the education system underscores its conservatism.

This tends to be the case in most countries, even though the methods of teaching and the subjects taught may differ markedly. The school system combines two different levels. The majority learn basic literacy and numeracy and other traditional subjects like history, geography, sciences and perhaps a foreign language, and then sit exams with the idea in mind that they will leave school to get a job at the first opportunity. In practice the jobs are no longer widely available, but the system maintains the fiction that they are – at best saying only that the lack of jobs is temporary. Circumstances have changed, but educational philosophy has not – indeed, as we shall see, it is all too often taking refuge in the past.

The exams are for the convenience of employers. They are a badge which the young person wears to show how employable they should be – the better the exam results the more employable for *any* job. These young people are not going to use their exams as a springboard for further academic purposes, nor did they sit them because the experience was enjoyable; they did so because the job market demanded that they should. In essence, school does the job that personnel officers should be doing, and it does it most imperfectly. It is a nonsense to suggest that the attainment of an 'O' level in history will mean that a person will be a better supermarket shelf-stacker than someone with no qualifications at all. Employers are using exam results as a sieve in a period when they are embarrassed by the riches of too many applicants. Inevitably this results in the educational under- or non-achievers making up the bulk of the unemployed, with no regard to their suitability or otherwise for employment. The number one rule in the UK job market is that *employers will always appoint the most over-qualified person for any job*.

The second level in the school system concerns those who intend to continue studying after school-leaving age. Examinations are passed initially to satisfy academic boards rather than employers; the badge is flaunted at a different judge. This is only a delaying device, however. The young person may go on to get 'A' levels, a good degree and perhaps a master's or even a doctorate, but one has to ask the question – why? Is it because he or she likes to take examinations? Highly improbable. Is it because the person likes to study for the sake of it or is totally absorbed by the subject? Possible but rare. It is primarily because the higher qualification is yet another merit award for an employer to consider. A recent survey in the UK showed that appointments at a junior managerial level were very influenced by prestige factors. Degrees were preferred to other equivalent qualifications, degrees from universities preferred to those from polytechnics and degrees from Oxford and Cambridge preferred to those from newer universities.

Employment is all-important and school is directed towards it from the earliest days. A primary-school headteacher recently told parents at a pre-school meeting that their children must attend on time as it would build up the habit that they would need when they went to work. This was aimed at five-year-olds. Primary schools do, however, tend to provide a balanced education and cater for the curiosity and innate appetite for learning that characterises the very young. They have an advantage in that there are no examinations in the state system to distort teaching at this level, although most of the evidence shows that when the 11-plus exams existed the quality of education was still very high. Secondary education, on the other hand, loses the interest of many children – and this is especially true in the UK.

Whether this is due to puberty, to the system of teaching, to the type of schools, to the lack of parental interest and reinforcement, to poor teaching, to irrelevant subjects or to the children themselves provokes discussions all over the country (education is rivalling the weather and beer as a universal topic of conversation). It is probably due to a combination of factors which includes class, demography and the political philosophy of the Local Education Authority concerned. Above all, there is the growing awareness that an increasing number of school-children regard their school and the subjects they are taught as irrelevant. For them the prospects of employment in the short term are remote; they must look forward to the dole, YTS or staying on to the sixth form in a school they dislike. *School prepares them for little except exams and hence employment.*

Examinations rule the education system. In the UK these have been set by university boards in the past, which gave an inbuilt disadvantage to the majority as the exams were seen as a stepping stone on the way to university, a non-starter for four out of five youngsters. The CSE examination has recently tried to break the mould by using school as a base for the examinee in a more constructive and relevant way. Not unnaturally, however (because one of the major reasons for the introduction of this exam was to provide one that was easier to pass, and thus remove the feeling of failure from many children), it is seen as second best. The latest plan is to replace existing exams with yet another at 16-plus, but it will be surprising if this too does not founder on similar rocks.

Examinations are not a good aid or stimulus to the art of learning. Most can be passed by committing facts to memory rather than exercising deductive powers or reasoning ability – the regurgitation of facts is all. This applies across the board up to a standard which includes most first degrees, and even some master's and doctorates, and it is certainly true of professional examinations in medicine, dentistry, the law and accountancy. If this is the be-all and end-all of the education system, we must ask whether this is what we need. At a time of fast change the answer must be no.

To cope with change a person must be capable of recognising a moving situation and, rather than freeze at the mere thought of change, adapt to it. This implies that the person has been taught flexibly, not merely how to recognise a given and static position. As I pointed out in the preceding chapter, the ability to deal with the dynamics of a movement is becoming crucial. Given that this presupposes an ability to come to terms with a series of new and changing events, it follows *that schools should be devoted to teaching young people how to learn*. This alone will enable people to approach something new, whatever it may be, with confidence in their own abilities to cope with it successfully.

This involves a different method of teaching, which will be more demanding on teachers and will require considerably more of them. When facts are taught they should be analysed. 'Why?' should be as important as 'when?' or 'who?' in history, and the development and philosophy of science as important as the equivalence tables in chemistry. Neither of these approaches are incompatible with examinations, although a change to a more thought-provoking and experience-based system would be an advantage for everyone. This is not a new theory. The Institute of Education of London University adopts it as a central feature in their teacher-training courses, but the reality in the schools – especially in London – bears no relation to the theory; the old methods and traditions hold sway.

It does not seem to matter whether the conventional examination system is nationwide, as in France; based on continuous assessment, as in the USA; or decentralised, as in the UK – the end ambition is the same. It is to use education to get the best available job. Everyone conspires to promote this end; teachers, school boards, governments, employers and, above all, parents and pupils acquiesce. It is natural for them to do so. Those in positions of authority have generally battled their way through the education system themselves, so that to criticise it fundamentally is to denigrate their own success; few people in such positions are strong enough to do so. But, with fewer jobs available, a debate should be starting on the uses and abuses of the education system in a changed and changing era – perhaps on a 'learning to learn' basis. Remarkably, however, this has not happened. Vocational training in schools has become fashionable, and training for school-leavers is supported by the entire Establishment from the government to trade unions.

The debate has been postponed by a reversion to older but irrelevant virtues; the Renaissance concept of education as a good thing in itself has been resurrected in a perverted form. We now practise *training* as a good thing in itself. The end product is subordinate to the fact that the training is given and virtue is acquired both by the provider and recipient, no matter how effective or pertinent the training has been. The trainee, however, is far from fulfilled and only too often far from employable at the end of it.

Training and education are quite different concepts. We train performing seals to amuse us, dogs to be obedient and horses to run fast. We use the same word when we talk of apprenticeships or the learning of a skill or craft by other means; we train typists and nurses, doctors and engineers, bricklayers and librarians. It is the imparting of a specific group of skills that characterises training, and it is basically a narrowing process. *Education*, on the other hand, is essentially mind-widening. In the real world there is obviously a need for both, but training should come *after* education and education should not stop at the end of schooldays – it should be a lifelong process.

There are many training schemes in the UK – some for school-leavers, some for young adults and others for older adults. The apprenticeship system has fallen into acute disrepair, with the numbers dwindling in all crafts and industries, and in great part it has been replaced by government-funded schemes, run mainly through the Manpower Services Commission (MSC), which are less industry- or craft-related. These are superimposed on a growing tendency to provide vocational training in the secondary school system. Of all the moves in education of the past fifty years, this has to be the most misguided.

The theory behind this move is that if a youngster shows little aptitude for the academic side of education then school should be about preparing that youngster for a job. But lessons in how to look smart, how to perform at an interview, how to write an application form or a CV are of limited use. Teaching should be about communicating with people, about literacy, even about fashion – none of these is an academic subject but all are skills which are needed throughout life. Instead of expanding in this direction, however, we are training young people to learn tricks to impress potential employers; this is narrowing their horizons, not expanding them. And the idea of training in specific skills is generally half-hearted, as schools have neither the facilities nor the monies to undertake this at present, and local employers do not do enough. In any event, fast-changing technologies need equally fast-changing skills. Schools tend to teach technologies that were available some ten years ago at the best (for example, word-processors have barely a toehold in commercial courses), and the twin constraints of lack of money and expertise inevitably mean that this will continue. Teaching old techniques (such as typewriting rather than keyboard skills) at this particular time is counter-productive. Possibly the best arrangement is to enable students to spend a day at a business, preferably of their own choice, and if the right chord is struck this can be interesting, informative and even educational.

The main drawback to vocational teaching is that it solves no unemployment problems, it merely shifts them. Even if some of these young people get jobs, when their school record would suggest that this would be unlikely, they will do so at the expense of other young people. The scheme does not *create* a single job, but assumes that any job – however unpleasant, dangerous, underpaid or dead end – is better than no job. It has also limited the education of those taking part, incurring costs but imparting little in the way of overall benefits. It is the antithesis of the 'learning to learn' principle. Vocational training lets the cat out of the educational bag, emphasising that school exists to prepare pupils for employment and little else. But school should be about preparing the pupils for life, of which employment is but one part – albeit an important one.

Leaving school to go into a job was something that the generation of people brought up in the fifties and sixties believed was the natural state of things, but nowadays it is only a minority of school-leavers who do this. The sixth forms and sixth form colleges now contain young people who do not wish to go on the Youth Training Scheme, and cannot get a job, but want something to do. For these youngsters, continued schooling is a method of killing time in familiar surroundings. Other young people need money (perhaps they've been ejected from the family home, or dislike the very thought of school) and they will go on the dole. Yet others will go to some place of further education. The remainder will either be fortunate enough to get a job or will go on to one of the Youth Training Schemes (YTS) programmes. These are the quasi-jobs that are provided for the young jobless, the schemes where training is provided for the sake of training. By the time that this book is published it is likely that the government will have made YTS compulsory in all but name by withdrawing the dole from unemployed school-leavers.

The YTS can be seen as a method of reducing the unemployment figures and keeping the young unemployed off street corners and out of sight of the populace. This theory would suggest that the prime beneficiaries of the schemes are adults, and there is more than an element of truth in this view. YTS is treated by youngsters as second best to a real job, and is all too often really third best – being on the dole would probably widen experiences more. The training can be rudimentary, the life skills courses laughable. In too many instances the employer sees the trainee as cheap labour and replaces an existing employee, or perhaps does not hire an extra one when he would otherwise have done so; the checks on this form of abuse are rudimentary. The YTS scheme is not a first choice for anyone except for this type of less-than-scrupulous employer. It is tolerated because the government and employers need it, the opposition parties would use it if they were in power, and the trade unions have a vested interest in that they have seats on the MSC itself. No one looks after the trainees (they have no union), health and safety requirements are flouted continually, they get a pittance rather than a wage and at the end of the year (soon to be two) they display all the symptoms produced by redundancy without ever having had a job.

It could be, with imagination and commitment, a splendid opportunity for young people – particularly if it applied to everyone, not just the 'second best'. There are a few examples of good courses which shine like beacons amongst the general murk, and which show what could be done if sufficient time and trouble were taken. They can also teach us some important lessons. Rank Xerox run several schemes for youngsters: YTS courses, apprenticeships in information technology (both hardware- and software-oriented) and 'office of the future' courses. Young people get the opportunity to handle and learn about extremely powerful computers and artificial intelligence, and the YTS courses run the gamut of the company's activities, competitions forming a key part of the training. One of them was to devise a way of using a room at head office for the benefit of the community. Four groups of four sixteen-year-old girls took part; they had all been to London schools and between them had very few CSEs or 'O' levels, so they were the relative failures of the system. They gave a remarkable presentation, however.

The ideas were good, the research most impressive, the grasp of detail excellent and the presentation itself imaginative if somewhat stilted. None of them had ever been asked (or made) to do a project like this at school, they had not been taught how to research, or to marshal the facts that they uncovered. None of them had ever had to make a presentation in front of strangers, and most of them had not even had to do it in front of their own form. The talent was there in these girls all the time, however; their schools had not tapped it, indeed they may have held it back. In truth, the girls surprised even themselves.

What would have happened if this was an ordinary YTS scheme? The girls would not have learned about themselves and nor would they have acquired new skills. They would have been left as they were after school, underachieving grossly. They were lucky, but far more youngsters are not.

One of the major problems associated with YTS is the letdown experienced by the trainees when the course ends and there is no permanent job waiting. This applies to at least half of them. A project in Glastonbury in Somerset is trying to remedy this; called 'Workface', it has taken over the largest shop in the town and converted it into meeting rooms, computer rooms, workshops and showrooms. The trainees are placed in craft occupations, leatherwork, sign-writing, implement-making or glass-engraving are examples – and the showrooms are for their use, as are some of the workshops. Anyone who is not taken on by the instructor or who does not get a job is set up as a self-employed craftsman or woman, or a new company or co-operative might take care of them with a central marketing effort. Tony Horrocks, who is the guiding light of the project, believes that only two out of more than six hundred have been disappointed so far. Workface also has a large computer facility which is not only used to teach the trainees about computers but also links together all the disparate parts of the organisation, which extend over six counties, using techniques that they have developed themselves.

Computers are very much the flavour of the month in education. Everyone believes that young people should be taught about them, without quite knowing what it is they should know. Schools boast that they have computers, but pupils who end up in a YTS scheme or on the dole have generally had little or no contact with, and certainly no benefit from them. Information technology centres provide facilities for people, not necessarily young, to play with and train on personal computers. Those who are interested will find such schemes useful, not to say enjoyable, but those who are indifferent are unlikely to be stimulated by the provisions. The strong feeling remains, however, that the new technologies demand that we have a computer-literate work force and that we must train our children with this in mind. This has almost received the status of received wisdom and, like all such statements, needs careful examination.

In earlier chapters I examined the types of jobs that would be available in the future and it is clear that most information and communication systems will be computer-driven. This applies to the home too. However, apart from a need for basic keyboarding ability, computer skills will not be at a premium in this area. Software packages will be purchased off the shelf or bespoke, and word-processor operators or workstation-users will need some additional non-computer skills, as will retail-workers on checkouts or bank-tellers. Drivers of cars are not expected to understand how a car works or to repair it if it breaks down, and the same applies to the operators of machinery – be it in an office, a factory or the home. Managers will need similarly limited computer skills, although they will need to understand database construction and retrieval mechanisms. Overall, however, computer design or servicing skills, programming knowledge or the ability to analyse data-processing systems will not be widely needed.

Some people *will* need to know about computers in more depth. The workers in the new knowledge industry, and employees who work with and upon the hardware, software and peripherals, are clearly among these – but is school the correct place to teach this knowledge? Despite the trend towards vocational teaching, we do not ask schools to train people in detail in other facets of employment. The main function of a school with regard to computers must be to demystify them by defusing the jargon and demonstrating how easy they are to use. Other than for those taking computer science as a subject, and the use of the computer for practical purposes in the school, little can be gained by accumulating great numbers of them. Unfortunately, school governors, teachers and parents alike tend to boast about the numbers of computers available, without knowing precisely why they have them. As a result of this confusion between quantity and quality, schools all too often use their computers in artificial and academic circumstances, but they should be used to solve problems, perhaps in the running of the school or in the local community. As the Rank Xerox competition showed, this is a marvellous way to teach. One reason why it proved so successful was that it was real – all the groups were going to have to put their plans and theories into practice. It was learning by doing.

We must rethink the educational strategy on computers and associated subjects by cutting through the waffle and hype that has surrounded them. A computer in every school, of course, terminals linked to local networks and mainframes if at all possible, but in a planned and reasoned way. The present course is charted more by a combination of hysteria and commercial need than educational or community benefits.

Community schemes are another government training initiative. The trade unions are not as keen as they might be, probably because the trainees are older and they see the possible exploitation more clearly than with the YTS. The training takes many forms in theory, from community environmental work to voluntary service and from electronic engineering to dry-stonewalling. Some organisations provide part-time work, training and a retail outlet. 'Brass Tacks' in Hackney is one which repairs and then resells electrical goods and furniture, rather like a London version of 'Workface'. Initiatives such as these are only too rare, however, and too many of the schemes are attempting to put a plaster on a local running sore with cheap labour, little commitment and no training at all. Training within companies is decreasing and many of the industrial training boards were disbanded by the present government. With education moving in the wrong direction by narrowing horizons rather than expanding them, and training becoming an end in itself rather than being used as a means to an end, the future of UK industry looks anything but secure.

There is an old saying that schooldays are 'the happiest of your life'. Many children and young adults would disagree. They find the discipline irksome, the subjects irrelevant and the company far from congenial, especially in secondary education. This is not a function of the type of school, it afflicts all types in the independent as well as the state sector. Many of these people – who drop out, to all intents and purposes – are bright and perfectly capable of doing well academically, and not a few of these regret their 'misspent youth' at a later date. If they could, they would turn the clock back to repair the damage, but as they cannot the next best thing is to offer them a way back into the education system by making it a lifelong consumer good.

There are few opportunities for a person who has missed out first time round, or perhaps wants to change careers at a later date, to re-enter the education system – although this varies from country to country. In some, like Sweden, it is encouraged – especially when it is felt that the person will never get another job with their existing qualifications, or lack of them. Indeed, the Swedish Labour Market Board has financed people to do all sorts of courses, especially languages, as a substitute for work. This is not the approach in the UK, however. We have been reducing the adult education budget over the past five years, we have reduced the number of places at universities; yet again the prevailing policy is moving in precisely the wrong direction.

There are two good reasons why this must be reversed. The first is the lack of flexibility in the current situation. Too many people have redundant knowledge and skills, and as the rate of technological change increases, so the number of people in this position will increase. This is not merely a training problem, it applies at least as much to the basic 'building-block' subjects like physics or biology, where new developments in knowledge are constantly being made. On a wide, societal level this implies a waste of talent which should be remedied; on a personal level it can lead to frustrations and neuroses. It can also be argued that life is nothing but a learning experience and that anything that can shift us along the learning curve or perhaps up onto a higher curve is to be welcomed. This assumes that education should be a means of allowing a person to fulfil him or herself and that both society and the individual have an implicit duty to take this as far as possible. As we have seen earlier, this is not a popular philosophy at the moment. The idea that education is something to dip into and out of at will is even further away from mainstream thought, yet this must be the ultimate objective.

A future where there is less work for all, or for some, will provide a different backcloth against which new scenarios may be played. Education could be seen as a panacea in such circumstances; there might be a temptation to raise the school-leaving age substantially, even to the age of twenty. Young people would marry at school, raise their children at school and possibly get divorced whilst still at school, but this would be a very mistaken thing to do. School is irksome to too many of the older pupils at present. Keeping young adults at school could prove to be a risky business for the teachers – and an expensive one in terms of building repairs! Whilst there may be a temptation to go along this route, it should be avoided at all costs; it would be another example of a policy ostensibly benefiting the young but in fact designed to benefit adults.

If increased awareness of the possibilities of education is forced upon legislators and educationalists by declining employment levels, this may be to the advantage of older people. Distance learning, using interactive cabling techniques, is a cheap option if there is already a cable link in the home. The Open University and Open Tech could be expanded and supplemented by a variety of other courses ranging from the vocational to the recreational, and weekend schools would complement these courses. Pressure may well grow to use the existing educational facilities to a fuller extent as attempts to keep people occupied and out of mischief grow. Should this happen, it would involve the use of buildings for fifty weeks of the year rather than the current thirty or so to bring them into line with other buildings.

Changes can and should be made now, however. Schools need to develop a far stronger base within the communities from which their pupils are drawn, and it would not need many extra resources to link together the main local community institutions – such as the hospital, the library, the school and the largest employers.

This could form a matrix within which pupils could develop a sense of purpose and awareness, as well as acting as a teaching aid. Local business, social and environmental conditions could be analysed, and unmet needs or gaps in the local economy could be identified; there is absolutely no reason why school-leavers, either on their own or in cooperatives, should not fill these slots. For example, the school itself probably buys furniture from suppliers who import it. Why not have existing furniture repaired or made locally instead?

Unemployed or underemployed managers are only too much in evidence in almost every part of the country. Their talents could be used by schools to encourage pupils to survey the local communities, teachers not in general being equipped to teach the skills that are needed in this type of endeavour. It is not good enough to wait for the youngsters to have left school, this should be an on-going series of projects starting with the fourth forms and including the academically inclined as well as those who will leave at sixteen. The local council, social services, community groups, voluntary agencies and clubs, transport authorities, commerce and business should all be closely involved. There is absolutely no reason why such a programme should not be instituted immediately; there are models to work from in the post-school field, admittedly on a very limited scale, but their existence demonstrates that some goodwill exists towards the basic notion.

If society has determined that education and schools are a good thing, and we wish to encourage as many young people as possible to make use of their facilities, it is clear that the 16-plus pupils will ultimately have to be paid. This should be treated as part of a case for some form of basic payment to all individuals as of right, and I shall explore the arguments for this later in the book.

Schools – indeed all our educational, training and retraining establishments – impart or reinforce the employment ethic directly and indirectly. School has the effect of structuring students' days and looking after their every need, a policy which has the effect of stunting the development of decision-making skills. In doing so it reflects what happens to most people later in life at the workplace. Once again, preparation for employment overrides education for living. This concentration on the employment ethic can be diluted by the simple expedient of educating people to appreciate the existence of the many other facets of life, and this amended ethic would be nearer to the original (pre-industrial) work ethic than the one that consumes us at present.

Confidence is a fragile but important thing. A report some five years ago on the education systems of Germany and the UK pointed out that, whilst the German system produced self-contained and confident young people, the UK system developed youngsters who were dependent rather than independent. This is a grave indictment. A considerable amount of the blame for this can be laid at the door of the low expectations of pupils and parents, regrettably reinforced by some teachers, and by the inhibitions produced by the unique UK class system. Without confidence there can be little chance of self-fulfilment, while the nation as a whole loses some of the potential benefits which would have flowed from these stunted talents. The same problem does not arise in France or in Scandinavian countries, and most certainly not in the USA. The American 'show/tell' system means that all youngsters are capable of standing in front of people and talking to them; in the UK the most widely remembered nightmare is that of having to make a speech in public. This sums up the difference between the two systems – one develops self-confidence while the other inhibits it.

The lack of self-confidence is reflected in many ways. It undermines risk-taking except in the most hopeless and institutionalised forms like betting, it restricts choice in leisure activities and it forces people to be subservient or deferential for no good reason. It is not a universal affliction even in the UK, however – the independent school sector prides itself on producing confident, not to say arrogant, young people. It is all a matter of the style of teaching and the fostering, rather than the putting-down, of ambition.

Education is our lifeblood; it is the major national investment in the future. This being so it should also be *of* the future, but it is not. It is of the past. The need to produce a steady stream of unquestioning (if not uncomplaining) employees is disappearing as employment declines, but the system still produces them. The need to produce an imaginative and flexible work force is apparent, but the system does not respond. The requirements to teach proper life-skills and to educate in the arts of living are being ignored; instead, we train for the sake of training. We are not treating education as an investment for the future, but we look at it as a current cost, to be reduced where possible. School rolls are falling, and the response is to cut the numbers of teachers and close some schools – despite the fact that we anticipate school rolls to be rising again within the next ten years. The idea that the teacher/pupil ratio should be improved and standards allowed to rise while we await this new 'bulge' is rarely discussed.

It is profoundly depressing, but it is also remediable over time. We need to train teachers to teach students (and parents) in the new ways. This will take at least sixteen years to have some external effect and it assumes that the objections of parents and some of the educational establishment do not delay the process. Those who are looking for a quick and easy resolution of the problem must look elsewhere.

It is vital that the problem be resolved, however; indeed it may be the only possible non-violent way of coming to terms with the future. But some governments, especially those with a repressive bent, may sense a potential danger, and this harks back to that Tory MP of the nineteenth century. A well-educated, confident and sophisticated young population with little chance of a job which they feel befits their talents can be a danger. They are not as easily bought off or repressed as the uneducated and timid – or, as the MP put it, 'the brutal and the starving'. The results of this are already apparent in some parts of the world; an abortive revolution in Sri Lanka was led by such young people and many died. Some governments may argue that this can be avoided by reducing educational provisions and replacing them with training or some other anodyne and thought-deadening substitute. This way lies a new 'dark age' which must be resisted at all costs. The answer is to adapt to the new realities, not to hide from them. Education is and will remain the key to prosperity and a better life.

10 Meeting people's needs

'We live in a society in which the majority are better off, but nevertheless there is a growing poverty and despair and a sense of powerlessness. People will say that if this can be shown to be the case, this is not a decent society in which to live. They won't accept that greed and self-interest are the driving dynamic of our society.' This is not a snippet from a speech by an opposition politician and nor is it a leader in an anti-government paper. It is a small excerpt from an interview given to *The Times* by the Archbishop of Canterbury, Dr Robert Runcie, late in 1984. Clearly he is suggesting that there is a growing amount of physical and spiritual need in the UK at the present time. It is an observation that only the most blinkered of government supporters would disavow, yet it goes hand in hand with an increasing amount of unemployment, and little has been done to remedy matters.

If the principal reason for working (and this includes employment) is to meet the needs and demands of both the workers themselves and other people then something is clearly very wrong in today's world. Those who are unemployed *should* be employed, as there is so much for them to do. Dr Runcie was commenting on the UK, but the people in this country are relatively well off compared to the millions of people in the less developed countries (LDCs) who live with little food and no shelter. This mismatch between wasted resources and expertise and the multitude of needs that could benefit from their application is one of the great scandals of the century. Although it is easily realigned in theory, in practice it will be far more difficult for logistical, political and economic reasons. Indeed, a lasting solution may not be available to us in this course of this century.

There are two competing political philosophies which affect this problem. The governments of the UK and USA are committed to the principle of 'the market'. They believe that the market allocates resources in the only optimal manner, and appear set on extending the range of goods and services to which this precept applies. This has been demonstrated by the privatisations in the UK, where state assets like the telecommunications network, aircraft manufacture and docks have been sold on the stockmarket. As in some instances (British Telecom is an example) the company is in a position of virtual monopoly, the benefit of market exposure is difficult to fathom; but the underlying philosophy is clear. There are, however, other strings to the market bow.

People who use some of the services which in the UK are provided by the public sector are being encouraged to 'go private', the encouragement being provided by tactics as diverse as glossy advertising, the withdrawal of subsidies or even the withdrawal of the service itself. Health is one of these, education another – up to and including university level. The care of the elderly is being transferred to the private sector, municipal house-building has virtually stopped, the cost of NHS dental treatment has soared, resources to special schools are being cut, and spectacles can be purchased anywhere – though at great cost. It is a wholesale transfer of dependency on to the open market.

Another possibility is to reduce wages to a level low enough to enable the not-so-well-off to pay for services directly or indirectly. In other words a nursing home will have to drop its charges to attract poorer clients, and they can only do this by paying lower wages, or dropping standards – or both. A third option is to increase the amount of voluntary work as a proportion of the whole. I am referring of course to the needs generated in what are often known as the caring services, or the person-to-person sector.

There is a confusion between needs and demands. Demands are for things that people want, and they generally concern consumer goods or services of one type or another. There is often no element of necessity associated with them; they are articulated and can be measured. Demands are met through the marketplace in the western industrialised countries, and whether people are satisfied depends on the distribution of income and the availability of the goods or services. On the other hand, needs may not manifest themselves in an obvious way. For example, there is a far greater *need* for health care than there is a *demand*, because many people do not know that they are unwell at any one time – for example, they may be unaware that they have an ulcer, or that they are about to have a heart attack. We can meet the demand but we can never meet the need. Although humans are mortal it is possible to spend the entire gross domestic product on keeping them alive, and the potential liability for health care is infinite. The same argument can be made about education. Needs are absolute and unconstrained; we *need* food, clothing and shelter to carry on living. The distinction between *needs* and demands is that over and above these needs we may demand smoked salmon, a three-piece suite and a nice detached house. There are of course some instances when one person's demand is another's need. A city-dweller with access to public transport may demand a car, but a villager may *need* a car to go about his or her everyday life because there is no public transport. Whilst both needs and demands are experienced by every individual, they are perceived in a different manner. Demands manifest themselves through the market price mechanism, while needs only become apparent indirectly and are expressed mainly through mortality and morbidity statistics. And they are far more politically sensitive.

The opposing political philosophy argues that 'the market' does not allocate services to those whose needs are greatest. This is because they are the people who are the lowest paid – the unemployed, the old and infirm, the disabled and the poor – and the market allocates goods and services according to price and the ability to pay it. A chronically sick person who cannot work, cannot pay; a mentally sick patient would need a wealthy family to be able to afford long-term private-sector treatment, as would a paraplegic or Down's syndrome child. The Labour party, and other social democratic parties across Europe, would take such services out of the market – so lessening the importance of income and wealth distribution in these forms of care. Indeed, nearly all the industrialised countries (with the exception of Canada and the USA) provide free or highly subsidised health care, and all provide a basic free education through to school-leaving age.

Because of the nature of the services themselves, they generate a considerable amount of employment. It is possible to have the most sophisticated equipment in the world yet find patients dying, or not recovering fully, because the essential human element and contact has been overlooked. Doctors cure as many people with psychology as they do with their medical expertise, nurses aid recovery as much by their presence as by their skill, and physiotherapists provoke movement by encouragement as well as by technique. People are all-important in health matters. It is possible to computerise many facets of medicine at the expense of medically trained staffs, but in the long run health will be promoted best by the use of trained and expert *human beings*.

Many of the other services which meet needs share this person-oriented characteristic. Helping the elderly, soothing the distressed, cuddling unwanted children, tending the mentally handicapped, running youth schemes – all these and hundreds more tasks need people to perform them. Quite clearly, therefore, the meeting of needs can be a great job generator. Equally clearly, these types of services have been curtailed all over Europe and the USA with the result that the jobs which might have been expected to materialise have not done so.

The reasons for this are twofold. The move to transfer some of the services to the private sector has reduced the total number of jobs in the welfare field, but the second reason is more significant in the long run. Public expenditure is considered to be generally undesirable by many governments (except when allocated to defence or law and order). To increase the number of jobs in the entire welfare area, and at the same time start to meet growing needs, there will have to be a reversal of the current economic and political philosophy which makes public expenditure the leper of economic policy. This, however, is only the first essential condition for success – it is certainly not enough in itself. And it may not be as easy to reverse the current tide of international opinion as many opposition politicians believe; in chapter fourteen I shall tackle this topic but the example of France has to be borne in mind at the outset. The Mitterand administration started out with hopes of full employment based partly on increased expenditure in areas of greatest need – it has failed either to meet the needs or create the jobs. The fact that France is dependent upon the international financial community has had no little part to play in these failures, and this dependency is shared by all the industrialised countries. Only the USA and perhaps Japan are strong enough to ignore pressures from this quarter.

The EEC Summit in Bonn in May 1985 reinforced this international view. It was agreed to concentrate on reducing inflation and providing 'sound' money rather than reflate economies and provide jobs. The prevailing economic wisdom in the UK and USA that market mechanisms are the only lasting salvation for jobs prevailed. This means, should the policy stand, that even more needs will be unmet, even more poverty will emerge and the misery of the unemployed millions will continue unabated.

The problem is that all the costs in this area are measured in money terms, whilst the benefits are completely unquantifiable. How do you balance health, happiness or contentment against billions of pounds or dollars? How does one justify keeping an old person alive to an accountant, as all that has been achieved is to ensure additional costs in the sure knowledge that there will be no financial gain in return. These sorts of arguments stem from the attitude noted by Dr Runcie of greed and self-interest being on the increase, and their logical implications must be unacceptable to any civilised nation. Nevertheless, an economic problem remains that cannot be wished away.

Sooner or later the costs of increased services in these caring sectors will have to be met, and they will be very considerable. Any offsetting gains will be in the future, if at all. Certainly health and education provisions for young people and those of working age can be looked upon as an investment with a guaranteed return, although as labour is needed less and less in the productive fields this argument diminishes in force. It is, however, a long-term investment, and the return may not be apparent for ten to twenty years, while national income accounting and the annual budget are measured on an annual basis. Politicians find this time-shift difficult to explain to the electorate, who tend to believe, after four years of restraint coupled with lavish public spending, that the government has had enough time to make its policies work. Much of the expenditure will have no financial return at all, especially in the crucial areas of chronic illness and disablement. To pay for these services and jobs, revenue will have to be created by productive industry.

Like any business or household we can borrow to do this; it is *not true* that we cannot spend more than we earn. Every generation has had to meet the national debt of their forebears. Up to a point the internal debt is a relatively small problem, but the external debt is quite another matter – we cannot put off paying this for ever. As the UK has to import many goods, it has to export to pay for them. Oil revenues have kept this balance healthy for six years, but the decline in the manufacturing sector combined with falling oil prices has put the pressure back on to sterling.

This pressure would be exacerbated if policies to meet other needs were to be pursued at the same time. These are the needs associated with the crumbling of the physical fabric of the UK: sewer reconstruction, railway and road updating and renewal, house, school and hospital building programmes, energy conservation, cabling, inner-city regeneration, defence system reviews and satellite development. All are needed; all will meet needs. To do them simultaneously (within a decade of each other) is not really feasible, however, given the deficit on the balance of payments which would ensue. The other domestic, economic and social constraints that surround this policy were discussed in chapter eight, and these add to the difficulties inherent in a 'dash for growth' policy. In turn this means that in the short term it is extremely unlikely that the millions of jobs that should be created in the 'need' fields, can be.

It may be possible to create, let us say for the sake of argument, one million jobs in one year. The rate of growth that this would need, and the non-cash productive areas in which it would have to be achieved, suggest that the economy would have to slow down (because of the reasons given in chapter eight) unless there had been a gigantic leap in productivity in that year. If this were the case then more jobs would have been lost in the manufacturing sector as a result, and growth in the 'need' sector would have had to be even higher to decrease unemployment. A slower rate of growth with a slower increase in the number of jobs is more sustainable and would appear to offer a better chance of additional and lasting employment.

Tom Stonier of the University of Bradford believes that if the need for education at all levels were met it would provide enough jobs to employ many of the unemployed. This is true in the sense that like the health-care sector, education could command limitless financial resources and still leave some educational needs unsatisfied. Education, like most of these other government service areas, has the dual advantages of being desirable in its own right as well as having the potential to create a considerable number of jobs.

Clearly there is no difficulty in finding places where jobs need to be done; the difficulty comes in the practical translation of these tasks into employment over a long enough period, bearing in mind that the technological changes will be reducing the number of jobs in all areas. Meeting needs is not really about employment, in that a great deal can be done by work outside the employment net. Much of this is done already within families and by the voluntary services. The extended family cared for the elderly and infirm at one time and this need, if not the extended family, still exists to a greater extent than is often supposed. The elderly need people to listen and talk to them, as well as physical and medical help and comforts; they need to be reassured that they have not been forgotten and they need to feel that their experiences are still of some value. The relationship of grandparent to grandchild is of decided benefit to both for these reasons. While it is possible to pay people, especially youngsters, to talk to older people, this would seem to be one of the many services where the need for genuine voluntary commitment is apparent.

It is possible to conceive of paying people to do any task. In his play *One-Way Pendulum*, N.F. Simpson has a woman paid to eat the leftover food in the 'hero's' household. If we are to pay people to perform the task of talking to others, we are not far removed from this theatrical caricature, but there are services which old people require and for which people should be paid. Home helps, visiting nurses and the like all provide physical comforts, not just a human response; they are people who are employed and obviously they must be paid. However, despite the number of the elderly in special homes, in hospitals and still within the family, we cannot truly say that enough is being done for them; that the quality of their lives cannot be improved. The amount of work that needs to be done is immense, but most of it is concerned with people making their persons – rather than their expertise – freely and willingly available. This is not an employment-expanding service. Imagine what it would feel like to be chatted at by a person you knew was only doing it for the money – it would be degrading. This is not social work that can be conducted by paid social workers, it is humanitarian work that must be performed by volunteers.

There are many instances of this type. The Samaritan service, which acts as a lifeline to some people, would lose its impact if the person phoning in knew that on the other end of the line someone was being paid to listen to them. The caller would rightly suspect the commitment and the genuineness of the responses. This is not to say that all the necessary additions to the caring services can be made through the voluntary sector and by volunteers. We need social workers to cope with the deprivations of poverty and help those who cannot cope. We need youth workers to stimulate and encourage the new generations. We need specialist workers to help the disadvantaged. There are needs to be met in providing relief or shelter for single parents and their families, fostering for needy children, company and accommodation for drug addicts. The mentally handicapped need to be cared for properly, perhaps in the community and perhaps in sheltered accommodation, the physically handicapped need special help and facilities. Each of these services will require professionals and experts as well as back-up staff: clerical, administrative, manual and domestic. There even need to be co-ordinators and employees to ensure that the voluntary services work smoothly. Hundreds of thousands of jobs should emerge over time, but the time period may have to be an extended one if these jobs are to be made secure.

Voluntary work comes in addition to this, and there are old-established as well as newer bodies which arrange for this work to be done. The WVS is an example of the older establishment type of organisation which is devoted to 'good works' and has performed precisely these over the years. The 'settlements' in the East End of London which endowed youth clubs, sponsored boxing tournaments and provided courses and evening classes are more organised and specific examples of the same philosophy. It is a rather paternalistic (and maternalistic) approach; duty and the financial capacity to help are the twin dynamics, and guilt is not far below the surface. Despite this it would be churlish to deny the good that has emerged from these efforts. Newer organisations like the Samaritans or the battered-wives shelters have emerged to help individuals overcome problems of a more contemporary nature, rather like

179

Alcoholics Anonymous did in its early days. Volunteerism extends into this sphere, where only a victim or a person with the same problem can counsel a fellow sufferer with any hope of giving relief.

With all these unmet needs in the UK it is surprising that the voluntary sector has remained so unorganised for so long. It is perhaps a function of its local and community basis, which also accounts for much of its effectiveness – for example, hospital-visiting tends to be done by people living near the hospital in a pattern organised locally. This immunity from national political pressures and aspirations is coming to an end, however. Umbrella organisations are beginning to emerge, professional administrators are making their mark and the resources of the organisations are increasing. Pressure groups have begun to work alongside the traditional organisations offering practical help – the voluntary sector is starting to come of age.

Bodies like Community Service Volunteers are now acting as a mouthpiece for the sector as a whole, as a lobbyist to central and local government and as a practical organiser and co-ordinator on the ground. They also act as 'think tanks' and may well drag voluntary services out from beneath their Cinderella image. If they do so it will be a process aided by political parties – both the Social Democrats and the Conservatives have their eyes fixed firmly on the advantages of voluntary work.

Voluntary service has been seen as a method of obtaining cheap community service while providing something useful for young people to do, a perception which has aroused strong emotions and intense debate. An organisation called Youth Call estimates that about 300,000 full-time voluntary jobs in social services, health and education could be supported. If these, plus all the other non-employed school-leavers (about another 150,000), would actually work in this way it would cost roughly £1 billion per year to run, including state benefits for the 'volunteers'. The arguments centre around two contentious points. Would these volunteers take the jobs of existing employees (or jobs that should have been created to meet existing unmet needs); and should the scheme be a compulsory or a voluntary National Community Service?

The first of these contentions can only be argued in the abstract. It is clear that the temptation to use cheap labour as a substitute for employees paid at normal levels is great for a government committed to the principle of reducing wages to increase employment. On the other hand there is so much work to be done on the personal level, which does not come within the category of employment but which meets the needs of the recipient and of the giver, that this scheme should surely be encouraged. For this to be done properly, however, two prerequisites have to be satisfied: *the person providing the work has to be financially secure and the work should be voluntary.* Conscription will not work in terms of the quality of service that will be provided.

An umbrella body of youth organisations called Youth Choice has been formed to oppose compulsion, and at the moment it is winning. A MORI poll in October 1984 showed that only 41 per cent of the population thought that a compulsory National Community Service was a good thing, 4 per cent less than the percentage who thought that military national service should be reintroduced. Only one in four of the 15 to 24 age group thought it a good idea, and they will be the age group most affected. However, nearly 70 per cent of people generally, and almost 80 per cent of the 15- to 24-year-olds, thought that the government should introduce a *voluntary* community service scheme. The young people themselves would like to be able to do it but will not wear being forced into it. But even the voluntary method will fail, however, if employees and their unions refuse to operate the new scheme, and they might do this if it were felt that it was nothing more than a method of getting very cheap labour. The possibility of the current government, with an unchanged economic philosophy, getting adequate cooperation from unions or from the young is not high.

The UK government is clearly toying with the idea of removing any form of payment from young unemployed people if they are neither in training nor involved in an approved project. This may be the first step on the road to compulsion. The Social Democratic party's think-tank, the Tawney Society, has suggested a national scheme too, and their costing is a net £$\frac{1}{2}$ billion per year. Shirley Williams has proposed a different financial incentive which would make higher-than-dole payments to people (not necessarily youngsters) who were doing 'voluntary' community work. The SDP also assume that for a truly national scheme to be effective and to be accepted fully all 800,000 school-leavers will have to take part; it cannot be treated as another YTS for those who are neither academically inclined nor good employment material. This may entail the delaying of entry into university or other forms of tertiary education until after community service has been undertaken. An academic who has researched in this area, Professor David Marsland of Brunel University, warns that these schemes must not be 'futile make-work'. Young people are already disillusioned enough by this type of scheme, of which there are certainly plenty.

For a government which is supposed to be operating the twin virtues of 'real money' and 'real work', an awful lot of thirties-style 'New Deal' activity is taking place. The community programme projects are organised on a local basis and are intended to benefit the community, especially the environment. The jobs only last for twelve months and part of their value is intended to lie in the fact that the employee is actually in a job, absorbing the disciplines that this entails. Too many of the projects, however, are of the singularly useless variety – the modern equivalent of the army making men paint coal black or digging holes in order to fill them in again. Some schemes are worthwhile, of course, but there is an operational rule that the project can only be undertaken if it can be shown that there was no intention to do it outside the scheme. This means by definition that it was an extremely low priority and the projects are too often specially cobbled together. So it cannot be said that they are truly meeting a need – if they were, then plans would almost certainly already have been in existence to deal with the problem. The employees know this and respond accordingly.

Community Industry, which is organised by a charity and provides temporary employment for 'socially disadvantaged' young people aged up to nineteen, suffers from similar disadvantages. It offers some of the features of YTS – the life skills course, for example – alongside rudimentary community work, but it is thought of as third best by many of the people involved in it.

The YTS deserves a book to itself, even at this early stage in its existence. Given that it suffers from the disadvantage of catering for youngsters who would rather be employed, it still has more than its fair share of poor courses and non-existent training. Needs are not being met, it is a procedure for marking time before the dole for many trainees, and they know it. The MSC appears to be concerned more with the quantity of places available than with the quality of the various schemes (although many companies and agents involved with them point to local MSC people as flexible, helpful and prepared to support a good idea) and some of the more imaginative plans fall foul of the regulations – which could easily be bent to accommodate them.

Increases in the amount of leisure time available will stimulate a need for all kinds of facilities. The British have not been good at educating for leisure, as I suggested in the previous chapter, but the needs of people will be immense. Information will have to be provided, confidence built up and language demystified; it is tempting to dismiss these types of needs as trivial but, as we shall see in the following two chapters, this is based upon a gross underestimation of the extent and depth of the problem. Let us just say at present that if leisure needs are met, then some new employment will follow in the industries created.

Most of the goods and services we use and consume are provided for us by the private sector; the market is allowed to do the allocation and – providing people do not fall below minimum standards of consumption – most people accept this position. However, we get what we are given – or what is available. As consumers we cannot force a manufacturer to make a product for us, or a retailer to stock it; whilst the theory of the market implies that all demands will be met, at a price, the price might be far too high for ordinary people. Economic theory assumes that the consumer is sovereign; in the real world Galbraith was nearer to the truth when he proclaimed that the producer is sovereign. Supply comes first, and market research and advertising create the demand subsequently. Many needs and demands are completely overlooked in this situation, but there are moves afoot to remedy this – especially in the realm of goods that meet personal and community needs.

Local Enterprise Boards are being developed by some local authorities in Britain. The largest of these is the Greater London Enterprise Board (GLEB) which serves the London area, although its future is in doubt as its main provider of finance is the about-to-be disbanded Greater London Council. One of the reasons for setting up the Board was to create jobs, but not jobs at any price. The goods and services that are being encouraged are those which have a community or other social basis, whilst the conditions of employment are carefully monitored and industrial democracy is actively encouraged. Over 5000 jobs have been created, and at a relatively low cost, although it is too early to say how permanent these jobs will be. Many of them are aimed at specific needs. The production of an electrically assisted bike, a cheap van equipped for minor household repairs for a standby emergency call service, energy conservation measures and travelling monitoring units, medical expert systems, a new chair for disabled children, ethnic and educational toys and a human-centred lathe (a modern lathe designed for human participation) are all examples of the work done so far. Some of them, like Airlec's new aircraft-loader or Whitechapel Computer Works's new work station, promise to be considerable commercial successes.

The virtues of recycling and of producing products which are durable rather than with an inbuilt obsolescence are being put into practice as well as preached. It is better in the long run, the GLEB argues, to employ car mechanics to repair cars that will last ten years than employ robots to produce a car that falls to pieces after four. This clearly fits into the pattern of socially useful jobs.

Technology networks are the other method by which the GLEB intends to meet needs by promoting socially useful goods. As Dr Mike Cooley, the Director of Technology, has pointed out, 'Mankind is advanced enough to put a man on the moon or land a missile within a metre of where we want it after a 10,000-mile flight, but the blind still have to wander about much as they did in mediaeval times.' The networks are an attempt to link academics, manufacturers and the public in order to use appropriate, though not necessarily high, technology to meet medical and social problems. Expert systems, third-world energy machinery, water transport, road/rail vehicles, computer technology and energy conservation of all descriptions are being developed. There is also a need amongst the public to find an outlet for their ideas, and these networks are attempting to provide workshops and technical help for such people. People are linked with the academic world through the workshops and their technicians in an attempt to get what is known as 'popular planning' off the drawing-board and into the practical arena. Whether this is merely a good but naive idea, or whether it will actually work, will only be seen over time. What *is* clear is that visitors from all parts of the world come in droves to see what is happening, and take away a most favourable impression. It is an experiment which deserves careful monitoring.

Whilst the GLEB devotes an all-too-small part of its resources to the problems of the less developed countries, it is merely reflecting the concerns and priorities of the industrialised world. Need is ever present in the LDCs. Hunger, starvation, exposure, lack of jobs, lack of communications, lack of industry, lack of money and lack of hope are only too common. It is possible to tackle these problems, but the industrialised nations of the North have fought shy of committing enough resources to the South to make a material difference.

The Brandt Report of 1980, which recommended no more than a form of global Keynesianism, has been rejected out of hand by the governments of the largest and wealthiest industrial nations. It argues that the LDCs need to be set on a growth path of their own in order to reach self-sustaining growth, and that aid should be given with this aim in mind. It argues that this increase in global growth will repay the North several times over as the volume of world trade increases, resulting in more shares from a far larger cake. This is called the policy of 'enlightened self-interest'; certainly there has been a secular slowing of world trade growth and it needs a stimulus. But the North's leaders at the Cancun Conference in 1981 not only rejected aid to the South, they also took the short-term view about their own economies. They were wrong on both humanitarian and economic grounds.

Technological change will have a great impact on the LDCs and NICs. At present much of the technology is used to split jobs into their component parts, and those that require manual assembly are being transferred to these countries. The lack of protective labour law and the low paid and 'captive' work forces make this move an irresistibly tempting prospect for large Northern-based companies. As the technology progresses, however, fewer of these processes will be needed, automation will replace people, jobs will go and companies will pull out. However, some of the LDCs are realising that they can manufacture products on their own, they have the design and the technical capability, and they will thus shortly become fully industrialised countries. South Korea and Singapore are amongst the latter, and Brazil and Indonesia amongst the former group.

There are of course some countries – especially in Africa – where technology is virtually irrelevant, where an integrated circuit or a heart-lung machine is useless because there is no likelihood of an electricity supply in the conceivable future. The main hope for such countries, most of which were converted from a self-sustaining group of communities to cash-crop countries by the North many years ago, is to receive aid – not emergency food or shelter but help in the form of resources, appropriate technologies and expertise to work with the indigenous people to safeguard their own future and to grow. On balance, the latest technological revolution is unlikely to help LDCs much, if at all, while for some it will have positively harmful effects, such as reducing employment in labour-intensive areas.

From the point of view of the industrialised nations, the needs in the LDCs could be an opportunity both to expand their economies and reduce unemployment. These needs could be met directly by exports to LDCs, as well as the transfer of people to encourage, to teach and to work; Voluntary Service Overseas is one organisation which arranges for these types of placements. Providing that the damaging political connotations of the old US Peace Corps are avoided, and the transferees work with, and under, local inhabitants, there is no reason why the scheme should not expand rapidly. Exports to the LDCs would consist of products which could be used to encourage growth; in turn this would go some way to expanding world trade, which in turn should lead to higher growth and perhaps a little more employment across the board. This is the creation of a virtuous circle. It simply extends an additional international dimension to the 'need' argument – working to meet need – that is what work and employment should be about.

Most post-war economic expansion was arranged through the manipulation of demand. Taxes were raised or lowered, savings encouraged or discouraged and the economy 'fine tuned'. High demand kept employment high, and increasing demand today will not necessarily create employment – as we can see from the experiences over the past five years in Europe. Governments will have to learn to switch their attack towards meeting *need* instead and this will mean that politicians will have to revise their received economic wisdoms.

Eradicating urgent need as far as possible, and keeping the rest under strict control both at home and overseas, should be the first aim. It should be the overriding reason for working. *Combined with this should be the realisation that the employment ethic is no longer relevant to the twentieth century.* We are reaching what has been called 'the post-industrial society'. In pre-industrial times we had a work ethic, and now that we are moving away from that form of industrialisation it should be possible to pension off the employment ethic. It has fulfilled its purpose. We need to campaign to reintroduce the original work ethic, along with the concept of usefulness. These are appropriate to the post-industrial societies and the meeting of people's needs.

This does not mean disposing of the employment ethic altogether – it means that it has to be amended. It also means that the boundaries between employment and leisure should be reworked so that the distinction is between working time and free time. Many of us are not employed, and many of us work far less than before. Free time is becoming a larger and more central feature of our lives and it is to this that we must now turn our attention.

11 'For the unemployed, leisure is a waste of time'

The Shorter Oxford English Dictionary defines leisure as 'freedom, or the opportunity to do something' or 'opportunity afforded by unoccupied time' or 'the state of having time at one's own disposal; free time'. It is a revealing set of definitions. The concepts of freedom and personal choice are involved, and it is difficult to think of two more jealously guarded gifts than these. However, 'unoccupied' carries the connotation of 'empty', and this diminishes the feeling that leisure is a good and worthwhile thing. In the real world people have this same ambivalent attitude to leisure time. They like it and they want to have more of it, but to do nothing with it is considered 'sinful' whilst the ethic surrounding it suggests that it is little more than a distraction from the serious business of life – being in gainful employment.

In any working week a person might spend 40 hours actually in employment, which leaves over three times as many hours to do other things. If we assume that almost 60 of these hours are spent in bed, then 68 waking hours per week are available as 'free time'. This of course applies to people who are full-time employees, but these make up less than one half of the UK population. The others – be they too young or too old for a job, part-time employees or not employed at all – generally have more time to spend doing the things that they choose to do. Leisure time commands a greater proportion of our lives than employment, yet it is considered to be far less important.

The definition implies that 'free time' is an escape from occupied time, but this does not always have to be employment. A person doing housework is committing his or her time, yet this is not employment – it is work. It is certainly not leisure. However, this is one of the exceptions to a prevailing rule. Most people treat leisure as a release from employment – 'Thank God it's Friday' is the heartfelt plea heralding the start of the weekend. Even if the weather is awful, television is dreadful and there is little to do, the escape from the restraints of a job makes leisure periods something to be anticipated with pleasure. Leisure exists because the unfree time, employment, also exists. Without employment there would be nothing to escape from; free time is the pleasure of no longer banging one's head against the wall of employment. The retired rarely talk in terms of having a totally *leisured* life, however – they do not feel that the word applies to them. Whilst they have *unoccupied* time for the most part, and by definition this should be leisure time, it is not an escape from anything at all. It is not leisure, but rest perhaps.

Holidays provide a similar ambiguity. These are periods of leisure, but we can spend some of the time 'working' should we wish to do so – for example, we can decide to dig the garden from ten in the morning to noon every day for two weeks. We are committing this time, but is it any less leisure time as a result? Clearly it is not. This is not a totally straightforward concept, however; some work can be described as a leisure activity but not all. Gardening, DIY and voluntary work are undertaken primarily in leisure time, but housework is always thought of as 'work' in work time. The best rule is to treat all time as leisure time unless it is spent at employment or the traditional equivalent; historically, housework and the rearing of the young has been the female counterweight to the male breadwinner's job.

Leisure tends to be measured against employment rather than work (except in this one case). Without the time spent at employment, leisure is not fully appreciated – indeed it may not be described as leisure at all – and we now look at leisure as a reward for working hard at employment. Holidays, days off, the weekend – all of these are savoured because we have earned the right to have them. Leisure, like money, has to be earned; this is part of the employment ethic. But it leaves the unemployed with a considerable problem. They do not believe they have unlimited leisure, despite the fact that they can decide to do as they wish with their time, because they have not earned the right to the leisure. It is tainted time. As one young man from Newcastle succinctly put it in a recent TV programme, 'For the unemployed, leisure is a waste of time.'

The 'leisured classes' are those people with enough money to spend it on what they like doing best; it may be jet-setting, sailing, riding, gambling or any other reputedly pleasurable activity. But the other main reason why the unemployed and pensioners tend to claim that they have no leisure time is that, whilst they share the free time with the jet set, they certainly do not share the money. Although there is a saying that 'the best things in life are free', most leisure activities cost money. If a person is cut off from these activities by a lack of finance, he or she will also feel cut off from proper leisure.

Despite the fact that employment is a minority interest and occupies only a fraction of our time, the number of books, academic and learned articles, journals and TV programmes devoted to it is legion. They far outnumber those about leisure as a subject in itself, although there is a growing literature about individual leisure pursuits. The number of magazines on home computers, gardening or camping, for example, grows every year as both free time and general availability of money increase. Overall, leisure is considered a trifling and non-academic (to the Establishment, therefore, unimportant) phenomenon – and moreover one that is neither easily analysed nor categorised. Despite this neglect, however, leisure is vitally important to the health and well-being of individuals as well as to the cohesiveness and affluence of society. The money that we spend in our leisure time on leisure pursuits keeps the economy ticking over.

Roughly 32 per cent of household expenditure, excluding food and energy costs, is committed to leisure goods and services; this includes tobacco, drink, 50 per cent of clothing costs and 40 per cent of transport costs. In addition there is public sector leisure expenditure, and the total amounts to an enormous amount of money. It circulates, it creates employment and it is money that would not have been created if it were not for leisure time. As the number of hours spent at employment over a lifetime falls, so the importance and potential of leisure-time spending increases in relation to total national expenditure. Leisure time is vital for economic growth in a post-industrial society, indeed it represents the only private sector area where both growth and employment growth is probable.

The people of Britain have very funny habits; where else in the world does one half of the population eat dinner at 12.30 and tea at 6.00, whilst the other half eats lunch at 1.00 and dinner at 8.00? Where else in the world are people divided into two bars in the same drinking establishment, the public and the saloon? Class rears its head almost everywhere, and nowhere does it have more effect than in leisure activities.

The way we react to advertising is class-based, the products that we buy can be predicted on a class basis, what we eat and where we eat out, when and where we take our vacations, the colour of our wallpaper and front door, what we say and how we say it, where we go and what we do in our leisure time – all are class determined. Class is with us at our places of employment to a great extent, and its manifestations there have been well researched and documented. Its effects on leisure activities are at least as important, however, yet little research has been carried out and scant statistics exist – except within the files of the opinion-testing and market research companies. In the workplace all sorts of mechanisms have been, and are being, tried to get rid of the pernicious effects of the class division; works committees, 'single status' conditions of employment, consultations, even management/worker social events, have all been tried. No one has thought it necessary to put the same sort of effort into the effects of class on non-work situations, but the loss in economic and social terms as a result of these divisions must be astronomical.

They start from a very early age; educational attainment is class-based to a large and unacceptable extent in the UK, despite the introduction of the comprehensive school system, and success in exams from 'O' level to University entrance is largely a middle-class phenomenon. These are the articulate people who will become the journalists, the musicians, the TV producers and the pundits, and they will shape fashion and taste. They become the cultural élite, and as the arbiters of taste they will not unnaturally try to keep one step ahead of the masses. Once the public starts to cotton on to a particular cultural activity it loses much of its value. One has only to look at the fashions in serious music or in the art world to see the exclusivity factor at play; Tchaikovsky is less well regarded than Webern, Picasso more over-exposed than Mondrian – and all four are old-hat anyway. It is true that the arts must always move on, otherwise they stagnate, but it is suspicious that the movement should always be away from popular culture.

These cultural values impose a straitjacket upon wider participation in many leisure fields, as well as a loss of potential jobs
in these areas. There is a widespread feeling that listening to
Mozart is 'better' than listening to UB40, or that reading Proust
is more uplifting than a Mills and Boon novel. This view
immediately categorises a person according to what he or she
likes to do with their free time, and it further suggests that there
are certain 'right' things to do, whilst others are a waste of time.
Why is it better to sit in a library than to go fishing? Why does a
person who spends an hour a day in their office chatting and
drinking coffee create a fuss about lazy British workmen when
they see them taking a five-minute break resting on shovels?
The answer is that these are class-oriented responses, they
reflect middle-class expectations and values.

The school system is defective, as we have seen, in not
attempting to widen the horizons of pupils or equip them to
expand and educate themselves at a later date. Curiosity is the
key to trying new things, but it is difficult to control; it is often
considered suspect and not encouraged outside a given syl-
labus. Self-confidence would be a great advantage in this
respect, but it can prove difficult for teachers, and later on for
employers, to handle. The result is that confidence is in very
short supply amongst school-leavers. We should ask ourselves
why working-class people do not go to the opera, for example,
rather than just accepting that this is the case. The little
research there has been into this suggests that a lack of
knowledge, plus a feeling of intimidation by the physical
surroundings and the expertise of the aficionados, puts people
off. Market research shows that some working-class people will
not go into a bookshop to buy a book, but will buy that book in a
supermarket or a station bookstall. The reason given is that
they are intimidated by the book-shop assistants, especially if
they are young and female.

Food is another area where a tremendous lack of curiosity
exists in the UK. Not only will many people avoid going into
'posh' restaurants (this is not a question of price, as some steak
restaurants are even more expensive) but they are loth to try
new foods, especially foreign food. Holidays are another indicator of class – where they are taken and when. What emerges
from all this is that working-class people restrict their own
choices, the most obvious reason being that they have not

been encouraged to do otherwise – at school or in adult life.

There are a number of traps that one can fall into as a result of this analysis. The first is that working-class choices are second best; this idea must be rejected out of hand. What must be accepted, however, is that these choices are made from a restricted range and so *the aim must be to widen the area of choice for everyone*. A lot of middle-class people might like to go to bingo or the 'dogs', but cannot bring themselves to for fear of being seen. A second trap is to glorify working-class culture as the only valid one and to suggest that the prevailing cultural values are actually valueless. This philosophy leads to the withdrawal of subsidies from the existing 'flagship centres of excellence' and the diverting of resources to local community groups. But this is as illogical, indeed philistine, in its approach as unconditionally supporting the *status quo*.

The danger here is that the people who take the decisions to do this are doing so on behalf of the working classes; the GLC and some London boroughs exemplify this problem to a nicety. The membership of the controlling Labour groups of these bodies is overwhelmingly white, male and middle class; their decisions are based on a romantic idea of what they think the working class wants, and the resulting community activities reflect middle-class mores. The authorities encourage local communities to define their *own* needs and their own ways of meeting them; the working classes must be able to choose for themselves. All that is needed is a larger menu with proper and intelligible explanations about each possible choice and a mechanism for making their choices known.

The following table is taken from *The Leisure Shock*. It is based on data from the 1977 General Household Survey and is the last government survey of this nature. Other than the probability that billiards and snooker will have a rather higher ratio today, there is no reason to believe that this table is no longer representative.

The ratio of (a) to (b) is a 'middleclassness' indicator, or perhaps a respectability factor. The higher the factor, the more acceptable is the activity in terms of prevailing cultural values. The numbers refer to the percentage of men (in official surveys women are assumed to take the class of their husband or father) who had participated in the activity at least once over the preceding four weeks, presented on an average annual basis.

Activity	Professional Employers & Managers (a) %	Semi-skilled & Unskilled (b) %	Ratio of a:b
Outings to seaside	9	5	1.8
Outings to country	8	3	2.7
Outings to pubs	4	3	1.3
Visiting historic buildings	13	4	3.25
Visiting theatre/opera/ballet	7	1	7
Visiting museums/art galleries	6	1	6
Amateur music/drama	6	2	3
Going out for a meal/drink	77	64	1.2
Dancing	15	11	1.4
Social and voluntary work	13	5	2.6
Listening to records/tapes	69	56	1.2
Gardening	61	43	1.4
House repairs DIY	60	41	1.5
Hobbies	14	8	1.75
Book reading	68	40	1.7
Swimming	12	3	4
Football	4	4	1
Golf	9	1	9
Squash/fives	6	1	6
Darts	9	16	0.55
Billiards/snooker	9	10	0.9
Walking (2 miles +)	25	12	2.1
Bingo	2	7	0.3
Gambling & pools	7	33	0.2.

There are few surprises in the table. Perhaps pub-visiting being more of a middle-class than a working-class habit comes as a mild shock, although this could be a reflection of money availability – drinking at home is cheaper. While it is obvious that the middle classes are likely to try more things more often, one worrying factor is that the working classes take less exercise. When combined with differences in diet and smoking habits, this has grave implications for health care.

It is quite clear that a lot of persuasion is needed, and information should be made available, to widen people's perspectives. It may be that attitudes will change under the impact of increased leisure time, but this cannot be relied upon. Campaigns are, however, starting as the authorities wake up to this problem; the Sports Council have started a Sport for All programme aimed at the non-doers, and local authorities are making a concerted effort to improve the quality and quantity of their leisure services. There are four sets of reasons behind this sudden interest in leisure time.

The first is commercial. Leisure markets are growth markets. Children want the latest brand of football shirts as worn by Arsenal, or the track shoes that make Seb Coe run so fast. Sport has to be promoted for this market to be cultivated, and other activities which require entrance fees, equipment, coaching and training have to be fostered and publicised. The tourist market is growing and good opportunities exist there for large profits, whilst the facilities that are available during high season can be used in the low season by the locals; hotels, theatres, museums and parks come into this category. Shops, restaurants, taxis and tours are other leisure-time provisions where increased free time has stimulated expansion.

The second reason is fear. There are more people with more time off than ever before, plus the unemployed with all their time their own. What are these people supposed to do with this time? Until recently they had been left to their own devices, but this is no longer the case. Increases in vandalism, petty crime and the 'street-corner syndrome' are persuading the authorities that leisure facilities must be made available. All sorts of initiatives are being taken with this defensive strategy in mind, and sport plays a disproportionately large part – presumably because it is assumed that it will tire out the youngsters and render them relatively harmless. For it is of course the youngsters that inspire the fear. Groups of pensioners on street corners tend not to send the alarm bells ringing, whilst the middle-aged unemployed are rarely suspected of stoning ducks to death in the parks or terrorising lollipop ladies. Their frustrations are turned in against themselves instead.

The third reason is that there are some people who believe that because we have a 'work ethic' (really the employment ethic) at times of full employment, then we need a leisure ethic to cater for the unemployed. Hence the preoccupation with leisure activities. It does not require much thought to realise that this idea will not work. It is not possible to have an employment and a leisure ethic running at one and the same time – they are mutually contradictory. The unemployed can point to the employed and say, 'Why is it me that hasn't got a job?' with a great feeling of being wronged. If there was a leisure ethic a person who was having to do a job would also ask, 'Why me?' This is only part of the reason why a leisure ethic cannot work, however.

The fourth reason is that people want to be useful, they want to be wanted, they need to be needed. Leisure activities do not fulfil this basic urge. To suggest to the unemployed that they can fill their time enjoying themselves, whilst those who have jobs are having a terrible time of it, will not be taken seriously. Throughout history there have been attempts to buy off populations with bread and circuses, although never the unemployed as a group, and never very successfully. Science fiction writers, however, clearly think that this will be the pattern of the future – given the number of books, TV dramas and films like *Rollerball* on the subject. It will be sad if they prove to be prescient.

The unemployed do have problems in filling their day; some cannot cope at all. Harry was a senior shop steward with a large production company until he took early retirement. He had spent a considerable amount of his time advising and counselling his members about this very thing, so he felt confident that he could cope. Within six months the high point of Harry's day had become tea-time. He got up later than ever, walked to fetch and then read the paper, had his first drink at eleven o'clock, slept through lunch-time and woke for tea. When his wife Marge and his son and daughter came home from their jobs he would not let them talk about their day in front of him, and flew into a paddy if they did. Harry was a fit, energetic man, but, if it were not for the fact that he has put on over thirty pounds, he could be described as a shadow of his former self. Harry is not only not unique, he is not even unusual.

In the early weeks the unemployed do jobs around the house like painting and repairs (if they are allowed to by the landlords), garden (if they have one), overhaul the car (if they have one) and generally make themselves useful. This wears off after two or three months and Harry's form of lethargy sets in. Certain things have to be done of course. Shopping is eked out so that as many trips as possible are made out of the house, but this involves buying small amounts and is the most expensive method of purchasing goods. Housework has to be done and basic personal hygiene has to be maintained. Other than a trip to the local Job Centre or perhaps to an interview or to post more job applications – and of course the customary grovelling obligations to social security or Employment Department officials – the week is devoid of incident. Few surveys have been made as to how the unemployed spend their time, although one is under way in London at present, and Harry was one of the pilot studies.

The reports and TV documentary investigations that have been published suggest that there is a large difference between tolerance of mornings and afternoons. Mornings are tolerated, but afternoons drag terribly because the limited work that was needed has been largely completed by then. Most unemployed men hate housework (and strangely hate making beds more than anything else); sex-stereotyped roles prevail, although not quite as strongly as amongst the employed. A 1982 survey by the Economist Intelligence Unit is one of the few which has looked closely at how the unemployed use their time.

Almost half the women and one in five of the men did housework in the mornings; shopping was the next most usual occupation for women (one in four compared with one in five men), but over one in five men went job-hunting or to the DHSS, compared with less than one in six women. Gardening claimed the attention of one in seven men and reading was the choice of one in ten. Over one in eight women spent time washing and ironing, but only one in fifty men owned up to this. Surprisingly, few men or women admitted to drinking, playing sports or cooking, although one in ten women went to visit a relative or friend whilst one in twelve men and women revealed that they stayed in bed.

The afternoons were used differently. There was less shopping and housework but more women than men went job-hunting, and almost twice as many men and women went visiting. Three times as many women as men cooked (but still less than one in five), TV was watched by about one in seven men and one in eight women, but reading declined amongst the men although it doubled amongst the women to one in ten. One in eleven men admitted to doing nothing except sitting around in the afternoons, although this is probably a gross underestimate. The unemployed in the higher social classes apparently will not admit to doing nothing, as this would be a double admission of failure. It also emerged that the younger people sleep more and that the longer the spell of unemployment the less interested people became in trying to get another job. Demoralisation sets in quite early and this shows up in other ways too.

One-third fewer unemployed than employed people take part in voluntary activities, despite the fact that they have so much more time at their disposal. Surveys show that one in five of the unemployed are severely unhappy and one in three of the longer term unemployed claim that their families had been badly affected. The unemployed tend not to use their time constructively. The small number of people who take part in sports, read or go on visits to towns and use the civic amenities suggest that they have lost the ability to take initiatives. Self-denigration and self-abasement are evident as they feel that without a paid job they are useless or worthless. Leisure cannot be enjoyed or used constructively in such circumstances and with such negative thinking.

As the number of the wholly and partly unemployed grows, so this syndrome becomes ever more apparent. This gives rise to a new need – to motivate the unemployed enough for them to use some of their free time in a positive way. The longer the period of unemployment, the harder this will be. The young unemployed have these feelings of worthlessness too, but add to them anger and resentment; they have illusions to be shattered, they have not yet built up the veneer of cynicism as a barrier against the outside world. Unemployment denies them a stake in their own communities as well as denying them their own abilities. It is little wonder that this can bubble over into random and senseless violence or self-destructive habits. *Leisure and leisure time are both seen as negative assets.* The leisure needs of this group will be different from those of the employed or from the older unemployed, and this diversity of need will be one of the thorniest problems of the leisure planners.

It promises to be a vastly overloaded system. The inexorable movement towards less employment time over the entire industrialised world will partly be met through leisure markets – but these will be unable to cope with many of the smaller groups. The range of people demanding and needing something to occupy their time will be larger than ever before, and certainly larger than anything we have seen this century. Given this diversity, and the fact that some of the groups will have little economic or political power, local and central government will have to bear more than a little of the burden. The only precedent is when the Victorian philanthropists and city fathers of the mid nineteenth century built parks, museums, theatres, libraries and galleries in an attempt to widen the interests of workers and provide them with much-needed recreational and leisure facilities.

For the Victorians, however, there had to be a moral rationale for this, which was self-improvement. Not only were the leisure provisions in the towns and cities educational (even the parks were 'botanical gardens'), but the seaside was health-giving and the waxworks mind-improving. If any single moral value underlies the current interest in leisure provision, it is to maintain peace and harmony in communities by giving people something to do. It is a defensive and pre-emptive strategy which holds the interests of those who need the facilities to be secondary to the wider view of a stable society.

The ascending star of leisure is international. The Germans have virtually lost their image of being born with a spanner in their hands and not releasing it until the undertaker prises it loose. Not only have there been strikes to get a shorter working week, but the polls are revealing that younger workers have a different set of motivations from those of their parents. They would like to spend more time with their families, they are prepared to trade off money against increases in their leisure time and they no longer believe that a job is the only purpose in life. The traditional German sentiment is summed up by the apoplectic headline in the magazine *Bild*: 'Germans outraged – we are *not* lazy!' The same forces seem to be at work there as in the UK; the loss of jobs due to the new technologies and the run-down of traditional industries have increased tension, indeed led to bewilderment as the old certainties have been swept away. Jobs have lost their allure as new, impersonal and worryingly different techniques and systems all add to the pressure.

Free time suddenly becomes alluring. Employment no longer reaches the parts that other activities do not, at least not the parts that the employees want reached. German workers are no longer held up by employers as something which the British should admire and emulate. This mantle has been handed on to the Japanese, but it may not be long before they pass it to the NIC workers as the fears about robotics and continual change start to upset the newly affluent workers. In France holidays are taken seriously, as are many everyday leisure activities like eating or drinking out, the theatre and cinema and visiting art galleries; none of these has the class connotations of the UK. Working lifetimes are getting shorter in France, as they are in every other European country, with unions to the forefront of the campaigns. Workers want to spend more of their time at leisure but, like other matters to do with employment, this leads us into a paradox. Employees want less of what the unemployed desperately need, and want more free time – a benefit which the unemployed would gladly put aside altogether.

Some of the unemployed cope well with enforced free time, while others do not. The major contributing factor in coping has been identified in recent research as our old friend the protestant work ethic. The reason for this may be that the researchers identified a strong 'work' rather than 'employment' ethic, which would clearly help a person find outlets for his or her talents. Work is perfectly compatible with free time, employment is not. A strong work ethic would also suggest that the person is more capable of setting achievable goals and structuring personal time, as well as being motivated by a strong sense of usefulness to others. As the research sample was exclusively made up of those with academic qualifications, however, it may not be applicable to wider interpretation.

In Victorian times the middle-class entertainment centre was the home. Soirées, large formal family occasions, musical evenings and singsongs, charades, parties and games – all were part and parcel of respectable family life. As affluence grew, along with living standards and expectations, entertainment was sought outside the home. Pubs and clubs, theatres and music halls, sporting events and charabanc trips all contributed to a widening experience. More people met other people than ever before, as the new forms of public transport made even the poor relatively mobile. Leisure activities and leisure expenditure were outward-looking; the seventies and eighties, however, have seen a sharp reversal of this trend. Once again the home is becoming the major leisure centre. The difference between Victorian times and today is that it is now based in more solitary pursuits.

Television and the explosion in home ownership have been the two major causes for this. Television, with the added attractions of the video recorder, has become the latest opiate; it is by far the most influential leisure-time provision, and takes up more of people's time than anything else. Despite an observed fall in hours of watching (which may have been caused by the use of videos), TV is watched for about sixteen hours per week on average (inevitably in the UK this is class-related, with the middle classes watching some four hours less). Television effectively ties people into the home for most evenings and weekends because there is nearly always something that appeals, though it is possible to envisage videos freeing people from this tyranny.

Home ownership has an entirely different range of effects. It ties up cash flow, thus reducing leisure expenditure, and encourages pride in ownership – which means that the home should reflect the status and the aspirations of the owner. In turn these made demands on money and time: money to pay builders and decorators or to buy materials which will be needed to make the house reflect this image, time to arrange these things and to indulge in the DIY that most house-owners attempt sooner or later. Ownership means that personal vanity is exercised so that gardens tend to be tended rather well and double-glazing becomes a necessity rather than a luxury. The net effect of this relative diminution of disposable time and money is that the home has to be the place to be. It makes sense too, if a person has invested all this time, effort and money in their home, that their return is maximised by using it more often.

The growth of the home as a leisure centre is well-recognised and manufacturers and providers of services have not been slow to take advantage of it. Drinking at home is facilitated by the use of cans, home-brew kits and the relative cheapness of these when compared to pubs and bars. Takeaway food emporia, which are growing apace, presuppose that the food is being taken back into the home, whilst there is even a resurgence apparent in the boardgames market, with new ones on the market every Christmas. It is all part of the growing 'self service' economy, where the home is acting as a substitute for what used to be external and job-creating economic activity. Washing machines replace laundries and launderettes, vacuum cleaners replace human cleaners, and frozen gourmet meals replace restaurants.

These trends are reinforced by the idea that out there lies danger, at home is safety and security. Inner-city dereliction fuels this fear, along with violence and muggings – both of which are assumed to be on the increase. 'Better to be safe than sorry' is the motto. This applies to what were previously regarded as safe pursuits like going to football matches or to the seaside on a bank holiday.

If the home is to continue developing as the major entertainment centre, and if the manufacturers of all the new electronic gadgets have their way it will, then we must change the way we look at leisure provision. With the home becoming a substitute for external economic activity and a work and business centre too, people are in danger of becoming isolated. We may be coming full circle here; in pre-industrial times social contacts were made at both work and leisure, and this changed slowly until by the 1960s employment was providing the main channel for human and social contact. With the loss of employment and the retrenchment into the home it is clear that leisure policy will have to be aimed at getting people to meet and relate to each other, and socialising might once again become something that we do in our free time rather than at work.

Of course the unstoppable march of home entertainment and values will mean inevitably that fewer jobs will be created in the leisure industries than might otherwise be expected. Nevertheless there is so much need, so much pent-up demand, covering such a wide range of places, persons and priorities that massive resources should be committed. We need, and will almost certainly get, a new leisure revolution to match the new industrial revolution. Whether this will result in a liberating or enslaving experience will depend on what controls are exercised and who exercises them. It will be a test for democracy and freedom.

12 The leisure revolution

When I lunge despairingly across a tennis court after yet another blistering volley from my opponent I am not thinking to myself, I'm taking part in a recreational activity in my leisure time – amongst other things I think I am playing tennis. The same applies to the more energetic among us who play squash, the walkers who play golf, the sedentary bridge addict and the prone sunbather. 'Leisure' and 'recreation' are words which an observer uses, they are not in a participant's vocabulary. This semantic division reflects the divisions that are inflaming the normally sedate debates between the different organisations which have a stake in the leisure industries. Should there be leisure planning or not, should the planners dictate or should the plans emerge from the potential participants, and, if the latter, what mechanisms can be used? Who plans, who pays and who plays? These are the basic questions that need to be considered.

The Marshall Islanders have an old saying, 'One man's rest depends on another's broad shoulders', which means that life requires many layers of interdependence. The reductions in the time spent at our jobs are throwing these layers into sharper relief than at any other time this century. The enjoyment of leisure time depends on other people (as well as ourselves) doing the jobs which enable resources to be made available for recreational activities. Actors, broadcasters, journalists, sports coaches and employees of clubs all do jobs which provide the rest of us with our leisure-time requirements. However, the industry itself is fragmented, planning (if it exists) is piecemeal, while the supply of leisure provisions is becoming less relevant to those who have the most free time.

The new industrial revolution has created a new employment revolution, which in turn is creating the new leisure revolution. There are not only quantitative differences but qualitative ones. More of the same, which is the prevailing philosophy of politicians and those who take the practical decisions on what resources are to be made available, will not be good enough. The newly emergent and different leisure needs must be met by the use of appropriate measures. It will be a true revolution; old attitudes will have to change along with old prejudices and even older practices.

The new leisure revolution has taken us unawares. Each change in employment pattern, each new shift arrangement, each shorter working day, week, month or year has been separately arranged in isolation from the others. Each redundant person, unemployed school-leaver or retiree represents an individual circumstance. On aggregate they add up to a clear trend, but because this has been built up from thousands of discrete decisions it was not apparent until problems started to emerge. The trend, however, contains many different, and at times, mutually incompatible needs, and the winning trick in this new game will be to devise a series of policies which will meet these needs. In short we need a 'win/win' strategy.

Employees spend less of their time at their place of employment than ever before; this is caused by a variety of factors, as we have seen. Shorter working weeks and more holiday entitlements have been introduced. Less overtime is being worked. More people are working part-time, or in temporary jobs, or both. More people are self-employed and can adjust their own employment and leisure hours. More elderly people are living longer, more handicapped and chronically sick people survive. There are more unemployed people with 100 per cent free time. Finally, there are an increasing number of people who, for one reason or another, cannot cope with the stresses and strains of modern society who need, although they do not get, increased free time.

Each of these different groups adds a different set of demands on to the leisure system. While, overall, leisure time is increasing, the times at which it becomes available are changing; this is a result of the other main feature of the new employment movement exemplified by changes in shift patterns, some of them highly unsociable, and flexitime arrangements. Completely new needs and demands are beginning to emerge, and in particular the new arrangements for the practical implementation of the shorter working week have resulted in different demands on the leisure and recreational system.

A shorter working week can be achieved in three basic ways. Let us suppose a decrease from 40 to 35 hours – in the real world this would be phased in over a period of three or four years but we shall suppose that a super negotiator has been at work and it is to be implemented instantly. It is possible to reduce each working day by one hour; it is possible to finish at lunch-time on Friday (or any other day) and it is possible to increase the hours worked in a day to nine and thus work a four-day week with an hour saved somewhere along the line. All three of these options can be introduced alongside a change in shift arrangements; indeed the last option would demand such a change. Which one is chosen will depend on the operational problems of the enterprise, on the feasibility of new shift arrangements, on the availability of labour, especially part-timers, and on the bargaining strength of the work force.

Each of these choices demands a different response from the leisure industry. An hour off the working day is not very much; it may enable parents to play a bit more with children, it may be used for shopping, gardening or for some form of sporting endeavour or on the other hand it may lead to an extra cup of tea and earlier TV-watching. It is possible to take it in the lunch hour or by a later start rather than an earlier finish but, being only one hour, it is likely to place less strain on existing facilities than a larger block of time such as the half or whole day off. Travel is possible with these longer periods, as are visits to cinemas, theatres, museums and art galleries. With regard to sports, in an hour only those that can be completed quickly can be attempted (squash and swimming, for example), but over a longer period pastimes like bowls, cricket and football, angling or cards become possible. If the half day or whole day off is taken on a Friday, longer weekends can be taken and tourism comes into the picture; if there are children of school age this will put pressure on the education system to become more flexible.

Even these categories only scratch the surface of the possible permutations. An extra hour's leisure on a summer's evening may allow the playing of a sport that was not quite possible before – a twenty-over cricket match, for example, or a sponsored walk can last for well over the extra hour. The hour releases existing 'locked up' leisure time. Less overtime worked has the same effect as daily hour reductions.

The effects of increased holiday entitlements are not totally straightforward either. Holidays may be chosen freely or they may be tied to the employer's requirements. The fifth week's holiday in the UK is often taken over the Christmas/New Year period when many plants and offices close completely or just open for essential annual maintenance work. This puts pressure on all the leisure facilities because such a large proportion of the population is on holiday at the same time. It is similar to the traditional French exodus from Paris and the other industrial centres in August, putting all the pressure on roads and holiday facilities; government policy there has been to spread these holidays over the rest of the year in order to avoid the congestion. The 'wakes weeks', when entire towns close for a week, still exist in the UK to some extent, but more often than not companies try to keep their plant running for as many weeks in the year as possible. Christmas time is not the only period when employees have constraints placed on their choice of holidays, however; some are instructed that they can only have two weeks of their annual entitlement in the July to September period, thus directing their holidays to other and less popular times of the year. This can tie people to their own neighbourhood as children may still be at school, or perhaps the spouse cannot get a similar holiday time arranged, a problem that is becoming increasingly frequent as more wives get jobs.

Holidays, tied or not, are relatively large blocks of leisure time. People often claim that they get bored with long holidays, partly because they have not been educated to cope with large amounts of free time and partly because of a lack of easily available things to do. Some people actually get temporary jobs in their holidays, and only partly because they need the extra money; that deep-felt need to be doing something useful is rarely eradicated completely. More people having longer holidays will add to the overall pressures on all sorts of institutions. Home life can be affected, the peace of the community can be threatened, and if people do try to use existing facilities they often become unpleasantly overcrowded – especially in the high seasons when overseas tourists are much in evidence.

Part-time and temporary employment add extra dimensions to these problems, and they are not just of increased scale – shorter working weeks and longer holidays writ large, as it were. Part-timers have singularly different problems and needs. They may well have children of school age and they may well be working odd hours with unconventional shift patterns. They are much more likely to be women than men, whilst others may be near to, or even past, retirement age. Temporary workers have the problem that by definition they work for only part of the time and cannot totally control when this may be. This uncertainty factor is very important. If the potential users of leisure resources do not know when they will be free to use them, it makes the task of those who supply the resources that much more difficult. Added to this uncertainty is the relative lack of disposable money, as most employees in these categories are not paid handsomely.

The self-employed come under a completely different heading, although there are many subdivisions in this group. A successful barrister may be turning away work and attempting to increase his (less often her) leisure time, while a builder might be struggling to get work and to all intents and purposes be unemployed. Any London taxi-driver will tell you that the only good thing about his (even more rarely her) job is the freedom – 'I can stop work when I've taken enough money', they boast. In fact they do not; most keep on working. The theory is that the self-employed can regulate their own working hours; in practice, by no means all manage to do so. The continual emphasis on work is probably the result of the chronic insecurity that afflicts so many of the self-employed, the little voice that keeps whispering that this is a good year but next year may be a disaster and there is nothing to fall back on. The importance of this group, and indeed that of the secondary workers, lies in the fact that they are expanding rapidly as a percentage of the labour force.

The unemployed are the final grouping in an employment-oriented analysis, and they too are growing as a group. Their problems are different from those of the people with jobs; lack of available money is one problem, and lack of motivation and confidence another, as we discussed in the previous chapter. If the unemployed do not believe that they actually have leisure time, attempting to provide for it becomes that much more difficult. Most of the groups we have been discussing have one thing in common: much of their newly acquired free time is in the period which has been conventionally allocated to employment. It is also the time when there are the least opportunities for leisure activity, and without positive action this will result in yet another classic UK mismatch. The new shift systems designed around new technology and the shorter working weeks add to the availability of free time at non-peak hours.

Split shifts, especially for women part-timers, are on the increase. Twilight shifts, which allow women both to look after their families and work, are becoming more common. Computers themselves need night-shift work by operators, whilst many of the new production-side systems demand seven-day week, twenty-four-hour day working and shifts have to be arranged accordingly. The current wave of shorter working hours combined with agreements which – at the least – maintain cost/output ratios have stimulated the introduction of new continental shift systems, most of which mean that these employees will have to take their increased leisure time when most others do not. The limited ability to amend the hours worked that is conferred by flexitime arrangements is swelling the numbers of people with free time at precisely the times when the social system expects them to be at work. A recent paper by Roberts and Chambers ('Work schedules, leisure and lifestyles') points out that 'Most leisure, educational and social/ personal services in the public and commercial arena correspond to the requirements of conventional work time patterns.' They point out that this can have adverse effects but that it may ' . . . permit the adaptation to, and the creation of, new leisure experiences and activities'. This is a consummation devoutly to be wished.

The elderly form another significant group with considerable free time. There are two forces at work here. Advances in medical and nursing care are enabling more people to live longer and at the same time remain relatively fit and active. Orthopaedic surgery gives mobility to thousands who would otherwise be housebound, physiotherapy and speech therapy alleviate the after-effects of strokes, and drugs can control some of the disabling symptoms of diseases like Parkinson's. The other factor is that expectations amongst the elderly are higher than ever before. A graceful decline out of sight of the more active public is no longer the ultimate ambition. Fitness, travel and improvements in the range and the quality of their overall lifestyle are now becoming commonly held aims. Highly desirable as these may be, they also place a strain on existing and finite resources.

Paradoxically, medicine has helped to increase the numbers of the chronically disabled. Many accident victims, or the congenitally handicapped who might have died ten years ago, are now living and are rightly demanding better lives and higher standards. This applies to many of the mentally handicapped too. The boundaries between the social services, medical care and leisure provision become extremely fuzzy at this point. Social workers around the country, most often in the high unemployment areas, are identifying more families, more children and more individuals at risk. Many of them are living a life of permanent tension, cannot get away from the family environment and may prove to be a hazard to themselves or others. But this need is scarcely articulated; it lies beneath the surface of what, to outsiders, may seem to be quite normal, if poor, lifestyles. Quiet despair was, until recently, the prerogative of the elderly, but it has spread rapidly. Here too the social services and the leisure providers should be working hand in hand to prevent this need becoming an engulfing flood of demand.

It is difficult to imagine a greater range of needs than those which are starting to emerge in the leisure arena. They affect the entire age range, but especially the young and the old; men, and considerably more women; the superfit, the able-bodied and the handicapped; the employed and the unemployed; the brilliant and the not-so-brilliant; the affluent and the destitute. All of them are clamouring (some more noisily than others) for more things to do in their extra free time. The times when people want these services are changing too; mid-morning, lunch-times, afternoons, or the middle of the night are now usable leisure periods. The old, rigid, employment time-demarcated system is breaking down.

Local government is in the front line of this revolution, although not always willingly. It bears the responsibility for the social services which should both identify and alleviate existing need, and anticipate future requirements. It has responsibility for the education system. It owns and manages much of the existing leisure capital in the country, and has to keep the local transport and physical infrastructure in good repair, especially in the places where tourism might be expected to bring in many visitors. It has a duty to the elderly and the handicapped. In short, it is the vital link between people and services.

There is an upheaval in local government in the UK. Councils come and go, and new bodies are cajoled into life only to be brutally smothered not long after, making long-range planning more difficult than ever. As the demands on local government increase, so their expenditure is under attack by central government – which makes meeting needs that much harder. Nevertheless, there are signs that local government is starting to take the subject of leisure seriously; some county councils, especially those along the coasts, have no option as they already have to spend considerable amounts of money on provisions for tourism. In some, like West Sussex, this expenditure is one of the major items in the budget and could, if leisure time continues to increase, become the largest.

The Association of Metropolitan Authorities (AMA), a national co-ordinating body for much of local government, has arranged seminars, held conferences and produced papers on the various aspects of the subject. The consultancies that work with local government are also arranging conferences on a leisure theme. So the interest is there even if the necessary money is not always available. Some councils are appointing leisure officers on salaries which match their newly acquired senior status, and there are even signs that a longer term view is being considered, in an attempt to foresee problems before they occur.

What has not yet filtered through to enough people is the need to link leisure policy with other decision-making centres. Social service departments are an obvious example. Where and what are the recreational needs of the clients? Can single parents get out of the house, and if not can anything be done for them? These are the types of liaison that would be effective. Housing is another department where cooperation is needed; the lack of garden or play space, petty acts of vandalism on estates or elsewhere in the neighbourhood are indications that something should be done. Education is another obvious candidate for a close and harmonious working relationship with leisure-planning organisations, as should be transport and other committees like those running libraries or parks. Leisure planning at a local authority level is still too isolated and too 'prestige project' oriented. An increasing awareness of their responsibilities is, however, a welcome start that some authorities can build upon, though the arbitrary division of responsibilities between the different layers of local government does nothing but hinder this. The entire question of co-ordination in this area is one that might in fact be usefully tackled by using the new technologies themselves, as they are, after all, communication- and information-based.

Leisure provision and management is creating a new range of skills in local government. Not only do leisure centres and other facilities have to be planned, built, managed and staffed but the service has to be monitored, complaints dealt with and customers satisfied. Research in Canada suggests that planners are muddling through rather than taking strong policy decisions, and this is especially true of the acquisition and disposal of land and other resources. Recruitment into local government is changing in response to these criticisms, and more officials are being taken on who have had experience of working in, and dealing with, companies in the private sector. These new officials are spearheading the drive for more joint public and private sector ventures. Councils are making land available for private developers, or are building sports and recreational facilities which are then leased to private sector managements which have a good track record in their particular field. This arrangement has the additional advantage of creating a fixed and certain operational revenue for the council. Sports and leisure centres, swimming pools and meeting halls, concessions for the catering or entertainment facilities in centres and parks are examples of this – as are the joint ventures in heritage and industrial archaeology sites. It is a new field, where both parties are cautiously feeling their way.

'Greening' the cities is one of the preoccupations of the eighties, much of it stimulated by the Liverpool Garden Festival project. New parks are being laid down in urban centres for the first time since the nineteenth century, and old parks updated and modernised. Where 'keep off the grass' signs were once as prominent as the flowers in the formal beds, now informality and some imagination hold sway. There are now gardens for the elderly and scented plant arrangements for the blind, as well as an ancestor-worship corner for the Chinese population in Manchester's municipal cemetery. It is slowly being realised that parks are for leisure activities and not for boosting the municipal image. Artificial ski-slopes, BMX tracks and all-weather sports pitches are starting to make their appearance, and there seems to be an attempt to improve amenities like lavatories and cafés. There is of course always the danger of trendy councillors being carried away by the latest fad and providing a facility that is out of fashion, and use, after twelve months; my nearest open space boasts a skateboard park, for example, but no one has seen a skateboard there for the past five years. Flexibility and easy conversion of capital facilities to take account of fashion changes is becoming one local government priority, and where it is not, it should be.

National parks and places of historic and cultural interest, National Trust properties and other tourist attractions need roads, parking facilities, policing, public transport systems and street lighting – all of which have to be paid for and provided and maintained by local government. The percentage of income that will have to be diverted to these indirect effects of increased leisure time will be felt by the other spending committees, unless provisions are made to subsidise councils, or some other method of funding becomes available. Net local authority expenditure on leisure facilities and activities in the year ending 1983 was just under £1 billion. The largest elements in this were parks and open spaces (£260 million), administration (£170 million), sports and leisure centres (£100 million) and swimming pools (£100 million). In terms of balancing income with expenditure, only golf courses and allotments came anywhere near breaking even, and only catering made an overall profit. So it is clear that even these substantial amounts of money are not adequate to meet fast increasing needs and demands. Indeed, in some of the areas expenditure actually fell in the preceding twelve months; museums, galleries and libraries all had less spent on them. If you have borrowed this book from your local library you should be asking the librarian (when you return it) about these cuts and how it is affecting the number and the range of books that can be loaned, and draw your own conclusions about the consequences.

Central government has direct and indirect roles to play in leisure patterns. It is a provider of finance through the Department of the Environment to museums, historic monuments, galleries, libraries and, through a subsidy system, to other bodies both voluntary and statutory. The Arts and Sports

Councils, Heritage and the National Playing Fields Association are examples of this type of payment conduit. Government legislation affects the ability of local government to provide services by constraining their income, and affects other provisions by taxation and legislation. VAT has had an adverse effect on theatre (a visit to a West End theatre is an entertainment in itself because so many of the audience are tourists from overseas), cinema and football attendances. Legislation will ultimately determine if and when UK dwellings are wired for cable, how the cable system will operate, and therefore what leisure patterns we will pursue. The government determines our drinking habits through the laws on licensing hours and duty on alcoholic beverages, our mobility through petrol taxes or the financial targets on British Rail, and our walks through protection of the Green Belt and other planning policies. From wildlife conservation to attending football matches, governments have an immense impact on our choices whether they (or we) like it or not. It is an inevitable consequence of having a central government of any description.

Discussions on planning for leisure are starting to erupt in academic as well as professional circles, especially the apparent paradox of planning for freedom and planning for individual choice. Whether the planning should be left to the planners is a key question, and several models are being produced which suggest strongly that the answer must be no – at least not on their own. In the past, providers of recreational activities and facilities guessed what the demands were and tried to meet them. Pubs and cinemas were situated in an almost random manner, clubs developed in basements, recreation grounds in open spaces where no one wanted to build, and later community centres, pools and playing fields where the council owned the land. It was a haphazard development. We now need to control these movements, partly because it is clear that some groups, often the economically weak, were treated badly under the old system and partly because the existing facilities are all too clearly inadequate. Another reason is the growing emphasis on market research, which in this context is called either community involvement or consultation. The capital and running costs associated with many new ventures are very high and, using precisely the same reasoning as a motor car manufacturer, this research discovers people's tastes, and if necessary moulds them, in order to avoid a commercial or social disaster.

The emphasis on the community is now highly visible in local organisations and politics. The Liberals first used 'community politics' in Liverpool in the sixties and, to most conventional politicians' surprise, struck a rich response. Cracked pavements clearly mattered – and deeply too. Since then, other parties have taken up the community theme and some London Labour controlled councils have actually tried to devolve such services as housing and refuse collection into local neighbourhoods in an attempt to get a better local response and input. There are of course problems involved in doing this. In large cities it is often difficult to identify a community, new developments and depopulation having destroyed what we fondly imagine were tight-knit and harmonious groups. It is interesting that all the most popular British soap operas, *Coronation Street, East Enders and Brookside*, are based on real-life but highly romanticised communities; we obviously yearn for this type of environment. To reinvigorate it will require work and commitment, as well as financial resources, all of which need to be made available.

People spend a considerable amount of time in their local neighbourhood – particularly women, children, the aged and infirm. Given this, it is more than logical to see the need for local leisure provisions. The local community is the yardstick by which success or failure is measured to a great extent. This is of great importance to the unemployed and partly employed who at present believe that their community holds nothing for them. Not only can work and employment come from community development but people can be persuaded that they have a stake in it, for themselves and on behalf of others. As we shall see, it is important to develop or even invent new communities, and one way of doing so is to bring people together in festive circumstances. Enjoyment is a good community-builder and spirit-raiser.

The Easterhouse Festival is a permanent event which takes place in a large new estate on the outskirts of Glasgow. It is not, and nor was it ever intended to be, a poor man's Edinburgh Festival; it has far more fundamental, important and serious motives. Easterhouse is one of the medium-sized new overspill towns where planners 'forgot' to include leisure facilities, shops in neighbourhoods, community focuses or places of employment. Unemployment is epidemic, money scarce, shops have shut, vandalism was rife, hope totally absent. The festival is about self-help. The local community group has taken matters into its own hands, ignoring the local council and councillors, and started to refurbish shops and flats using local labour as far as possible. A splendid mosaic now covers what was one of the uglier expanses of wall in the western world (it was assumed that this would be vandalised almost immediately, but it remains unblemished), and there are plays, concerts (pop and classical), children's parties and competitions. The people meet each other, enjoy each other's company and see some improvement. Hope has started to trickle back, and some of the people – especially the children – are learning that the environment can be improved and that they have a degree of influence over their own futures. As the success of the project has become apparent and its fame widespread, the local council has been forced to attempt a partnership with the Festival. At the time of writing the outcome of this approach is not known.

Studies are being made on these types of initiatives. An arts festival in central Pennsylvania has been analysed in depth, and case studies on the board members reveal the changes, conflicts and interactions between themselves and the hundreds of volunteers; at the same time a commitment to the community bound all these differing people together. The process of organising an event or a festival must in itself add to the developing sense of community, a lesson learned by too few educationalists and planners. Councils or other organisations tend, most unfortunately, to exert the dead hand of bureaucracy over such projects; it may be the filling in of forms (necessary if public money is involved), it may be that there are rules which must be kept, or it may be the age-old division between 'them and us'. Whatever the inhibition, community development works best when spontaneity is allowed relatively free reign and when the community relies on its own efforts. A man helping to run one of these events in a Suffolk village was witheringly scornful when the village decided to borrow the next village's band; he thought that even if their own was terrible they should have tried. 'It is no longer our own festival,' he said.

Community entertainments have been a feature of rural life for hundreds of years. The village fête on a common, village

green, or perhaps in the grounds of the big house, defined the
community, and some of the stranger customs like cheese-
rolling or the Dunmow Flitch were arranged as a result of local
community exercises. Towns and cities are now attempting to
recreate these events. Boroughs in London or New York, not
generally known for their artistic endeavours, have arranged
festivals and concerts, whilst attempts are made through events
like marathons to promote a city-wide perspective. This is
possible in terms of an abstract pride in one's locality, evident
among country-dwellers, but a city or large town (or even one of
its boroughs) is too amorphous for an individual to identify
with. Nevertheless, neighbourhood entertainments are taking
place where there is a nucleus of people who have the commitment and energy to galvanise the rest, and communities that
scarcely existed except in the minds of the organisers have
developed surprisingly strong and successful fêtes, fairs and
events. Goodwill obviously exists for such ventures, but even so
organising these activities remains one of the great tasks of the
future. A focus like a festival, a football team or a good school
play is of great help in starting to impart the strong sense of
identity without which this movement will be stillborn.

There are case studies showing how, in practice, the people
in small neighbourhoods can be brought in to influence the
planning process. The neighbourhood watch schemes in the
UK and the USA show that people will band together when
they have something to defend; there is some sort of basis there
for urban togetherness. The Swedes are developing a 'political
programme' for leisure, which is in fact a plan to reach the
community and to explain the rationale of leisure and recreational provision. Common goals are set, for example a sports
field, a new changing-room or a bus shelter, and people discuss
why these are needed, and try to make sense of the trendy
jargon so often involved. For example, what is 'a meaningful
leisure activity' and if we suffer from a 'weak cultural heritage'
how does it affect us? The final phase puts the theory into
practice. The scheme which was operated in Stockholm
cooperated closely with the local voluntary bodies and 'popular
movements', a potential difficulty in the UK when dealing with
formal organisations like unions and local government.

In the UK the planning and the financial aid for much of the
formal leisure sector comes from statutory bodies with chair-

men or women appointed by the government. As with all similar committees, they consist mainly of the great and the good; much expertise at a top level is included, but radicalism of any description is frowned upon. The Arts and Sports Councils are the major committees in this area. It would be unkind and harsh to say that neither they nor their devolved regional and city associations are doing a good job. The problem lies in what their job is defined to be; how it is being done is a secondary matter. The Sport for All programme is certainly a good thing but suffers from inadequate penetration (I have not seen or heard any publicity about it in my part of London) and a confusion about how the ideas should be delivered to the people in practice. Whether to use the limited resources on a sporting élite for youngsters to look up to and emulate, or to spread it wider at the grass-roots level, is an unresolved argument – perhaps it always will be. However, the greatest problem is that the Sports Council works through formal Establishment organisations. Many of the most pressing needs come from unemployed youngsters, often black, who have no place in this structure, and if they do they are easily and continually out-argued and out-voted. Women too are very under-represented, especially at local levels, whilst there is little effort to encourage employers to provide sports and recreational facilities for their employees.

The Arts Council, like its sporting counterpart, also tries hard. The arts, however, suffer from an ambivalent and inconsistent attitude from government. John Pick, in his paper for the 1984 National Leisure Conference, has isolated and summarised four headings under which governments justify their subsidy of the arts. Glory, a national interest argument; welfare, arts as the means to a social end; fulfilment, personal fulfilment for some; and economic, the arts as a component of economic advance. These very different reasons are given on different occasions to very dissimilar proposals. This makes the job of the arts organiser doubly difficult as he or she has no idea what will appeal to the grant-giving agency at any one time. The Arts Council, being the largest of these suffers from these cultural and political vacillations inordinately.

If the Arts and Sports Councils, along with the other national leisure and recreational bodies, were to be reinvented today with present and future demands in mind they would no doubt be very different bodies. They would be far more deeply rooted in local areas, be considerably less élitist, have members drawn from potential consumers as well as experts in the delivery of the service and they would widen the range of their interests. This assumes of course that a different set of people would be deciding on the requirements and appointments. Changes of this nature, and in the way the bodies interact with the multiplicity of groups at all levels and strata of society, need to be considered now. The very fundamental questions of what exactly these bodies do, and for whom they do it, must be asked – and if the answers do not include meeting the needs of people all over the country at a very devolved level, then remedial action should be taken swiftly. All revolutions require decisive action and this is one of the most important areas in which it should be taken.

Governments and quangos are not the only providers of resources to the leisure, recreation and entertainment sector; sponsorship and ordinary commercial practice provide a considerable percentage of the total resources. Much of the London theatre and cinema world is completely at the mercy of the box office, although without overseas tourists many would have closed some time ago. Most sports now rely on sponsorship. In football the League, one of the cup competitions and most of the teams are sponsored, cricket has all its competitions sponsored, and it is virtually impossible to race a Grand Prix car without sponsorship; horse races, show-jumpers, athletics meetings, snooker, darts, golf, tennis players' clothing – almost every sport has become a gigantic advertising hoarding. Without this massive cash boost we would have a very different, some might say better, sporting structure in the UK, and it could indeed go too far. The 'Sherman Carbuncle Cream Test Series' against the West Indies does not have an authentically cricketing ring to it, but then ten years ago would you have believed a 'Cornhill Test Series' was just around the corner?

The arts and other activities find sponsorship too. The large banks and insurance companies, retail stores and cigarette manufacturers all sponsor cultural events. In this respect there lies a problem which is similar to that found in the sports sponsorship. Not unnaturally, sponsors treat their expenditure as a commercial venture and, this being the case, flagship events which attract publicity and, they hope, TV coverage are the favourites. The small community venture is starved of cash and the rising young artist neglected in favour of the established star, and the unemployed and working class probably get nothing at all. Resources are put into areas where resources already exist, and those areas with none stay that way. Some organisations do go out of their way to help young sports enthusiasts, artists and performers in the playing of minority sports or the performing of difficult plays and music. The decision by the Dairy Council to stop funding the Milk Cup and to spend this money on schools football instead is an example of what can be done. For the most part, however, this area is left to government subsidies. The policy of the current UK government is to encourage a switch from state to private sector funding, but given the drawbacks inherent in linking advertising with sport and culture, this may result in the loss of a considerable amount of talent.

There are all sorts of leisure activities. There are active and passive ones, constructive and destructive ones, participatory and voyeuristic ones. In one of those magazine test-yourself quizzes it would be clear which leisure activities would score the most points, but quite which activities fit the above descriptions is a matter of personal definition and judgement. Is playing chess passive – it is certainly not as active as a game of badminton – or does 'active' refer to physical activity or the mere fact that a person is actively taking part in something? It should probably be the latter definition. 'Constructive leisure' refers to work – it may be voluntary work in the community or family, or it may be gardening or do-it-yourself, but whatever form it takes it must have a useful component. Participation rather than voyeurism is an obvious distinction.

It has to be recognised that the encouragement of these activities may mean a loss of jobs in the service sector. DIY often replaces the services of a decorator or builder, an allotment can partially replace the products of a greengrocer, whilst cooperation in baby- or granny-sitting can lessen the dependance on baby-minders and the social services. A considerable amount of this work, however, either does not come under the heading of employment, like talking to and cuddling children or walking with an elderly person, or is so low on any list of priorities that the jobs would not get done. Clearing canals, mural and mosaic preparation and a great deal of general environmental work comes into this latter category. Their low ranking is not because they are unimportant but because with so much to be done it is always possible to find more pressing matters on which to expend the limited resources available.

Many household tasks are not considered to be leisure activities. Housework in the form of cleaning, cooking and infant child care has long been allocated to women as their form of 'employment'. Many of these tasks are being made easier and faster to accomplish by technological advances, such as programmable washing and drying machines, cookers which have automatic timing mechanisms, dishwashers, more efficient vacuum cleaners, microwave ovens and the growth of convenience foods. For the women who can afford them, their use can result in real increases in leisure time. This release from the tyranny of housework, supplemented by the number of women now at work on a full-time, part-time or temporary basis and who now feel that they need leisure facilities equal to those traditionally available to men, open up a new range of challenges.

The first challenge is to the decision-making structures in the leisure fields. For example, who decides what is or is not acceptable to women? When this has been decided, who pays for the facility? – important if a woman does not have her own disposable income. What transport is available? Fewer women than men have access to cars and the juxtaposition of young children and public transport, especially anywhere near a peak period, can be a nightmare. At what times are facilities provided, are there child-care facilities or special coaching facilities, are facilities open after dark and if so what safety measures, if any, need to be taken? The statistics on the use of free time by women are marginally worse than those for men, and research on why certain facilities are used or not is limited and rudimentary.

In schools girls are traditionally pushed into 'women's areas' like sewing or cookery. Some educationalists see this in terms of a challenge which the school system will have to meet, and it is resulting in some good and some bad practice. Teaching boys about housework and girls about DIY activities normally done by boys, like car repair or woodwork, is excellent, but putting an end to proper football and cricket and substituting hybrid games for both sexes on the grounds that the traditional games are too competitive for girls will probably undo all the good works of the first series of changes. The first thing that schools must do is to widen the horizons of both boys and girls, not have one sex blaming the other for their miserable time at the school.

Fashions in leisure activities change, much as do other fads. Five years ago jogging started in earnest, but it has become less popular now as possible health dangers have begun to emerge. Women-only health clubs started about three or four years ago and are just starting to show signs of failure, and dance studios with their aerobics may go the same way as jogging. Football attendances have slumped, while interest in ice-hockey, basket-ball and American football has waxed considerably. Reading has increased in popularity, more women than men read weekly magazines but fewer people are reading books for pleasure – vocational and technical reading has increased to take up the slack. Theatre-going is rising while cinema-going is continuing to decline. Squash and tennis have become popular with men, and swimming is making a come-back amongst women, who are also starting to play squash in greater numbers.

Through all these changes the public perception of the idea of leisure still retains an aura of hedonism. This is unjustified. There are many enjoyable leisure activities and the idea that free time is symptomatic of laziness and self-indulgence is one still held by some, not all of whom are apologists of the Protestant work ethic. If people do nothing it is often because they have all too little information about what there is to do. There are magazines which tell people what is going on in towns (London has at least four), but these are more about events and less about facilities. When David Minton and Anne Vernon Griffiths started On-Line, then Kids' Line, and now Sports Line, they knew that there was a considerable gap in the information networks. They operate around the London area and provide information to the thousands of people who phone them every week about entertainments, events, what sports to do and where to find them. London radio and TV are now following this lead, as are local radio stations in other areas; regional TV, covering wider areas, is not as useful. Until they started there was no central clearing-house for leisure informa-tion; people who lived in the next street to a leisure centre probably had no idea what it had to offer. Much of the under-utilisation of resources is due to ignorance. If people do not go to the library they have little chance of finding out what is on offer – and this assumes that the council has firstly produced a list and secondly makes it easily available to libraries. Some do, most do not.

The leisure revolution is complex. Normal academic approaches which use comparative-static techniques will not be able to describe adequately the changes taking place. There are a complex series of interrelations between employment changes, social changes, physical infrastructure changes and the changes in fashions and expectations. Research must use dynamic techniques to trace not only the results of these interactions but also the ways in which they took place, if we are to be able to learn from our mistakes. The selection of activities from which we can choose is getting ever wider, bewilderingly so at times, but where are the leisure counsellors (other than On-Line), where is the commitment to change the pattern of people's leisure time and where is the political lead coming from?

Specific individual leisure activities are difficult to select from this multitude of choices. If people, especially the young ones, could be persuaded to take a positive and constructive approach to leisure for at least some of the time, the welfare of individuals in the community and the environment in which they live should be enhanced. This should be the main aim of the leisure revolution; it cannot be compulsory. The idea of compulsory sports and games, community and social work or home-decorating and gardening cannot be taken seriously; the uncertain quality of performance and how to enforce the compulsion would be only two of the difficulties. Encouragement is the key, and this will only be successful under certain conditions and circumstances. Amongst the most important of these are financial security for individuals and families, a direct input into the planning of the activities by the participants and a recognisable result in terms of the area becoming better to live in and the people happier.

13 Thinking the unthinkable

The first steam railway trains were thought to induce heart attacks because the human body could not survive the strain of travelling at speeds in excess of twenty miles per hour. To do so was unthinkable. The early motor cars had to be preceded by a man with a red flag walking at a steady pace, because to go faster than that, terrorising people and horses, was unthinkable. Prior to the suffragette movement the prospect of women having the vote was unthinkable to nearly all men and, as a famous astronomer and physicist once remarked in the 1950s, it was unthinkable that a man would ever walk on the moon. It was even unthinkable that a man could run a mile in four minutes. What was yesterday's unthinkable thought is today's commonplace. We call it progress.

There are always some people who are thinking the unthinkable, who are attempting to push back the technological frontiers or who believe strongly that social or political patterns must change. The great thinkers and philosophers like Plato, Socrates and Euclid, the great scientists like Galileo, Newton and Einstein, the explorers like Columbus, clerics like Luther, naturalists like Darwin and anatomists like Harvey all fought against the established wisdoms but finally had their views accepted. Battles were fought and entrenched positions defended desperately by the people whose views, and therefore position and power, were threatened. The industrial revolution which changed the face of Europe succeeded because inventors, entrepreneurs, city fathers and bankers believed the unbelievable – whilst Karl Marx certainly thought the unthinkable as far as this new establishment was concerned.

More changes and unthinkable thoughts have probably been in evidence in the second half of this century than during all previous centuries put together. Nuclear weapons and the prospect of Armageddon, space travel, famines on a horrific scale, antibiotics, heart transplants, cloning, the dissolution of the old empires and a host of technological, social and international changes. We have lost the capacity to be astonished amidst this kaleidoscope of changes. We are appalled at the horrors, but forget quickly, while television trivialises the wonderful and makes brilliant inventions seem almost a matter of course. Despite this constant movement and variety we take the basic fabric of our society for granted and believe that it will not change.

Employment remains the great motivating force in society; only sex comes anywhere near its power. The family continues to be the basic living unit and marriage is supposed to provide the cement which binds it together. Religions still give solace and comfort in increasingly uncertain and unpredictable times, although they may not be the same religions that our forefathers adhered to. In the UK we still live and work in roughly the same places as we did at the start of the century, albeit with very much higher expectations from life. In the UK the parliamentary system has prevailed almost unchanged but in Germany, France, Italy, Eastern Europe, Austria, Greece, Russia, and Turkey various cataclysms have brought overwhelming political changes in the course of this century. *The current wave of thinking the unthinkable concerns the very things that have been stable over this lengthy period.* We are about to embark on a period of very substantial change.

People have never cared to admit to themselves that changes might occur to the fundamental certainties on which they have based their lives. Life can be cruel – deaths to loved ones, sickness and injury and disappointments all place a strain on an individual's resources – but if the routine certainties of life (such as employment, living conditions and political stability) are under threat as well, a considerable number of people will not be able to cope. Uncertainty can be stimulating but total uncertainty can be unnerving. Although we need some degree of security, however, when it is based on false premises and misinformation people will sooner or later see through it and be mistrustful.

More often than not there have been no indications that elemental change is on the way. There is a feeling amongst the Establishment that it might be destabilising if people were to be alerted to possible changes which would affect the entire pattern of their lives and expectations; better just to let them happen. Changes of a fundamental nature normally take some years to accomplish or, on the rare occasions when they occur suddenly, as with revolutions, they have normally been preceded by a great deal of debate so that the element of shock is diminished. This has generally been possible because there have been urgent and pressing reasons for the change – the political reform acts of the nineteenth century or women's suffrage, for example.

We are now passing through a time of very great upheaval, yet a casual visitor from another planet would be hard put to detect the fact. Business as usual is the watchword, even though there is less business. It disturbs politicians to dwell on the time when they might have to change the political responses of a lifetime and base policy on less than full employment or on a different definition of work and employment. It disturbs them to think of the possible responses of the electorate. It worries both trade union officials and employers to admit that the enterprises in which they have an interest will never again be increasing their employed labour force. The whole *raison d'être* of trade unions is employment, and employers like to hold out the prospects of further employment even if they have no intention of ever adopting more labour-intensive methods. It disturbs ordinary people to believe that the things for which they have been working and saving will not be there forever and that their basic values might have to change. Conservatism is based on the attitude that if it was good enough for my father it is good enough for me, which, while it adds to stability and defines tradition, is unhelpful at times of rapid change. Security, which is one of the great motivating factors behind the employment ethic, would be threatened as never before if full employment was publicly announced to be a thing of the past, and few politicians and no civil servants will court such a risk.

This all adds up not so much to a conspiracy of silence as to a dampening of curiosity. This self-denying ordinance concerns two hypotheses. The first is that the current level of unemployment is more or less permanent in most political and economic scenarios. The second concerns the effects that unemployment, and all the other changes that are happening, will have on many of our more cherished and stable institutions. Speculation is only tolerated in the guise of drama or fiction, and all policies and all thoughts are channelled into trying to return to full employment as fast as possible. People who challenge this position are given some credence for a limited period before the conventional juggernaut rolls again.

Both politicians and the media are committed to the short term in industrialised countries, and both tend to concentrate on single issues – preferably of a sensational nature, at any one time. The effects of technology and unemployment are spread over longer periods, however, and as they also involve complex interrelationships they are rarely, if ever, given an airing except in the most trivialised of ways. We know that various trends are evident in the UK but we do not analyse them or attempt to draw any conclusions from them.

Let us take towns and cities. We know that there has been a decline in some areas of the inner cities, commonly called dereliction, in the UK and the USA, and we know that there has been a reduction in the number of inhabitants in cities. Conversely, we know that there has been an increase in the number of minority groups living in the inner cities and that their unemployment is far higher than average. We also know that there is a new technology waiting to be implemented in all the commercial areas which, many people believe, will reduce overall employment, while another technology, already partly in use, will enable people to work anywhere in the country rather than have to use the city. We know all these things but we do not attempt publicly to put them together in any rational analysis. Some companies have done so, however, and as a result have decided to move away from the inner city – which in turn adds yet another dimension to the analysis. The arguments are roughly as follows.

If the number of people living in the city falls then the local tax (or rate) revenue falls, although the amount of services needed are increasing because of the high unemployment and other problems in the physical infrastructure. If the number of people travelling into the city starts to fall because of technological changes (especially in the commercial field) the demand for transport into the city will fall too. This means that to maintain transport revenue and maintain services either fares have to rise or a local subsidy has to be increased, or both. If fares rise or the service is cut then fewer people will use the system and this will mean further cuts; so the drift into the vicious circle has begun. If subsidies are required then local taxes will have to rise, but fewer people are living in the city so that each household, individual or business has to pay a disproportionately higher increase. As these taxes are already at a high level because the inner city inhabitants need so many extra services due to the dereliction, this acts as an extra incentive for people to leave the city, thus adding to the net emigration. This further reduces the local tax base and the employment base.

Fewer people and places of employment inevitably mean that the enterprises which service them have to close. Restaurants, theatres, cinemas, shops, sandwich bars and pubs, professional firms like solicitors and accountants all move away. The city loses a lot of its attractiveness and fewer people want to live or work there. The local authority can no longer provide adequate local services. Roads are unrepaired, street lights are broken, the refuse disposal service becomes less efficient. All this deters visitors and tourists who were already disturbed by the higher prices and bad transport. This results in more service industry leaving, less tax revenue and fewer visitors – which again results in even fewer services.

As the school system cannot get the money it needs because of the lack of revenue, so the middle classes move their children and often themselves away from the city. The minority groups either do the same or lose faith in the system, which declines further and leads to yet more emigration from the city. The difficulty that employers have in recruiting suitably qualified staff locally or those who would care to commute on the by now run-down but expensive public transport services (roads are poor and highly congested) impels them to move their offices out of the city. Their alternative is to use the new technologies to arrange for their employees to work from home or from near where they live, in the new office shops. This means less revenue and a smaller tax base for the city, along with increasing unemployment.

This is where we came in – except that the problem has become considerably worse. The city is on a spiral of decline that can only be halted by positive action or a fall in prices, especially property prices. The latter case would involve the insolvency of many companies and severe damage to a host of pension, insurance and investment trust funds. It is unlikely that the financial institutions would allow this to happen, but if they did the result would almost certainly be the resurgence of tourism rather than the traditional commercial or industrial activities.

The new technologies will make cities as irrelevant as the market towns became in the wake of the first industrial revolution. Before this the centres of power had been the ports and market towns, along with the capital city which acted as the commercial centre and seat of government. The new industrial towns and new ports changed this. From being centres of influence the market towns subsided into pleasant rural hideaways for the middle classes as the new heavily industrialised towns were first developed and then linked by the railway network. In the same way, the second industrial revolution does not need to use the older industrial or commercial centres. The new technologically based systems can operate in smaller units, need fewer employees and can thus be sited outside the large centres of population and can electronically distribute the work to remote places away from conventional offices. Given these advantages, enterprises will move to the areas of lowest cost – which will not be the city – only prestige offices will continue to flourish in cities in the medium term.

Some of our present urban areas are irrelevant to today's, and certainly tomorrow's, needs. The immense amount of capital tied up in towns and cities, mainly in the form of property, will earn less and less return. Most of the symptoms of the decline have already started, and the preconditions for collapse exist; they are called 'inner city problems' but are in fact spreading beyond that small ghetto area. The difficulties in funding local government in the UK and the recent financial problems of New York, coupled with the diminishing urban populations in industrialised countries, are the forerunners of the change. We are merely waiting for the nineties and the introduction of the electronic telecommunications network to act as the touchpaper for the technological explosion.

Towns and cities will still exist, but their function may well have changed. Many will have fallen below that critical daytime population level beneath which it is impossible to keep services running at an acceptable standard. But as prices fall developers will move in and new housing, new amenities and new light industry and small commercial enterprises will emerge. Parks will be expanded and the centre of towns may well become more like Paris than New York in that it will be fashionable to live right in the centre. Towns could be the places where people want to live and come for recreation, rather than areas where employment is the main attraction. Tourists will use the towns as somewhere to spend an entire holiday rather than just as a base for sleeping. The study of industrial history and archaeology will probably become ever more important as a leisure and cultural pursuit and tourism will be built up around it. The old industrial towns will stand as monuments on the grand scale to the age of steam power and labour intensive industry, dinosaurs in the age of the mammal.

Many of the large office blocks which have sprouted like so many glass and concrete stalagmites in our cities will be redundant too. We can already see the decaying hulks of old factories and warehouses in the towns and have watched at least as many be demolished. In the future this could happen to the empty office blocks, or perhaps they may be converted to other uses like cheap student flats, cheap hotels or even large dog kennels for security firms. Offices will still be needed but they will need to accommodate a far smaller number of people and this means that the buildings themselves should be smaller.

The activities carried on in the building will change too. Routine work will be carried on elsewhere, in homes and office shops, and head office will be used only for conferences and entertaining clients or customers. Managers will meet there to discuss strategies and gain the psychological benefits from meeting each other. Electronic companies today (Digital is one) that have tried teleconferencing discovered, to their great surprise, that their managerial travel expenditure and the number of meetings both rose rather than fell. The inability to gauge human responses using teleconferencing methods, and the discovery that there were all sorts of other subjects which teleconferencing didn't cover adequately, are the reasons given for this. It does suggest that, whatever the new technologies may be able to do in the way of routine work, they will not replace essential human contact at a managerial or sales levels. Staff who would have met at an office every day should travel in perhaps once a month to meet and maintain a corporate spirit.

If and when these changes happen, architects and builders will have a new set of specifications to work from. The offices, occasionally with a small productive capacity alongside, will not only have to be smaller but will have to be designed with the new technologies in mind. Work stations rather than separate offices, electronic carcassing of the building so that communications can be received anywhere at any time, and the ability to change the use of parts of the building at any time will be vital. Provisions for satellite aerials, secure rooms for computer installations and databases and electronic network back-up systems will all be needed. Employees working in the building with all the new equipment, much of which will be screen-based, will need more regular rest periods than ever before, which will mean bigger and better rest facilities for the staff. Alongside these will be the kitchens, bars, bedrooms and entertainment suites for the customers and senior management. The fact that conventional electric wiring will be replaced by electronic boxes, and that heating, cooling and safety systems will be controlled by a systems computer will raise standards and lower costs.

Prestige for both the enterprise and the architect will not be conferred by size, fountains and mahogany, as at present, but by compactness, style and efficiency. For the planners it will bring a new lease of life, especially in the conversion of existing buildings, for the architects and builders it will be a new challenge.

Many of the people who were employed in these offices will have no job at all and will spend much of their week at home in the suburbs. Many others will be 'patched into' their office from their homes or from their local office shops in the same suburbs. General typing, programming and managerial tasks are already being done in this way, as are specific professional duties that accountants, lawyers, secretaries and brokers carry out. When the new electronic systems reduce the costs and increase the efficiency and reliability of the telecommunications network these employment arrangements will really take off. For an enterprise the cost savings could be enormous, for an individual the savings on journeys, clothing and meals can be considerable. There are, however, potential disadvantages in working from home.

Homeworking can be a solitary experience; anyone who needs the social contact of companions at a place of work would find this very difficult to tolerate. The lack of variety in the physical environment can act in much the same way. On the other hand there may be too many people at home; a spouse or partner, children and pets can be using the house at the same time or perhaps wanting to play with the electronic equipment that makes the system work. They can not only make it difficult to do the job properly, but the close proximity of people over very long periods can damage close relationships. A large house with a separate room (or rooms) for the networker is clearly a great advantage, and it is difficult to see how this sort of work could be done from a small flat. The obvious way to deal with the problem is by developing the office shop.

These are in the process of development at present, with the first one scheduled to be open in late 1985. They will really be neighbourhood clerical centres and should be pleasant places from which to work. Some temporary-help companies may well use these shops rather than an individual worker to provide a service to their clients. They will overcome some of the difficulties of working from home, while still allowing for almost all of the advantages, and may well prove to be the most popular means of dispersing jobs.

As the cities subside, so the suburbs will take on a new lease of life. They will not be able to remain as dormitories with few of the facilities that make a town a complete place to live; they will have to cope with a large influx of people during the daytime, and services will be needed. Restaurants and cafés, bars and shops, theatres and parks – all these will be demanded by the new neighbourhood workers, and indeed the new unemployed and early retirees. The jobs lost in the service sector in the cities may be provided by their new counterparts in the suburbs, whilst new development and building should create construction jobs. Property prices will move inversely to those in the city centres; and there will be a suburban property boom the like of which has not been seen since the development of the commuter railway networks. The nineties will be the decade of the suburb.

Living close to one's employment, or indeed working from home, will mean that families will see more of each other. This may create problems as close proximity might well breed disenchantment. It is clear that marriages amongst the unemployed come under considerable strain, although how much of this should be attributed to penury or depression and how much to the fact that the partners are thrown together in this way is not clear. The unemployed admit that they tend to be bad-tempered, with themselves and with their families, and research in the USA and UK shows an increase in divorce and separation. Indeed, in America, 'terminal separation' (or murder) within the family increases considerably among the unemployed. Overall it is likely that the number of divorces will increase, and that the number of single-parent families will increase too. The current housing and welfare policies that make it worthwhile for very young unemployed girls to get pregnant as the only way to get accommodation will ultimately lead to a reinforcement of the single-parent trend and an increase in the number of children in local authority care.

The social customs that surround families are changing even now. Alcoholism is on the increase, or to be more precise the number of noticeable alcoholics has risen; again this has been positively correlated with increased unemployment in the UK and America. Alcohol is the great anaesthetic, it numbs the running sores of life. If living close together whether with or without sufficient money, abrades family life sufficiently then the chances of increased drinking are high, which in turn predisposes the breakdown of relationships. The frustrations generated by unemployment, and perhaps drink, can also lead to the terrible cases of child- and wife-battering.

The new employment systems will, in all probability, lead to a less stable population. Mobility will be slightly enhanced, relationships will be shorter and there will be more of them. Child abandonment or maltreatment will be increasing, as will both alcohol and stress-related diseases. Without changes in their prospects, young people will use their energies in destructive ways; they will vandalise the suburbs rather than the city centres, where the empty offices will be well guarded by security firms. If this sounds a less than appetising scenario it must be remembered that these fundamental changes will have happened without the consent of the people who are affected – without their consent because no one will have asked them if they approved, not because they withheld it. People will feel less in control of their lives than ever before, which means that even the consequences I have suggested may be wildly optimistic.

Instead of sedating themselves with drink or a depressed lethargy, some people may choose to give vent to their bewilderment and assert their individuality by becoming more anti-social and violent. Gangs of youths, mainly unemployed, may terrorise neighbourhoods; crime, especially against property, could rise, whilst the parks and open spaces might be made unusable. This is a less optimistic but still not very pessimistic view of the future. Pessimism arrives when to this scenario is added extreme right-wing political groups, who are currently engaged in cultivating the sympathies of this group of young people. (The evidence provided on the terraces of some football clubs bears testament to this.)

Society is based on a link between employment and a wage or salary. Some people are lucky enough to have sufficient money not to have to find a job, while others want, but cannot get, employment. To these we give some form of payment, but only grudgingly. The welfare state safety net, or its equivalent, in industrialised countries is supposed to prevent the worst effects of poverty but there is disturbing evidence that it is failing to do so. Diseases associated with malnutrition are increasing among the children of the unemployed in the USA, and children with no shoes to wear to school – though they have to go there for their one meal a day – have been reported in England, as indeed have rickets and other vitamin deficiency diseases.

Unemployment pay, social security payments, housing benefit, supplementary benefit, family income supplement, rate rebates and a host of smaller payments – in kind or in money – are available to some, and a complex series of 'means tests' complicates the situation even further. There are so many of these that few know where to look, whilst the employees of the government departments concerned are deliberately not as helpful as they might be – though this is policy rather than their own hard-heartedness. Combined with this are the rules which penalise people in part-time employment, or even the low-paid full-time workers, by putting them into the 'poverty trap'. Once entrapped, a wage increase can lose them more in benefits than the increase itself.

There are two ways of coping with this absurd situation. The first is to cut welfare benefits and so make low wages appear better by comparison; the UK government is clearly contemplating such a move. Apart from its dreadful effects on the truly poor, it will also depress demand still further (as there will be less money in circulation), adding to unemployment and thus the aggregate welfare bill; it is counterproductive in anything but the shortest term. The second method is to simplify the entire system by having, as far as is possible, one basic payment. One way of doing this is to use a negative as well as a positive income tax, and another would be the introduction of a national dividend or something similar.

The principle is based on the idea that each person or family deserves a payment as of right and employment, or the lack of it, should not affect this right. The national dividend is paid weekly or monthly to each man, woman and child. Income tax is levied on an individual's income (the family is not considered) and is progressive. No one falls below the poverty level, everyone is financially secure and one of the major effects of unemployment – poverty – has been removed. It is, however, expensive. Keith Roberts, head of theoretical physics at UKAEA, Culham, estimates that half of the national income would have to be devoted to the dividend and the other half to wages, profits, rents etc. As he points out, the sheer size of the dividend means that the revenue would have to be raised through taxation, both direct and indirect. It is a very radical idea, challenging most of our long-held assumptions about remuneration, and because of that is not likely to commend itself to the public, and most certainly not to the civil service, in the near future.

This scheme does have the advantage, however, of being able to cope with part-time and temporary work. As both of these, along with contract labour and services, are increasing, such an attribute is necessary for any new welfare or tax system. Negative income tax, a Milton Friedman idea, also copes with these new conditions admirably. A target income figure is announced, which must be well above subsistence level, and anyone earning that figure (which can be adjusted monthly with the retail price index) would neither pay tax nor receive benefit. People earning over the target would pay tax, people earning under would receive a payment to bring them up to the target level. In practice it would, however, be somewhat more complex. The code given to an individual would take into account personal and family circumstances, as it does now, and the target income for each coding would be different according to the needs of the family unit. Changes in these circumstances would be recorded on the new Inland Revenue computers and changes in the tax or benefits paid announced almost immediately. This system has the advantages of simplicity, of using existing methods, of efficiency and of a modicum of support – even the TUC have gone on record as saying they were prepared to discuss it, with safeguards. It means, moreover, that part-time work, job-splitting and job-sharing suddenly become viable options.

The cost of such a scheme is not as great in net terms as might be supposed. All the existing welfare payments and benefits would go, as would unemployment pay and state pensions, and a huge amount of administrative costs would be saved. But the question that has to be asked, and answered seriously, is whether in the long term we can afford *not* to have this or a similar system. With high unemployment and 'flexi-working' putting ever greater strains on the existing system, and the need for financial independence so urgent, something radical will have to be attempted.

Pensions are already becoming a source of worry to governments. The fact that fewer people are working and paying contributions has to be matched against the fact that more people are living to retirement age and then living longer to receive the pension. The unemployed retire too. The West German government tried to reduce pensions some five years ago, and met a storm of protest, and now the UK government is doing precisely the same. It cannot see how, under the present arrangements, it can meet all its future obligations, and there is a large private occupational pension sector in the UK which is facing similar problems. The reason for this is that by, say, the year 2020 there will be too few young workers to support an increasingly elderly and retired population.

Because pensions are funded on the open market they depend on the percentage rate of increase on the investment being higher than the rate of increase of pensionable earnings. Many people who have taken early retirement are not only receiving a pension for a lengthy period, but are not paying in their expected contributions. These two problems – diminishing income coupled with increasing outgoings, and the possibility of falling interest rates combined with increasing incomes – are making some schemes decidedly rocky. It may not be long before a small to medium-sized fund will default on its obligations, with its holding enterprise not being in a position to bail it out. Pensions are designed to meet the needs of a period when people stayed at one job through their working lives, and even if they changed would then find another full-time job. The lack of proper transferable pensions holds back mobility and penalises the redundant who can find other jobs. The entire pensions industry requires an overhaul and a total redesign to make it suitable for the late twentieth rather than the late nineteenth century.

Pensions and the other economic and logistical changes, such as how and where we will live and where our jobs will be, are only part of a wider set of disturbances. The current wave of changes is trailing a cloud of wariness and doubt above the industrialised nations; people are looking for certainties that no longer exist. Some take the quiet route and immerse themselves in familiar territory – their home, their friends and family and their job – avoiding risks and the outside world as far as possible. Others are turning, in small but increasing numbers, to a series of alternative lifestyles; these people are thinking the unthinkable in that they are challenging the current mores and ethics.

The Green party in Germany, and the other environmentalist parties around the world, are symptomatic of a deeper dissatisfaction with conventional politics than is usual. The political dimension is the subject of the following chapter but the lesson of this political evolution is clearly applicable to the other 'alternatives'. There is a feeling developing that politicians and governments have failed, and more in hope than anger people are starting to look elsewhere for their salvation. Nowhere is this more true than in religion.

Traditionally, religion gains converts during difficult times, and we are living in the midst of these at the moment. The conventional religions are making little headway, however, compared with the fundamentalist religions and some of the more esoteric sects. It is as though the orthodox religions are perceived to be too involved in the established procedures which have resulted in difficult circumstances to be considered as a bulwark or a consolation against them. Born-again fundamental Christianity, fundamental sects of the Moslem faith, Bahaism, Buddhism and Taoism, Hindu swamis and charismatic sect leaders are all making converts in the Western world. The faith that they inspire presumably acts as a shield against the blows that the world is dealing. It is clear that the established Western religions cannot provide this, and nor can they provide the guidance that these people appear to need. The scandals that have surrounded some of the sects concerning sex, the compulsory tithing of members' worldly goods, and even mass suicide have not diminished their attraction; indeed they may even account for some of it. There is a challenge to the Establishment in the growth of these religions; power is being eroded and other and potentially uncontrollable power centres are growing. It is a movement that both established religions and governments view with disfavour.

Alternative lifestyles provide another, although perhaps less dangerous, challenge – less dangerous because of the relatively small number of people who will take part and stick at them. The sixties saw an increase in this form of movement. Communes, freedom and mind-expanding drugs all promised to relieve the young of the drudgery of the job, the millstone of the career and the effort of responsibility. The attempts of the writers, artists and philosophers of this movement failed to promote any coherent pattern to which the young could attach themselves, and the movement died in squalor and violence, though not before the state had had to endure some difficult moments. The Vietnam demonstrations and the violent Chicago Democratic convention of 1968 rocked the USA, the Paris student riots had the French government reeling momentarily, the German terrorist movement alerted the state to the dangers within, and UK students created many confrontations, with authority – though they rarely followed them through.

The alternative lifestyle has been blighted since then, although a trickle of people are still making the attempt. Some try to make a self-sufficient life on remote Welsh hill farms, while others form new communes and some older established ones like Findhorn in the Highlands of Scotland have been revitalised. The ideology of these people is very easy to caricature as 'macrobiotic, crochet your own yoghurt', but this hides a nervousness or suspicion about anyone who has the strength to eschew what the rest of us find addictive – formal employment. These are people who are taking a positive decision to live their lives outside the normal rat-race, presumably on the grounds that the 'rats are winning'; they wish to pursue their own goals in their own way and in their own time. Providing they are not too successful and do not attract too many others, the Establishment is relatively happy to let them carry on, thinking perhaps that not only do they pose no threat at present but they act as an example of ungracious and at times comical living – certainly not one to be copied.

The people who take part in these exercises (they are still known as drop-outs in the sensational press) generally do not possess a strong employment ethic, although they might well have a well-developed work ethic. Part of their work often involves the setting up of alternative methods of production and the production of alternative products. Cooperatives are very much the 'in' method of enterprise formation at present, despite the fact that they are one of the hardest forms of organisation to manage and to keep on an even keel. Handmade and crafted goods, and organic and natural farming are practical examples of the type of practical contribution such groups and thinkers are making.

Other people are taking a less positive view. The number of homeless men and women who live rough, drink meths or anything they can lay their hands on, and have a completely anti-social lifestyle is increasing alarmingly. Theirs is also an alternative life style, but not the type so genteelly disinfected in the *Good Life* TV series; these people are, however, more a danger to themselves than to others or to the state. Drug addiction and glue-sniffing are signs that people need to escape, and both are on the increase – affecting young people in particular. Again, it is a negative statement of an individual's protest against society, and it is interesting that a surprisingly high number of reformed addicts turn to a fundamentalist rather than a conventional, religion. It is unthinkable for the majority that youngsters should behave as they do – for the moment at least.

It is at present also unthinkable, at least in political circles, that unemployment should continue to remain high. We have here yet another paradox. Why, if all politicians agree that employment is so vital, do they do so little about providing it? Other questions follow on from this. Why does the UK government spend billions of pounds on social security and YTS schemes on keeping people out of jobs? Why have there been so few civil and political disturbances all over the industrialised world, given the importance of employment to the unemployed? Why is there such political inaction at a time when action of some kind is so desperately needed? These are all questions that should be asked, even if we are not confident that simple or comprehensible answers exist.

The way that the questions are answered will be revealing in itself. We will soon find out which politicians are capable of thinking the unthinkable – and then learning from and acting upon it.

14 Political action – and inaction

Politicians are good on rhetoric but not always quite as sharp on action. The well-turned provocative phrase – 'on your bike', for example – can influence debate for years. Regrettably, this influence does not seem to apply to deeds in quite the same way; one certain thing about politics and political action is that there will be no agreement as to what action to take in any given set of circumstances. Disagreement and conflict are built into the system. At the same time, politicians are only too human; they compromise, they make mistakes and they change sides – in essence they are amateurs, as are we all. As Robert Louis Stevenson put it, 'Politics is perhaps the only profession for which no preparation is thought necessary.' It is important to remember this and to remind ourselves that we are as expert as they are, if not more so, in many respects.

It is perhaps a combination of these human frailties on public display and the concentration on the short term that explains the lack of initiative, or, worse, constructive thought by politicians the world over. Unemployment is a universal scourge, yet not a single effective new policy has been produced to deal with it. The new technology has manifestly changed production, information and employment patterns and most governments are urging their industrialists to produce and use more of it, yet it is assumed to have no political impact whatsoever. Legislators have had to come to terms with all sorts of technological changes and the effects they have had on society over the years. Why is this time so different? Is it because the problems that microelectronics bring are so all-embracing and so fundamental that politicians try to pretend that no problems exist, or is it that there are no easy short-term answers?

The present Conservative government differs from almost all its predecessors over the previous fifty years in that it embraces a long-term political philosophy. This seeks to change the underlying motivations of people and institutions. Entrepreneurs should be motivated to be more efficient, people forced to take responsibility for themselves and their families, unions shorn of power, markets freed and capital allowed to be invested in areas of highest return – with government playing a gradually decreasing role. We shall emerge out of the darkness of this transition period into sunlight, where a healthy competitive industry and a flourishing and profitable small business sector will employ a highly motivated work force. These workers will scrap good-humouredly for the available jobs, undeterred by the low wages, and their families will provide for their own health care and look after their aged relatives. It is, in short, the return to the Victorian values that are so beloved of the Prime Minister, but never really existed.

This is the theory, but it is not happening in practice. Although the government claims to stick to its 'medium-term strategy', it is forced increasingly to tamper with interest rates, manipulate taxes, raise money in the short term or back down on pieces of legislation. And central government is constantly accreting more power to itself – over local government, over unions, over people. The gap between the rhetoric and the action has seldom been greater.

Politics has of course always existed on the two levels of theory and practice. The theory is about capitalism, socialism or communism; the practice is concerned with party political rivalries, the difficult business of running a government in a modern industrial state, the trimming of policies, the alliances and the compromises. At a theoretical level there is a possibility that the present Tory government could be correct, in its own terms, but the time they need to prove it is highly unlikely to be made available to them. As this is a parliamentary system the electorate is likely to vote them out of office before their job is finished, if indeed it could ever be said to be finished. There are two reasons for this. The first is that the more radical the policies and the greater the hardship, the less popular the government becomes; the second is that TV and other modern communications make lengthy spells in government more difficult. This is partly due to familiarity with government figures developing into boredom, and partly because it is easy to oppose policies verbally – and the conflict this produces is meat and drink to current-affairs producers. The only saving grace for the government could, however, be the split in the opposition parties.

It is highly probable, however, that any government will have been blown off course well before the election date. The short-term difficulties caused by matters outside the government's control – such as an ultra-strong dollar, oil price rises or an EEC financial crisis – can wreck completely the best-laid plans, long or short term. The policies themselves may be misguided and need corrective actions. There is a strong case for saying that a combination of these factors have led to the present government being in the difficult position that it is in today, and that the high level of unemployment was to be expected given the actual policies that have been implemented. *If the political economy which underpins the government strategy had been interpreted correctly, and adhered to strictly, unemployment would be higher still.*

Governments in western Europe, the USA and Canada have between them taken almost no steps to reduce unemployment. Some tinkering around the edges in France and the Benelux countries has taken place, but the priorities are sound government finance and the avoidance of inflation. The theory is that the achieving of both goals will, in the long run, reduce unemployment. All political parties have, however, thrown up their hands in horror at the large number of unemployed, especially amongst the young. Even ministers of governments who have presided over these policies weep crocodile tears over the 'tragic waste of young lives', and then carry on as before. 'There is no alternative,' is the Conservative government's reply to critics. This has to be the most arrogant nonsense imaginable – of course there are alternatives. Some may work, some may not, they may not be palatable to an electorate, but they exist.

Remedial measures have not been taken because it has been assumed that once an economic recovery gets under way increased employment will follow, as it has in the past. In 1985 a limited recovery began in the industrialised countries, yet unemployment has continued to rise in all OECD countries except the USA, where the economy is just beginning to slow down! It is clear to an increasing number of economists and political commentators that the structural changes that I covered in the first half of this book are responsible for this unexpected turn of events. Unexpected to politicians, that is. It is equally clear that politicians, be they in government or opposition, are still not prepared to concede that any fundamental changes have taken place. They are still selling their patent nostrums as a cure for unemployment and other pernicious diseases, as did the carpetbaggers of yesteryear.

All the parties agree that they want to see the restoration of full employment, and all proclaim that they will deliver it – generally over a short period. The Conservatives would do it by letting the market work, driving down wages and converting the UK into a larger, northern Singapore. The social consequences of this would be appalling and almost certainly would not be tolerated. The inequalities that would arise between the rich and the increasingly large number of poor, highlighted by what will be necessary cuts in unemployment and other benefits, would polarise society in a potentially dangerous way, as we are already beginning to see. The conjunction of the new high-productivity technologies and these capitalist market-oriented policies add an extra dimension to these dangers; the worst and most troubled decades of the Victorian era could be repeated.

Fortunately, these policies will probably be prosecuted in a diluted and barely efficient form, one major reason, amongst others, being that the captains of industry prefer to keep their companies' government subsidies and cosy purchasing arrangements. Profits are secure this way. Only politicians prefer the icy winds of open competition to the snug fireside of security, and they do not actually have to brave the elements themselves – they merely volunteer others to do so. The consequence of the failure to pursue government policies to their fullest extent is that both unemployment and de-industrialisation will continue to increase. It is the worst of all possible worlds.

The concentration on free market forces leads to another problem. Investment is allowed to go to the areas of highest return, and it is assumed that this will benefit the nation. In the early 1970s, money flooded into the property market during the 'Barber boom' – it was money moving to get the highest return. It resulted in a secondary banking collapse (the Bank of England had to mount the 'lifeboat' rescue operation), several new millionaires, the birth of gazumping and a massive increase in house prices. Not only did it not benefit the country or 99.9 per cent of the people, it was actually counterproductive in that proper investments that should have been made were not, and we have been reaping that whirlwind ever since.

Today a similar problem is being created. The abolition of exchange controls has resulted in vast amounts of money leaving the country to be invested in our competitors. We lose twice over: first, because we do not invest in ourselves and, second, because we are enabling our competitors to modernise. The major problem, however, arises because we have limited resources in the electronics field – specifically a shortage of personnel, especially good design and production engineers who are also good systems analysts or computer specialists. The projects giving the highest return may well be 'candy floss investments' – the development of electronic fruit machines and arcade games, for example. If this is the case, and there is some evidence to suggest that it is so, then scarce human resources are being taken away from the vital areas which directly concern people's well-being, such as research to help the disabled.

At this point may I offer a word of warning? As a rule, beware of politicians who use the phrases 'the national interest' or 'it benefits Britain' frequently and carelessly. It is legitimate to ask precisely who or what in Britain will benefit, and this stricture applies to the debate about whether the new technology should be used or stopped. It is suggested that not to use it would damage our competitive position; this presupposes that it would keep out imports and help our exports. Why then invest in a new supermarket check-out system? No one will go to Paris to shop at Au Bon Marché simply because Tesco use an old-fashioned check-out system, so where is the national benefit? Why print *The Times* with a computerised system? No one will read *Der Spiegel* just because the old methods prevail at *The Times*. There is not only no gain for the country (and no saving in unit price), there is a loss. The experts who designed and then installed these new systems, who operate and service them, should be working on products which *do* benefit the people of the country. Protecting the balance of payments is one thing, saving life and preventing pain another. It is not true to say, however, as most politicians do, that all uses of new technology are good uses and that all uses are as good as each other. Some are clearly better than others – the trouble is that the market mechanisms are incapable of distinguishing them.

The policies of the Labour party would certainly create some jobs. The renewing of the decaying urban areas and the expansion of the caring services will see to this – but for how long? It will be necessary to fund these schemes and they carry no immediate financial return to offset against the costs. Taxation and public ownership are the two main sources of revenue for the state, but neither can be expected to raise sufficient money for a sufficient length of time. To create the competitive manufacturing industry that is necessary will require a large increase in investment and, moreover, one which would be highly capital intensive and employ fewer people than at present. This industry is needed to keep the balance of payments somewhere near to parity. Whilst import controls can reduce the import bill, they are both inflationary and restrictive, and this will mean that an incomes policy is on the cards. It will also mean that products and materials which will be needed in the task of regenerating industry will be kept out or become more expensive, thus adding to inflation. Some of these products could be made in the UK, but new capacity would have to be installed first as so much of ours has been lost. Import controls will also run into a hostile campaign from the consumers' associations concerning the sensitive area of restriction of choice. In the short term, a partial success in reducing unemployment is the best that can be hoped for. As with Conservative policies, negative social pressures would probably assert themselves well before the time needed for success had arrived and the policies would have to be amended or dropped.

In theory, however, socialism appears to offer better prospects than capitalism; indeed capitalism appears to offer only certain conflict and very uncertain benefits. The only way of avoiding the inequalities that can be caused by implementing the new systems is to share the benefits widely, and the only way to ensure that resources are used efficiently and humanely is to plan for this. The best way of creating a genuine employee interest in enterprises is to introduce industrial democracy. The best way to ensure a well-educated and capable population is to bring as many people under the education umbrella for as long as possible, and to raise the base standards. The easiest method by which the government can raise money is by owning profit-generating enterprises, and the only way to guarantee that technology is used in the 'people important' areas is to direct it there. The best way to rid the country of discrimination, whether against women, race or religion, is to educate and legislate. These objectives will be met far more readily in a socialist than in a capitalist environment.

It is not easy to characterise the Alliance response. It appears to take a pinch of reflation and a dash of competition, and it is unlikely to provide enough of the former or stimulate the latter sufficiently to have a significant impact on employment. However, there are some Alliance politicians, Shirley Williams for one, who have grasped the fact that structural changes need more radical responses, but in terms of what will be placed before the electorate their views will be ignored.

All three parties are very strong on training and retraining. I suspect that all three covet them as a means of keeping people off the streets and the unemployment statistics, at least as much as for the practical skills that they confer. This quasi-employment policy is the easy option. Training *is* needed, there can be no doubt of that, but there must be doubts about the government's intentions when looked at in the context of the cuts in industry-related training and in the school and university programmes. Their training policy is going in precisely the wrong direction – it is mortgaging the future. Both Labour and the Alliance see the need for proper training, however, and might be persuaded to put such schemes into operation; these would be based upon needs rather than the availability of instructors and courses. As the technology changes rapidly, so the skills required change – today's need may well be to-morrow's redundancy. Politicians and administrators are notoriously slow in adjusting to change, however, and this will make the promotion of a successful national training scheme that much more difficult. This is compounded by many of the potential employers not knowing what skills they will require in two years' time. Future training will need a large high-tech input and different, more imaginative, personnel. Politicians have the task of making certain that these pre-conditions are met.

If the political controversy surrounding training (for example, the YTS schemes and the abolition of most industrial training boards) is greater than one would believe necessary, then that concerning the idea of voluntary services is staggering. By and large the Labour party mistrusts voluntary bodies and workers; they are redolent of the days of charity and good works, and trade unions believe they may be used as a substitute for proper jobs. The volunteers who broke the strike in 1926 are still remembered, and reviled. Conservatives, on the other hand, have always seen voluntary work as part and parcel of life, filling the gaps that the state, employers or perhaps the family have overlooked. With the exception of a minority of their backwoodsmen, they do not see it as filling any substantial need in the long term, except perhaps in a compulsory scheme. The Alliance gives voluntary work and organisations a high degree of prominence and would probably institute a voluntary national social service. This is far nearer to work than is YTS or the other training schemes and would almost certainly prove to be more popular and more useful. It is one of the few positive initiatives that have been made by a political party on the assumption that unemployment will remain high. *Training policies assume that it will fall.*

With this exception, political parties (except for the Greens and environmentalists) will not accept the proposition of a continuing high level of unemployment. Nor will most of the media. Despite this, nearly two-thirds of the British people believe that technology will create additional unemployment and four out of five think that unemployment is the most serious problem facing the government today. By not accepting this challenge, politicians are losing the chance of taking any useful remedial or any effective pre-emptive action.

All three major parties are committed to employment, as are their backers. The Conservatives, with employers and companies as their paymasters, believe in the employment ethic; as Mandy Rice-Davies once said, 'they would, wouldn't they'. The continuation of this ethic unchanged will guarantee them a supply of as many employees as they need, though some employers are starting to realise that the coexistence of high unemployment and the employment ethic is a double-edged sword. Certainly they can get willing employees on favourable terms, but the cost of this luxury is the potential dislocation that this 'reserve army' might cause. Little sleep is being lost over this realisation, however, and the ethic is alive and well and living in the Institute of Directors' dining-room.

The Labour party is actually *named* after the work process. Whilst in principle this need not mean formal employment, in practice the binding link with the trade unions ensures that it has to be. Trade unions are dedicated to employment. They look after the interests of their members at their place of employment, and indeed their membership, income and thus power is dependent on employed members. To doubt the employment ethic would be to doubt their own reason for existence, and this is unthinkable to most unions; it is therefore unthinkable for the Labour party. The 'right to work', which is a lovely and excellent slogan, does not mean what it says – it really means the right to employment.

The Alliance appears to believe in the employment ethic. A large number of its backers are middle-class professionals who have achieved their position, status and assets through their own endeavours and see no reason why others should not do the same. While their children may be experiencing some difficulty in gaining employment, the class bias in the education system suggests that most will have enough qualifications to satisfy the majority of employers. Business contacts or membership of select groups take care of the rest. The employment ethic is an undiminished part of their lives, and so it remains with the Alliance.

As these political parties dominate British politics at both national and local levels, it is little wonder that so little imagination has been shown in the employment field. The government has tried to stimulate the small business sector with a little success – but whether many of these new companies will last is another matter. Over 150 enterprise agencies and 100 bodies providing finance and some practical help have gone into this effort, but it is very unlikely that the UK unemployment problem will be solved by small businesses alone, as on average they employ no more than ten people. To get rid of unemployment this would mean more than doubling the number of small businesses to about 650,000, a scarcely credible proposition. Aside from small businesses and recent related initiatives like the enterprise zones and freeports, neither of which have been conspicuously successful, the government has relied upon training as a substitute for employment.

A far more serious case can be made against the government, however. It is that unemployment has been used as a weapon against the trade unions and against high wage settlements. This has certainly been the *effect* of unemployment, but whether it was a deliberate aim of government policy or just a side effect of its main policies is a matter open to question.

Certainly some employers and indeed some Ministers have not been slow to seize the opportunities offered to them.

Local government has shown more imagination and practical sense. The Greater London Council led the way with its avowedly job-creating Greater London Enterprise Board and this was followed by similar, but smaller, efforts in the West Midlands and South Yorkshire, amongst others. It is no accident that these are Labour-controlled authorities and, what is more, nearly all are on the left of the party spectrum. Even now there is no real recognition, except in the formation of cooperatives, that these bodies have added anything new or even valuable to the political vocabulary. They have done so in a most unequivocal way, however. They are attempting to change the pattern of new technology use by showing that it does not always have to be used to increase productivity at the expense of employees. They are trying to use new technologies to enhance skills and to make employment a more satisfying experience. They are trying to create jobs which will meet local needs and are actively attempting to discover what these are.

This is a far cry from the current national campaign of the Labour party based on the slogan 'jobs and industry'. Any one job is as good as another in this programme. Many of them, in hospital laundries or in sewers, for example, are not pleasant, but the people who developed the policy are unlikely ever to have to do them. It is not a gripping slogan – indeed it harks back to the Wilsonian days when the white heat of technology referred to steel furnaces. If the Labour party and the unions at a national level cannot understand the importance of the GLEB experiment then there is precious little hope for the labour movement; it will not be able to cope with the new situations which the use of the new technologies will bring. Symptomatic of this conservatism is the attachment to regional policy when a more locally based set of proposals would stand a far greater chance of working. The Labour party has never realised that a region is an administrative nicety; it is too big for local identities to develop and too small to be self sufficient. It is, on the other hand, a perfect arrangement for the civil service – a non-threatening, completely controllable unit of government.

Political inaction is a charge that can, and should, be laid at the door of opposition parties as well as those in government whose actions influence our every day. Opposition parties have a duty to oppose, which is negative, but they also have a duty to propose new policies and place them before the electorate. Both the Labour party and the Alliance are guilty of rehashing old policies and regilding the old rhetoric. They both base these on the key fantasy of abolishing unemployment in the lifetime of the next parliament. Neither party feels strong enough or secure enough to turn to the electorate and argue that fewer jobs in a different set of circumstances will lead to a far better life for everyone, and that they are the party to create the right circumstances. In Australia Barry Jones, a science minister in the Hawke government, has shown that it is possible for a relatively senior politician to espouse different views about employment and not be pilloried or made to look foolish. He has not convinced his party, however. It is strange that in a world when employees clearly want to spend less time at the workplace, a political party does not make a virtue out of necessity and propose a radical alternative.

In Germany this has been done with greater success than elsewhere. The Greens argue against the politics of inevitable economic growth and for a society based on work rather than employment. Their successes over the past five years have been considerable, and they have obviously touched a deep-seated nerve somewhere in the German psyche. However, conventional political problems are beginning to emerge. The Greens are splitting on Marxist/reformist/fundamentalist lines as it becomes clear that implementing policies is quite another matter from developing them in abstract, while the discipline of having to play the game by the existing rules is proving to be too much for some members. The crucial period will be between now and the next German elections. If the Greens can survive with only small losses they will have established themselves as a credible radical alternative, but if they do not manage to do this they will have to start all over again.

The Ecology and Green parties in other countries are making some slow headway, if only in terms of media exposure, though disenchantment with the existing traditional parties has not yet reached the point where a very radical party can succeed. The disenchantment is growing, however. In France the extreme right-wing National Front party made large gains in the last elections, in the USA only half the electorate bothered to vote in the Presidential election, whilst in the UK opinion polls have indicated that the public do not believe that any of the parties can solve current economic problems. Despite these straws in the wind, however, it is unlikely that the Green or alternative economic movement will achieve much success through the ballot box, though this does not mean that they will be totally without influence or will see all their objectives ignored.

The aims of the alternative political parties must be twofold. The first is to influence and persuade the existing political parties to take ecologically sound positions in their policies. This can be done by infiltration into parties or by using the wider media coverage of public scandals, for example nuclear power stations, the slaughter of whales, or the acid rain issue. The other aim must be to act as a pressure group, standing in elections to force their message home but also acting as an extra-parliamentary force between elections. Demonstrations, marches, meetings, lobbies and petitions are all part and parcel of such a movement.

Politicians are increasingly responding to public opinion rather than leading it, as they once did. The Reagan administration relies heavily upon very frequent private polling of the 'what if' variety to enable it to tailor its responses to almost any conceivable situation. The Conservative party operates in a similar, although considerably less sophisticated, way, whilst the Labour party has also started to use polls and surveys. This information tempers the pressures that political supporters place on the parties, which often tend towards the extreme.

It is partial misinterpretation of these polls that is reinforcing the traditional response on employment. Because unemployment is rated as the most important contemporary issue, so consistently and by such a wide margin, it is assumed that this means that the public must want politicians to promise to get rid of it. This is rather like assuming that polls which say that rates and local taxes are too high also imply that people want services cut. Frequent polls have shown that people are inconsistent in this matter – they want to pay less but receive more. The same polls also show an acceptance of unemployment as a natural by-product of the new technologies, and this would imply that new initiatives would not be received as unworldly or be unwelcome. How good their reception would be depends on the policies themselves.

Pressure groups do have an effect upon politicians. At one

time the Church had a great moral influence, sometimes for good, sometimes not. It declined along with church attendances but interestingly has started to make a come-back. The outspoken Bishop of Durham and those archbishops and bishops with big city dioceses like Stepney, Manchester, Liverpool and Birmingham are making their voices heard across the ecumenical divide on the inequities of unemployment. Not only are the lords spiritual making their presence felt in Parliament and in the media, but task forces and working groups around the country are trying to grapple with the need for a new work ethic.

Trade unions are another pressure group. They have been arguing for the use of new technologies across the board, although individual members may not agree, and have also argued for negotiations about their introduction and effects. Whilst there are some good technology agreements between employers and unions (an idea first floated in *The Collapse of Work*) most are little more than productivity agreements with few employment safeguards. The best that has been achieved is the promise of no redundancies, which, as we have noted, allows for a considerably smaller work force over time. Unions have also been arguing for a Keynesian reflation of the economy to create jobs and a return to the tripartite consensus politics of the sixties and seventies.

The employers have been arguing, as ever, for tougher laws against trade unions, for low interest rates but sound money (a puzzling combination), for easier employment legislation and – more recently – for a very limited reflation. A new and most interesting addition to the realm of pressure groupies and pundits are the entrepreneurs (especially in high tech) and senior managers. Their representation on radio and TV chat shows has increased at the same rate and at the same time as that of trade union leaders has decreased. The Clive Sinclairs and Iain Barrons are listened to with respect, as are the Harvey-Joneses and Arnold Weinstocks; their views on employment do not always coincide with those of the CBI, yet each of them would not hesitate to shed labour if they thought it an advantage for their companies.

The worthwhile nature of employment binds together what on the face of it are two unlikely allies, Adam Smith and Karl Marx, although it should be remembered that Marx based much of his analysis on traditional classical economics. This alliance is reflected in politics. Capitalism has always depended on the use (some say exploitation) of other people's labour, while communists believe in valuing products in terms of labour – this has been vital to both philosophies. I put this in the past tense because, while capitalism is moving into an era of using fewer employees wherever possible, communism still relies on total employment as the lynchpin of the state. The new technologies, if and when they are implemented in the Comecon countries, have the capacity to create havoc.

They are countries where efficiency has been deliberately traded off to maintain full employment; without this the value system based on the labour of these people would have broken down. What happens when a completely new technology arrives which, if used optimally, will increase efficiency – how will the state cope? One answer is not to use the technology, but this will increase the gap between East and West in terms of the price and quality of goods, and certainly discourage any further thoughts of trade liberalisation. Another method, and surely a better one, is to use the people released by the technology to improve services; the problem is that services do not enter into the Eastern bloc accounting systems. This technology is going to create problems and pressures in the near future, ones which these governments will have to confront. It cannot be ignored totally, if for no other reason than that it underpins all the new defence surveillance and weapon-guidance systems.

Lest apologists for the capitalist system should chuckle and mutter, 'I told you that communism would never last,' consider Marxist analysis. Marx predicted the collapse of capitalism, and this has patently not yet happened; even where communist governments do exist they did not arise in the way that Marx would have expected. Peasants have revolted, wars have intervened and conquest has absorbed – but no truly Marxist revolution has occurred as yet. Surely we should ask why, since so much of his analysis has been borne out in other areas. One possible explanation is that he made a very fundamental error. He assumed, and at the time it was logical that he should do so, that capitalism was efficient and that companies profit-maximised and would continue to do so. He also assumed that capital would become increasingly efficient, i.e. that it would increase the rate of 'surplus value' and so reduce the number of people needed in the production process. Neither of these assumptions has been anything like correct, until the past five years.

When Marx was writing there were no paid holidays, no sick pay, no facilities for employees and no pensions or other non-wage benefits. Employees worked for 51 weeks of the year, 6 days a week, 12 or 14 hours per day, for as many years as they were of use. Each move to shorter hours, each additional cost per employee and each duty laid upon employers by governments has moved capitalist enterprises further away from a profit-maximising position. None of these things was given freely, they were squeezed out after long struggles by trade unions and later by government legislation. Companies have different motivations, as do the managers who run them; some want to optimise their market share, others their cash flow, others power and others profits. Shareholders interfere very little, providing that a relatively competitive return to their capital is forthcoming. Capitalism is not efficient and, though Marx's predicted conflict exists – albeit in a considerably weaker form than he anticipated, there has patently been no revolution in the Western industrialised countries.

However, along comes a technology which, when used to increase productivity (and productivity alone), will suddenly enable companies to profit-maximise with few employees to reduce this efficiency. Will the conflicts become sharper? Will we witness the coming-to-pass of one of Marx's key predictions at just the time when communist countries are coming under pressure from precisely the same technological causes? It is more than a possibility *if* the prevailing capitalist free market theories are continued, refined and actually practised.

In the meantime, Parliamentary democracy still exists throughout the industrialised world, but it too is coming under pressure. A fast-changing technology needs fast responses and the system is not geared to such speed in peace-time. As the pace of change quickens, so the social problems caused by these changes come ever faster too and the system of government is in danger of being left behind. Old attitudes prevail in new circumstances and debates are held on last year's questions rather than this. A government elected for a five-year period makes its case through a manifesto, but in a fast-changing world many of the manifesto priorities may have changed or been overtaken by events, whilst subjects unthought-of at the time of the election may have come to the fore less than two years later. In such circumstances the electorate start to lose faith in politics as a method of problem-solving or creating the best circumstances in which people can live their lives. As in the nineteenth century, a change in the system might be the answer.

Several types of change spring to mind. The first is to use the potential of the new technology to enable people to vote on any particular issue by using an adapted alphanumeric pad attached to their TV set. This would assume the existence of interactive cable, a universal Prestel system, or both; or alternatively the voting could be done from the local post office or library. Government by referendum would have the advantage of the widest possible participation, but it would be unstable, short term in outlook, devoid of direction, and would leave little time for considered thought. The demagogue and the populist campaign would win almost every time, whatever the merits of the case. It is no accident that when novelists or playwrights use such a system it is always in the context of supporting a dictatorship or propping up a particularly nasty regime – it will certainly be possible, but it is highly undesirable.

Another method is to allow the electorate more opportunity to make their views known and bring the latest problems to the attention of politicians. This can be done in two ways. The first is to reduce the life of a parliament to two or three years; if there were an elected second chamber whose members were elected for a six-year term this system might provide the combination of stability and flexibility needed. The other method is to elect MPs for five years but to have 20 per cent of them stand for re-election every year, a system that used to be used in some areas of local government. This has the advantage of allowing the electorate a chance to let the government know what it thinks of their efforts in a practical way, even to the extent of putting them out of office.

All these methods have the disadvantage of being essentially short term in nature. Not only would a government find it more difficult than ever to plan ahead but there would be even less guarantee of continuity to carry out such plans – though if these plans are based on yesterday's problems anyway, this may not be quite as severe a loss as it appears to be at first sight. Subjects like security, privacy, employment and job security, selling-techniques, education policies, the responsibility for expert systems, cable TV and health care are all being changed by technology to a great enough extent to require new policies and perhaps new legislation. And these are only the tip of an iceberg at present.

There is a great deal of government inaction at the precise time when there is most need for action but, whatever we may think about politics and politicians, they are necessary in this complex world. Legislation provides the framework in which the activities of society take place, and the statements and actions of politicians create an environment which influences other people's actions. With technological and social changes starting to arrive thick and fast, the need for cool, efficient and imaginative politics has seldom been greater.

The old slogans and outdated policies will simply not do any longer. The changes we are experiencing are as climacteric as those of the first industrial revolution. We made many mistakes in that one – we have a duty to ensure that our current politicians do not repeat them.

15 Facing the future: the new industrial revolution

It is difficult to overemphasise the importance of the first industrial revolution. It changed the world in so many different ways. New towns and cities grew where none had been before, and people had to adapt to different places to live and different places to work. Lifestyles changed from the seasonal rhythms of the countryside to the artificial cycle of the industrial production process. New skills were developed and learned, new products appeared, new concepts arrived. The creative genius of the engineer was allowed full reign, and was matched by a flowering of other talents in the productive industries. The whole world was affected as the industrialising countries acquired and consolidated their empires, using the goods they had made as instruments of subjugation or trade.

Political thought and systems developed to match the demands of these changed circumstances, and new societies and groups developed. An industrial working class emerged, followed by a middle class. New divisions superseded the older rural distinctions. It was a time of violent change, of great affluence and the most abject of poverty, of genius and of drudgery. In short there were two nations – the haves and the have-nots. We live with the legacy of that revolution, and this is not only reflected in the towns and cities with their emblems of municipal pride – the city halls, the galleries and the parks. The standard of living that we enjoy today is built upon the foundations of that era, our system of government was refined then, our urban and transport infrastructure laid down in that period. Above all, it was a time when – although mankind mastered technology – many people were enslaved by the machine.

The new industrial revolution has within it a propensity for change just as great as that of its predecessor. Microelectronics is a technology every bit as powerful as steam – and it works

257

over an even wider range. It too can affect where we live and work, the skills we need, our social relationships and our accepted notions of class differences. The pressures will be felt by individuals and families within the home as well as in the workplace, and as a result past certainties and the security that accompanied them will be shattered. No stabilising influences appear to be taking their place in the foreseeable future, *although positive actions could be taken to provide them.*

The analyses and scenarios in this book have so far been based on the assumption that, as in the first industrial revolution, the machine has become the master and the overwhelming majority of humans the servants. I have also assumed that the motives behind introducing these new technologies are those of increased efficiency and productivity, cost (and employee) minimisation, and a desire for better quality and enhanced speed. The first assumption is not necessarily true in all cases, but although there could be other reasons than the ones I have stated for using the new technologies, I do not believe that they will play a significant role in events.

The work being done on human-centred lathes by the GLEB and the Centre for Alternative Industrial and Technological Systems is pointing the way to high-tech machines designed to enhance human capabilities. The newer production groups at Saab car factories, deliberately organised to move away from conventional Taylorist production lines, show that traditional production methods are not immutable. However, in general the probability is that the new machines and systems will dictate to people, rather than the other way around; the forces of market capitalism and the lure of cost-cutting must not be underestimated and will be strong in this particular respect. This is precisely what Marx predicted would happen.

Given these conditions, other routes will have to be taken in an attempt to make the new industrial revolution valuable and enjoyable as well as profitable. Some of the changes are of a psychological nature, and I shall deal with these in the second of these two chapters; the others are practical. The overall objective is partly to avoid as many of the conflicts and disagreeable side-effects that will stem from the introduction of the technologies as possible, and partly to use the opportunities opened up by these technologies to make life better, happier, richer and more complete than ever before.

It is possible to reduce – if not completely to eradicate – unemployment, and it is certainly possible to provide sufficient 'work' for people. Throughout this chapter, as indeed I have tried to do throughout the book, I am distinguishing between employment and work. 'Employment' is a paid job, 'work' is a useful activity undertaken in free time (although it could be employment in another context). If the matching of people with 'work' can be accomplished then some of the problems that arise from unemployment will disappear. There are no easy options on this route, however.

The existing policies of the major political parties fail almost completely to come to grips with the nature of this industrial revolution. As someone remarked about the 1983 Labour party election manifesto, it contained proposals about fox-hunting and almost everything else – but the word 'computer' did not appear at all. The Tory approach is to see microelectronics as a source of sufficient efficiency and power to amount to a second industrial revolution, which is presumably why they are attempting to implement the same policies as their ancestors did during the first one. The Alliance realises its power but wants some form of diluted Keynesianism to control it, while the Labour party appears to believe that it is similar to any other technological development – the machine tool, for example – that can be contained by its normal interventionist and Keynesian policies. None of these inspires overwhelming confidence, although the last has the virtue of having had some partial short-term success in the past.

The dangers arise from pursuing unsuccessful policies well beyond the time when they should have been dropped. The use of unsuitable strategies can not only exacerbate the difficulties but also divert attention away from alternatives. We cannot keep believing that there is light at the end of the tunnel when, if it is there at all, it is the lamp of an on-coming express. Sooner or later, preferably sooner, a series of decisions will have to be made which acknowledge the magnitude of the current changes and take responsibility for their continued development.

We are looking at a revolution, and moreover one that has barely begun in the industrialised countries. The technology that has been developed has not yet been implemented in most instances, whilst in many cases where it has been it is not being used to its fullest extent. In addition there are all the new fifth-generation systems to come, all the artificial intelligence and expert systems to be made operational and all the biochip avenues (the combination of microelectronics and genetic engineering) to be explored. A revolution is a profound change, a discontinuity; by definition it is not merely the development of an existing trend. A revolution needs to be confronted by equally powerful ideas, some of which might be described as radical in the conventional sense.

I would argue that there is no one magic formula, no single philosophy or course of action which is going to create employment and solve all our other problems. There is a range of actions that can be taken, some of which depend upon each other – although others can stand alone to be accepted or rejected. None of them will be easily acceptable to the vested interests of the Establishment; their power may be threatened and their influence decreased.

The four basic building blocks are also the hardest to achieve. These are to amend the employment ethic, to reduce working lifetimes, to provide financial security for all regardless of circumstances and to encourage community growth and initiatives. The first of these means returning to the old work ethic (the usefulness ethic) and bypassing the existing employment ethic. This is not a utopian or abstract appeal, but is aimed at a specific purpose – to provide work and employment for people that doesn't appear to be a second-best option.

If it is possible to produce and deliver the goods and services that we demand using fewer people in the process, then we can use the released time to meet the many needs of others which depend on the imparting of our humanity rather than our practical or intellectual skills. Ideally this will be shared around as equitably as possible, though in practice it will be very difficult because of the mismatch of needs, demands and the availability of people. The high unemployment areas will have more needs to be met, though not that many more, while the low unemployment areas may not have enough people to meet their own needs.

The task of changing from an employment to a work ethic lies partly in the province of the school system, partly in the attitude of government and partly in the response of communities. Schools have to reorientate their teaching towards a wider view of life, rather than concentrate on a preparation for employment. At the same time the school should become one of the focal points of the community, both giving to it and receiving from it. This is made far easier by the recent moves to restrict the intake into schools to children from the local area. In practical terms this interchange can be arranged on several levels.

The school should be open to the community both in and out of school hours, and rooms should be set aside for various activities and members of the community. The elderly should be encouraged to come in and talk to, even teach, the pupils about the local area and what it was like when they were young; this would take the grandparent/grandchild relationship into a new dimension. The library could be open to some of the younger unemployed, as could many of the sporting and workshop facilities to a wider range of people. The school should be available all year round for both pupils and adults. Longer holidays taken at off-peak times by parents will put a strain on the existing system of terms, and these will have to be replaced by a more flexible system which enables a pupil who misses some time to get back into the course without missing an entire term or even year.

Schools should also act as a major focus for community action. Young people at school should be encouraged to study the local community closely, indeed much of their teaching can be based on it. The interdependence of one group upon another, what needs and demands exist and are unfulfilled and how to meet them – these are valuable life- and ultimately work- and employment-enhancing lessons. It is also a practical rather than a theoretical method of learning, and it amends the employment ethic in demonstrating that work need not always be in the formal sector. Because it is a practical and useful exercise the opposition that might be expected from local businessmen (and even unions) because of the possibility that work might be taken away from them could be weakened; indeed one would hope that local managers and professionals would do some of this teaching. Nevertheless, such a programme would take a considerable time to achieve even moderate success as hostility could be considerable.

Education is a key to the adaptation process but unlocking the door is only a prerequisite to taking the first steps into the future. Employment should be reduced to 32[3]: a 32-hour week worked for 32 weeks per year and over a 32-year working lifetime – in all a 32,768-hour employment lifetime, or less than half the present amount by the year 1995.

It is an extension of part-time work for all. This is a modest overall ambition, not a fixed or ridiculous target, but it is not possible within the economic and business context in which we work at present. If the removal of people from the labour force (to the equivalent of half the present working lifetime) is done in blocks of at least a day, so that replacement labour has to take over some of the work, the number of jobs that would therefore be created in the UK could reach two million. There would not, however, be a doubling of the work force for many reasons. Some jobs are almost impossible to share, and others need a degree of personal expertise that cannot be duplicated. The scope for increasing productivity with the current technologies is still very great and the move to reduce working hours would stimulate this and the use of short-term contract labour. However, there are reasons why even two million may well be an overestimate.

Overtime would have to be constrained severely. This would not only require domestic legislation but almost certainly EEC directives, along with a minimum standard annual holiday of 60 days and perhaps a 6-month sabbatical leave every ten years. Changes such as this will certainly stimulate the introduction of new labour-saving systems based on microelectronic technology and other productivity-enhancing techniques. They will almost certainly mean a removal of some types of work done in the EEC by the transnational companies to the newly industrialising countries where it will be cheaper, but EEC legislation could make such moves unprofitable for the companies concerned. Another reason why this might be an overestimate is that some techniques will pass out of the orbit of the industrialised country altogether; certain textile and clothing operations, assembly of microelectronics and some database preparation will go to the NICs and LDCs.

To reduce employment by this amount requires some major changes and the luxury of time. The reductions would have to be phased in on an annual basis, and even then several exceptions will have to be made. The mismatch of unmet needs not co-existing with available surplus labour will have to be catered for, and the difficulties caused by skill shortages (where those who are skilled will have to work overtime until education and training meet the demands) will have to be overcome. In itself this entails a proper employment forecasting system for the skills needed, and in turn this means that both government and employers will need to break with tradition and make joint plans. Some jobs require continuity, however (breaking off a surgical operation because it was the end of a shift might not be in the best interests of the patient), while the increase in the numbers of the self-employed will make overall planning more difficult. The flexi-year approach would appear to be of value in these areas. How to monitor and enforce the system without it being too authoritarian is another problem, although the new technologies themselves will help solve this. The new French 'smart cards' which work out flexitime and can 'bank' holidays could be a considerable help.

The major difficulty arises with earnings, however. People will obviously want to be paid for a full lifetime's earnings even if they are working only half the time. Although productivity increases could enable part of this money to be paid, a competitive open economy would soon lose its edge if some of the competitors did not follow suit. There are several alternative routes that can be taken, however. The first is to close off the economy entirely, have a non-convertible currency and become a one-state Comecon. The resulting hardships and fall in the standard of living, together with the loss of choice and international movement, make this an unacceptable option. Another is to compel the employer to pay the full amount, but it is probable that marginal firms could not compete and would go to the wall; others with a healthy cash flow would automate as far as possible.

An alternative method is to use the negative income tax principle to ensure that everyone has a sufficient income no matter how many hours they work, even if they are not working at all. As pensions would have to be paid in part or whole at an earlier age, this method of payment could replace traditional pension arrangements. The advantage of this method is that it equalises the burden on tax-payers and extends and simplifies the welfare system, while enabling a company to retain employees on sabbaticals or indeed over a lengthy training or educational period.

Some people believe that the incentive to find employment

will be lost if there is a decent income available without a job, and this is used as a counter-argument to providing a reasonable payment for those who are either unemployed or who work part-time. There are three responses to this particular approach. The first is to agree and to drop the entire concept of negative tax, which would be a great loss. The second is to amend this idea so that no one will get more than 80 per cent of what they would have earned had they been employed full-time at their particular type of skill or trade. The third is to disagree with the objection entirely. It is strange that the prevailing government philosophy assumes that the well-off need more money and reduced taxes to act as an incentive for them to work harder, whilst the poor must have less money as their incentive.

The prevailing ethos would suggest that one of the first two options would be chosen, although most of the evidence suggests that, providing people do not actually lose money by doing a job, they would rather be in employment than 'do nothing'. A carefully constructed negative income tax should be able to maintain the traditional principle of a paramount link between financial reward and employment whilst providing financial security for all those who need it.

The fourth element of the model is the community. Jobs – paid and unpaid – are to be found in the community, as are companionship, identity of interest, and peer group competition. It is the area in which the employed, unemployed, partly employed, never-employed and wanting-to-be-employed meet without actually coming together. If a person or family group is financially secure, however, there is far more likelihood that they will be amenable to working within the community, for the benefit of themselves as well as others within it, whether or not they are directly paid for their efforts. People's 'good works' have always been made possible by financial security at the least, affluence at the best.

Communities do not just develop out of some mysterious ether. Initially they have to have some form of separate and unique identity, and beyond this there has to be a mechanism by which they can function and express their local and independent interests. This must mean some form of community council. However, local authorities and the councillors elected to them have not been known as the most generous of people when the question of sharing their authority, and with it prestige, has arisen. Community organisations, by their very nature, must challenge local government. The easy solution is for the local council to act as the parent to community organisations, as some of the London boroughs I referred to earlier have done, and then to claim parental control at a later date, but this would destroy proper community development. The acid test of a democratic system is that it is capable of tolerating ideas which are alien to mainstream thought, and this will be only too true of the most locally devolved of institutions, the community.

Communities should be encouraged to develop organically in their initial stages around schools, hospitals and local groups – using festivals and other events as a catalyst, in rather the same way that a crystal grows around a central core. From that point onwards the community must be allowed to express its own views about its own future, given that it has constraints as to the financial and other resources available to it. It should, however, be empowered to raise its own finances as far as possible.

Within the community the needs identified by the pupils at the school can be the object of a concerted campaign. The humanitarian needs, like talking to older people, may be met by some form of voluntary labour, while the more physical jobs, like building, will have to use the paid services of local people. The areas where there are the most unmet needs are, in general, those with the lowest *per capita* incomes and the least access to capital sources. Small businesses will have to be risk-sharing and this will mean co-operative development; local authorities with organisations akin to the GLEB should have a considerable role to play in the inauguration of such enterprises.

It would be courting disaster, however, if a group of people (especially young ones) with a good idea were given some initial funding and then left to their own devices, to sink or swim as it were. Schools do not teach young people about the real world of business; at best it is assumed that they will work for someone else, not for themselves, whilst few employees are encouraged to explore the financial and managerial aspects of the enterprise for which they have been working. Local managers, especially those who have retired early, should be encouraged to pass on their expertise and their experience; if managers cannot fill this gap then the banking system or the providers of capital for the enterprise should step in to do so.

The community base need not be a collection of worthy but excruciatingly dull projects. Entertainment must come high on the list of priorities and part of this can be built around modern technologies. Why not have a community TV service? It could be based on a school or technical college, provide news and information about transport (why there is a delay on the 253 bus route today, for example), local authority services, activities, local messages and advertisements, as well as making videos for distribution on a far wider basis. The equipment is becoming cheaper and easier to use by the day. Community newspapers and radio could be linked into the network with exchange facilities between different areas. A professional technician would be needed, and other workers would get on-the-job training, although the school could well take the opportunity to run a series of courses.

A resurgence of arts and crafts should be encouraged at a local level too. From glass-engraving to knitting, and from sign-writing to agricultural implement-making, there is a constant demand for handmade goods and services, which is not always satisfied. There are several advantages, and one clear disadvantage, in promoting expansion in these areas. Working with one's hands appears to give great satisfaction and meet a deep-seated need for many people. The goods can often readily be sold far away from the base where they were made, and often to export markets if there are good marketing and advice organisations available. The crafts keep older traditions going at a time when technology is tending to sweep away such roots, though it is a mistake to believe that crafts have to be old; a new generation of computer-based crafts is emerging, from art and clever print-outs to music, programmed graphics and do-it-yourself program kits. Finally, the community benefits from an additional focus for pride, jobs, income and interest.

The disadvantage is that it becomes all too easy to believe that these sorts of initiatives will solve all the unemployment and social problems of a community. There is a limited market for this type of product, even if it is somewhat larger than the pessimists might believe, and the areas of highest unemployment probably provide the worst potential market in this respect. Large organisations – be they in the private or the public sector – provide, and will continue to provide, the bulk of employment in the UK.

However, if communities can encourage these sorts of commercial activities and dovetail them into the social and person-to-person local authority services, a new dimension could be added to everyday life. Both jobs and work could be created – and, moreover, tasks which need doing by men and women of all ages. There is a view amongst the 'new economists' that each community should attempt to be as self-sustaining as possible and attempt to draw all strands of commerce, trade and culture into itself. Not only is this impractical in the urban context, it is also highly undesirable. The wider the spread and the deeper the mesh of these initiatives the better.

Much of the work or employment within the local neighbourhood will be part-time and match the decreasing hours worked within the formal sector. The simplified social security system based on something like a negative income tax would enable a person to operate successfully in both areas. There will still be a world outside the local community in which the majority of the labour force will find their employment, although, as we have seen, the suburbs will become employment stations and have to metamorphose themselves into proper communities. Within this universe of employment there will be changes.

Careers will be shorter than ever before. Fifteen years will probably be the time span in which a person will start, climb, peak and finish; a second career should then be a viable option although the education system will have to adapt to cope with this. In the high-technology areas this time scale will probably be even shorter, whilst in the more settled professions like medicine the constant training and retraining needed will constitute a change in direction, if not career. As promotion patterns will be relatively haphazard, and stability within large organisations a luxury, the employment climate will be characterised by high insecurity. In such a climate trade unions or similar collective organisations should show a marked recovery as employees feel exposed and run for cover.

Employment should be defined increasingly by domestic and personal circumstances. Some Swedish employers are pioneering this trend by enabling couples to work part-time in order to spend more time with their young children. If we use a flexi-year system it is possible to take this even further. Years could be taken off, whole summers or winters could be used as non-employment periods – an infinite variety of combinations would be possible. The change in promotion and career patterns will hasten this process as fewer people bother to compete in a race they know they cannot win.

The secondary labour market, or flexi-work sector, will continue to be the main employment growth area; indeed its proportion of the work force will increase from the current one in four to nearer one in three over the coming ten years. Much of this increase will be caused by the use of sub-contractors in the new technology and computer areas, as well as the fixing of permanent manning at a level marginally below normal output. The employees in this sector will be unprotected and it will be necessary to extend the legislation which confers employment protection rights to full-time employees to part-time, temporary and casual workers too. Whilst this will attract a howl of protest from many employers, and the politicians and academics who argue that in order to create employment it is necessary to reduce both wages and working standards to Victorian levels, it is a necessary move. If a wide division between primary and secondary work is allowed to develop it will have unfortunate social repercussions in terms of a 'two nations' schism, especially as men start to be recruited to this sector in greater numbers.

Meeting needs and demands will remain the main basis for job creation within society. As the manufacturing and indeed the service sectors become ever more capital intensive, so the main area of formal employment growth appears to be in the person-to-person service sector – and most of this in the public domain. Health services need to be more oriented towards preventative medicine and primary care and, whilst the growth of expert systems will siphon off some of the potential employment growth amongst ancillary staffs, the entire strategy is labour intensive. Doctors, nurses, technicians, secretaries, porters, orderlies, dentists, and ancillaries like speech therapists and physiotherapists will all be needed in greater numbers. The staffing of specialist hospitals in the mental health and psychogeriatric fields should be improved, as should the levels in children's homes, elderly people's homes and homes for the disabled. Can we say honestly that we give any of these a good service at present? The people concerned try hard, but there are too few of them working with scant resources.

Education should be revamped and expanded. A workable

method for re-entering the education system at a mature age must be introduced to cater for the people who need to change careers, not just retrain. An industry- and skill-oriented training scheme must be implemented to cope with the fast-changing technologies. In both instances there needs to be proper manpower-planning with a national computer-based network enabling information to be disseminated and exchanged across the different areas of the country. However, this information will be useless without enhanced mobility, which can be made easier by reducing the reliance on owner-occupied housing or municipal accommodation. A person who wishes to move from a high unemployment area to a high employment area generally has to pay considerably more for a house, or is placed at the bottom of the local authority housing list. A crash programme of building good low-rent housing is needed, ideally by housing associations, so that there is a flexible stock of housing.

Education and learning must be distinguished from training, especially at the school level. The vocational education system is a poor substitute for education unless you are looking for 'factory fodder', although it must be admitted that the present school system is losing the confidence of teachers, parents and pupils. A move towards smaller, neighbourhood schools – which maintain more of a teacher- rather than subject-base in the first two critical secondary years – may be a partial answer.

Some people would like to see the school-leaving age increased; others, including some politicians, would like it to fall by two years to fourteen. The former would keep unwilling young people at an institution which they found irksome, the latter would discard young people and leave them to a bleak future in an era when more jobs will be knowledge intensive. There seems to be a need for a 'post-school' education, part or full time, which could be arranged through schools, education authorities, the community, local employers or any combination of these. These new bodies, which could run parallel to the sixth form colleges, or even be a part of them, would attempt to avoid all the traps that so clearly turn many British youngsters against the existing school system. It would not be training as such, which is a necessary but separate need. The government role in this would be to create the environment in which these schemes would be given a fair chance, and provide the finance to ensure that they did not collapse.

Studies suggest that the falling school rolls will be reversed in the early nineties, so it appears shortsighted in the extreme to close schools and reduce the number of teachers. If we are serious in attempting to compete internationally then we need a better educated population (adult as well as young) which means that more resources need to be made available. The new technology will provide some capital additions to what is basically a labour-intensive process. Open University and Open Tech can be expanded and augmented by community programmes based on night-school classes and national or regional interest courses – history, geography, languages etc. Education can be, indeed should be, offered to adults as a consumer product to be savoured as school rarely was. Teachers, trainers and lecturers, teaching aides, dinner ladies, people to publish both books and videos, caretakers, builders – all are needed in an expanded education system capable of meeting the challenge of the next century.

As unemployment takes its toll, and the strains on the employment sector in a modern society increase, so do the casualties of the eighties. Social services are needed to cope with child abuse and other forms of physical violence, increasing alcoholism and drug addiction, poverty and poor living conditions. Social workers, community nurses and all the back-up staff that these experts need are required now, and the demands on their time will probably increase through the nineties. These are not jobs that can be performed by interested and well-meaning volunteers – a high degree of expertise is needed. Other jobs that should be created in this sort of sector are in the leisure and entertainment industries – in sports and community centres, parks and rivers, galleries, museums and concert-halls.

Most of these facilities were laid down in the nineteenth century and in recent years there has been a reduction in the resources made available for their maintenance. This means that many new projects need to be undertaken. Roads, sewers, railway electrification, schools, hospitals and housing all need to be repaired, rebuilt, improved or started afresh. Most of this money will need to be found from the public exchequer and this involves a massive change in current political attitudes. These projects will, however, along with the expansion of the caring services, create jobs – indeed they are almost the only areas about which one can say that with certainty, other than the knowledge industry itself. But, as I have suggested, the jobs created by public expenditure in these fields can only be sustained by economic and political measures that have been rejected by the electorate after too short a period in the past.

Life in the future will of necessity be less concerned with employment, however. Even the most optimistic scenario, with all the job-creating and working-lifetime-shortening actions fully implemented, will leave us with something like 15 per cent of the available work force not required to be in employment at all. In addition, another 20 per cent will not be in employment at any one time. The 32^3 life, which plays such a large part in this view of the future, allows for a far more sensible approach to free or leisure time than we have at present. For example, is it not foolish to give people their only long block of leisure at a time when they are least equipped to use it, at retirement? Would it not be more sensible for us to take mid-career breaks of two or three years to spend time with growing families or to recharge our batteries with a totally different education course or with travel? As careers will last for less than a lifetime such breaks could be institutionalised, although compulsion might be impractical as well as undesirable. With more free time there will have to be a more imaginative and coherent policy towards leisure.

There are a variety of avenues that could be explored. Why not have trains and coaches equipped in part for education? Some commuters already conduct French or economics classes on their way to work – why not do the same for ordinary, non-commuting travellers? Why not issue vouchers for the use of the empty seats on trains, buses, or aeroplanes? These could be tied to local tax or rate payments and be interchangeable. When London Transport and British Rail arranged for free or almost free travel for pensioners, the horizons of this group were widened dramatically. The under-utilisation of these forms of transport, especially at off-peak periods, is an economic and business lunacy; correcting it would provide a very enlightening service. There appears to be no reason why local authorities should not run their own hotels and exchange holidays with other areas, as they often control local transport too, complete packages could be arranged. Some form of rate equalisation might be needed if the increased free time led to heavier burdens on seaside ratepayers, for example, but several local authorities are already beginning to operate this type of scheme.

If one of the aims of the 'new leisure' is to get as many people as possible to participate in something rather than just be voyeurs, the controlling bodies of many of our leisure institutions will have to be amended. Both the Arts and Sports Councils will need to cater for ordinary people at a local level, rather than only the excellent as at present. The arts in general will have to be made more accessible to the public, whilst the fact that 'culture' is only available to the few (like 'positional' goods – bought only for their status value – art ceases to be cultural or coveted if it has a mass appeal) must be made irrelevant, even if it cannot be eradicated completely. The Sports Council will need to provide a wider range of participatory events, in a wider range of sports than they have covered in their Sport for All campaign. Community games which are often invented because of a lack of proper facilities for other sports, like street hockey, should be encouraged rather than frowned upon.

Appointments to the local bodies concerned with leisure can be made in many ways, including elections, though local participation is declining. This does not add to the ability of committees to reflect local opinion accurately and faithfully. The communities themselves should be enabled to nominate members through the new community councils.

Free time needs to be filled somehow, and all too often information about how this can be done is not easily available. Leisure shops in high streets, or in department stores or supermarkets, might meet the need. These would be a combination of a travel and booking agency, a sports goods shop and an information service. There would be assistants who could make suggestions and counsel clients, as well as help find the facilities, events or places required, whilst interactive databases run by organisations like On-Line and local authorities would be available for consultation, bookings and reservations. The extremely wide range of people who, at any one time, will have money and free time to spare will make the demands on such a shop very high. Whilst it would be possible to make this service available from the home through a cable or Prestel TV receiver, the person-to-person counselling might avoid some errors of direction.

The general trend towards working from smaller offices, office shops or from home in the suburbs will lead to two additional features in this scenario. A considerable amount of development will be needed in and around the suburbs, which will create employment; some of this will be for the provision of proper facilities for free-time use and local transport systems. The conversion of the suburb from a virtual dormitory to a complete neighbourhood with working and playing facilities will be one of the features of the late nineties across Europe. At the same time the cities will be undergoing a transformation. Decline will have spread and some of the redundant office blocks will have been demolished. Most cities will find a fall in property prices makes it feasible to renew building, but this time for dwellings and recreation, parks and leisure facilities. The conversion of Battersea power station into a large leisure theme park is an early example of what might happen across Europe.

Strangely, although London will bear the brunt of this second wave of unemployment in the mid-nineties, its dereliction will be far less than that of most other UK cities. This will be partly due to the fact that it will still be the centre of government, it will still house most ministries, the Royal Family will still be based there, the City and other markets will still have influence there and the international data and knowledge industry could well have its base there. The other reason is that it will still attract overseas tourists. The unemployment problem will, however, be acute especially amongst the educational under-achievers and the unskilled – most of the skilled will have moved away long before this happens.

Changes of this magnitude (indeed, the changes we are undergoing at present in the way we work) need additional institutions to deal with them – the present ones are not coping. Our political system is too short-term in outlook, too long-term in operation and too conservative in all respects and at all levels. The situation might be improved by a long-term think tank which is independent of the formal political parties – a role not fulfilled by the new Employment Institute, which is compromised by its campaigning function and overtly political ambitions. This UK-style Brookings Institute would study the potential hot spots in the running of the economy, such as employment, energy, population, raw material availability,

273

technological developments and religion. Their reports would contain no recommendations (the political parties and other interested bodies would fill that gap only too quickly), but they would at least be providing agendas for discussion on what the future might bring. Quite clearly such reports would link up with research in other countries, and hopefully a European picture could be pieced together as a result of which individual studies would be refined. Attempts to do this sort of thing in the OECD or EEC fall foul of governments wishing to put the best gloss on their particular efforts or withhold damaging information. Such short-term hypocrisy merely makes the case for an independent body that much stronger.

This is not to argue that the EEC has no role in the matter at all – it does, and a most important one. Supranational legislation on employment matters such as working lifetimes, the restriction of overtime, minimum standards of holiday entitlement, health and safety, and the secondary labour market will be invaluable. From the point of view of the EEC, it is necessary to maintain equality within the competitive elements. Other legislation constraining the activities of multinational corporations, especially in their use of LDC labour which does not meet the minimum EEC standards, would also be welcome. Finally, there is a role to be played in setting European standards and conventions regarding the use and development of the new technologies themselves. Do we need a European-wide information-added tax? We tax other sources of power. Do we need a European systems tax? This would tax an employer on 50 per cent of the savings made by replacing workers with a computer-based system. The rationale for this is that the cost of the former employees has been passed by the employer directly on to the state; and such a tax would be an attempt to recoup some of this extra expenditure. It could go into a special fund to create jobs for school-leavers.

I have so far ignored one particular think tank's report in this chapter, but it cannot and should not be omitted. This is the Brandt Report, entitled 'North – South'. While it has not exactly commended itself to the leaders of the industrialised world, it acts as an uncomfortable reminder that one group of people did think that something could be done to help the LDCs. There are signs that it is about to be disinterred by, amongst others, the Socialist International.

The Brandt Commission proposed that aid be given to the poor countries of the South. It believed movement towards equality, however limited, to be the most important factor as it would stimulate both economic and trade growth. In other words, it reversed the current conventional thinking which seeks to create wealth, knowing that this will create greater inequalities, and then attempts to redistribute the fruits of this at a later stage. Brandt argued that the redistribution itself is the mechanism by which world growth will be stimulated – it is Keynesianism on a global and heroic scale. It must be done. Over a time-period of perhaps twenty years, more jobs will probably accrue to the industrialised countries through this operation than through domestic policies. Apart from these motives of self-interest, humanitarian grounds alone should dictate that the Report be taken seriously.

There are countries in the world today which have no conceivable chance of ever servicing their debts (paying the interest on the loans that they have from the world's banks), let alone repaying any of the capital. The banking system, exclusively the property of the richest countries, is thus in a difficult, if not impossible, position. It has bad debts which it cannot recover – to do so would mean that some of these countries would declare publicly that they were in default, and then no one would bother to pay any interest at all. The countries concerned have few assets other than people; most of their other assets are in the hands of private or multinational corporations. The banks need to be let off the hook, the alternative being that sooner rather than later one of them will get tangled up. There could then be a domino effect, imperilling the global banking structure.

The banks should have a vested interest in the expansion of world trade to protect their investments. Loans made for the purpose of expanding the LDC economies along with a moratorium on debts would have several effects. The first is that these countries would need to import goods and services from the industrialised North to provide training and schools, roads, transport, factories, ranches or whatever. This would create jobs and temporarily export people from the industrialised nations. As the LDCs started to achieve economic growth they would start to trade. Their imports, as well as hopefully some exports, would start to rise. World trade would grow and, despite increased competition on certain product lines, employment in the North would grow too. To deny this argument is to deny the rationale behind the UK entry into the EEC or the part that the move westward played in the growth of the USA. Both of these are accepted truths – why does this not apply to the Brandt Report?

It is unclear which countries would benefit most in terms of increased employment – so much would depend on the pattern of development and growth and the resurgence (or otherwise) of old trading links. Given that there is a considerable amount of money lying dormant in the North, especially in the London stock market, the cost to governments of providing this aid would be relatively small. However, governments would need the persuasive or legal powers to control those monies, most of which are in non-government hands. Alternatively, of course, monies could be made available as loans through the private system.

We might be forced to make such a move anyway. This book is based on the assumption that the new technologies will be used, and used effectively. This assumes that firms and other organisations will have been investing in new systems, that we will have been training and retraining employees to use them and that we will have developed an approach where we feel comfortable with them. The first two of these require the expenditure of a considerable amount of money and, given the reluctance of banks to lend in the long term and the difficulty of getting finance for high technology purposes, some form of National Investment Bank may well have to be created. This would be based on the moribund but wealthy pension and insurance funds with, of course, guarantees for the individual integrity of all pension entitlements and policies.

The new industrial revolution is different from the first in that we are partially aware of what is happening. Newspapers and magazines, TV and radio tell us about individual changes as they occur, but rarely bring them together in a serious analysis. Technology is changing, employment is changing, products and services are changing – but the one key change has not yet occurred. As happened eventually in the course of the nineteenth century, we need a revolution in attitudes to match that in industry.

16 The hardest revolution of all

Many countries around the world have shown how easy it is to have a successful revolution, but many have also demonstrated, not long afterwards, the ease with which counter-revolutions can take place. What is clearly much more difficult to achieve is the one thing that would prevent a counter-revolution – and that is a revolution in attitudes. It really is the 'hardest revolution of them all'.

We are surrounded by changes, the mood of the nation is volatile and uncertain – not to say violent – and life is altering perceptibly, yet old attitudes die hard. Matters are not improved by the lack of guidance in these matters; the best we have is an invitation to return to the nineteenth century, a wholly inappropriate notion. Facing today with yesterday's attitudes is difficult enough, but facing tomorrow bolstered by the attitudes forged the day before yesterday is a recipe for disaster. There will *have* to be attitudinal changes because the one certain thing is that the technology on which the transformation of society is based will not go away, and indeed we shall be encouraging it to expand and develop.

The revolution in attitudes must start with the realisation that employment and work may be different things and that the ethic that we call the work ethic is really the employment ethic, as I have emphasised throughout this book. In the previous chapter I suggested how we could make a start in reverting to the older, more traditional work ethic, but running alongside this must be a gradual change in our attitudes. As parents we shall continue to worry our offspring about the sort of job they want to do; we shall still regard examination success as a stepping-stone to a better job and we shall still pester teachers about academic standards. We shall do all these things unless we stop, think and ask ourselves what we are doing and why we are doing it. These are difficult questions to answer, but it is a difficult revolution.

We have to take the attitude that employment is an important part of life, but is still only a part. We can be fulfilled in other ways – one of which is to be useful to others, whether or not this is in the employment sphere. As I suggested in the previous chapter, this change of attitude will not take place unless financial security is provided at a higher than subsistence level. Employment must be seen as desirable for part of the time, rather than essential for all the time.

The industrialised world has outgrown the employment ethic. We are living in a changed industrial age where machines operate themselves, and other machines control the strategy underlying the use of these and other machines. Human beings become increasingly irrelevant in this system of production, but they are as relevant as ever to other humans. As a species we are gregarious, we thrive on each other's company and it is in these directions that we should turn our energies. *The machines free our time. This is a positive feature, not a negative one, and we can use the time to make our own lives and those of other people more tolerable, and indeed pleasurable.*

Our attitudes towards the sources of our employment and work will have to change. Self-employment and co-operative development will have to be thought of as permanent features of community life, although in all probability people will be involved in them on a very part-time basis. We shall have to realise that hobbies can become jobs. Bee-keeping can be turned into honey or royal jelly production, model-train enthusiasts can put on exhibitions in local halls, pop enthusiasts can start discos, tennis-players can coach, gardeners can sell produce, knitters their socks and computer buffs their programs. Again, all these activities and countless others are viable on a part-time basis, and they could all form the basis for a form of barter economy.

Employment is traditionally supposed to be performed in a shop, office or factory – anywhere in fact other than the home. This attitude will have to change too, as the new technologies make home-working more of an economic feasibility. Homes themselves may well have to change. Ten years from now developers may be offering new houses with a work/communications room, and advertisements for houses in trendy Islington will add 'carcassed for communications' to the 'jacuzzi and his and her washbasins'. At the same time, attitudes to the types of jobs we do will change. Part-time, temporary and contract employment will have to be considered as normal rather than second-best, and the old long-term career pattern will fade into office folklore.

The division between employment time and free or leisure time will have to be blurred, if for no other reason than that the conventional working day or week is breaking down. It becomes blurred even further when free time is used to do useful work (in terms of the original work ethic) – in the garden perhaps, or visiting people in hospital. The arbitrary division, which developed so strongly in the first industrial revolution, no longer fits the needs of the late twentieth-century industrial and commercial processes. Flexibility rather than rigidity is the glittering prize of today's generation, so it is not surprising that the Establishment is weighing in heavily on the side of this particular change in attitude.

The concept of leisure as sinful and wicked will have to be changed. It is a product of the firm grip that the employment ethic exerts, to the extent that not being at a job, when we think we should be, fills us with guilt. We must ask the fundamental questions – what is so wonderful about employment and who actually enjoys it? Leisure time should be at least as desirable as employment time, and we must make every effort to ensure that this is widely accepted. The change of emphasis which the schools will impart over the coming years will, I hope, go some considerable way to seeing that this is done.

Our attitude to status will have to change. Status is generally conferred by a combination of personal income and wealth, the type of job and, more rarely, the accident of birth into the 'right circles'. For most people their income, if not their wealth, is dependent upon their employment (as of course is their job title). This means that the type of employment is crucial in status games, and the unemployed clearly lose every hand in this respect. One of the first questions asked of a new acquaintance at a party is, 'What do you do?' If the answer is, 'Ah well, mm, actually I'm unemployed,' the conversation tends to be short and not very sweet. Only resting Thespians, nursing and pregnant women and the retired escape this unspoken condemnation.

This is a trivial manifestation of a far more fundamental difficulty. Because status and self-esteem are so entangled in Britain, the unemployed lose the ability to recognise their own worth. Unless the link between status and employment is broken and replaced with something different, this will continue to create misery on a grand scale. It is not impossible to conceive of several factors which could replace money and employment as the measure of status. Being a good wife and mother was society's way of measuring women at a time when they were not encouraged to get a job; why not revive this and judge people in terms of whether they are good husbands or wives, parents or partners. Status and self-esteem can be measured in terms of value to the community based on the help one gives to others. It may sound terribly altruistic but it is a viable and pleasant alternative to the present situation.

With or without this adaptation there needs to be a change in attitude towards the unemployed or partly employed. They should not be considered failures or scroungers but people who are an integral part of their community and whose presence adds to its diversity. No doubt there will be people to whom this description does no real justice; they might be malcontents, psychopaths or just plain bloody-minded – but so they would be if they were employed. Given, however, the present class nature of the education system and the fact that the new technologies will almost certainly reinforce these divisions, it is likely that current attitudes towards the unemployed will be reinforced, and they will have a larger chance of being race-related too.

This will happen at a time when the existing class expectations will be breaking down in one respect and being strengthened in another. Middle-class beliefs will be shaken as both career and financial security come under pressure, so that all the consumer goods that are purchased on the strength of these twin pillars will have a shaky basis. This will force the middle class away from one of their marked distinguishing features, that of taking a long view, and push them into more short-term standards and preoccupations. They will attempt, however, as a class to prevent this happening. With education being the key to employment the middle classes will ensure that their children get the best available chances; the existing state school system will be under threat as demand grows from a vocal and articulate section of the population for a reversion to a more élitist system. This will be an attempt to re-establish the middle-class way of life through the next generation. It is unlikely to succeed because the nature of the technological revolution is such that these old values based on old employment patterns and prospects will never again re-emerge.

Everyone's expectations will need to change, however, not just those of the middle classes. More people could be able to buy more goods and visit more places on a regular basis. Overall there could be a revising upwards of expectations, although some of the higher paid may not have the security that they once anticipated. Whether or not these benefits appear depends on how the technology is used and how we, as a nation, adapt to that use.

People's opinions do affect the attitudes and reactions of politicians, especially those who base their policies on opinion polls. In the USA, before the last Presidential election of 1984, it was discovered that people had a most ambivalent attitude towards the unemployed and their problems. They realised that many of them were very poor and needed help, and also realised that the Democratic candidate Walter Mondale intended to provide this help. They were quite happy about this until they realised that their taxes would have to rise as a result. 'I'm not paying for those bastards out of my money – I have a difficult enough time as it is' was a typical reaction, even though people did realise that something had to be done. This attitude was far stronger amongst the working than amongst the middle classes, and their view was that in different circumstances (the employed and unemployed changing places) the same reaction would have prevailed. We all know the result. Reagan had a landslide victory, offering the poor and unemployed nothing but continual poverty, and reassuring those in work that their money would remain in their pockets.

This raises the question of how you arrive at the policies of political parties, the attitudes that underpin them and the acceptance or otherwise of these policies by the electorate. Fashion plays a larger part in the conventional wisdom of politics than those involved in it would care to admit. Public expenditure is unfashionable at present, not for the first but hopefully for the last time; there is something intrinsically wrong with a theory that claims that only private money is good, while government money is tainted. As we saw in the previous chapter, most of the large areas of potential employment will only be exploited by using public money. This will require changes in the attitudes of both politicians and the public.

The present Conservative government has consciously attempted to change the attitudes of people, not merely to govern; it has not been given sufficient recognition for this fundamental political act. A consensus had previously existed on matters like the state funding of the National Health Service, local authorities providing their own labour forces, the state providing free basic education, and state monopolies in the public utilities. All these certainties are now being challenged, and in one respect this has to be a good thing. If it means that we re-examine why we provided these services in the way that we did, and this forces us to adapt to the new circumstances of today, a series of healthier and better institutions should emerge. However the dogma which lies behind this government's actions does not stem from this view; it is based on the premise that private money is somehow purer, cleaner and better than public money.

In practical terms, services like health and education that were taken out of the open market some forty years ago are slowly being returned to it. This is of course an optional method of job creation in these sectors, but a poor one. Those who need the most health care are generally the least able to afford it, and private education is certainly beyond the pocket of the majority of parents. This would suggest that if the private sector does take resources from the public sector (thus gradually starving it of money), there will be a limited demand for private services, while the state services will worsen and overall employment will not be increased. Some of the changes that have occurred will be difficult, if not impossible, to reverse, but in general terms overall employment and the meeting of need will depend on public expenditure to a greater extent than ever before.

This bald statement hides the most fundamental of political conflicts. If public expenditure is increased, a method has to be found to get the income into the central exchequer in the first instance. Taxes are *never* popular, although they are usually grudgingly accepted. In the future, however, there will be a smaller number of people in employment who will be taxable, which will make tax rates extremely high if the same total revenue is to be gathered, and alternative forms of revenue will have to be contemplated. A progressive consumption tax – a variable-rate VAT which taxed higher priced and luxury goods and services at a higher rate than essentials – could be introduced. Corporation tax, to be effectively collected, would have to be levied on an EEC basis and this will challenge the national control of taxation, but in view of the terrible social crises and violence so evident in recent years, the attitude that taxes are a method of purchasing civilisation may strike a receptive chord. Public ownership is another way of allowing profits to accrue directly to government, although the monolithic single-industry nationalisations are no longer appropriate. There are, however, many other ways in which the state can control enterprises or parts of companies – by use of majority share ownership, loan capital etc.

Local government and community expenditure will be crucial too, perhaps even more so than higher profile national spending. To enable community councils and organisations to flourish money will undoubtedly be needed, but where it should come from is another matter. The areas of greatest need have the lowest tax bases, whether this is measured in property or rateable value, income, purchasing power or company profits. It follows from this that some form of local tax equalisation scheme will be needed, especially in the cities and towns with high overall unemployment. Again, a progressively based sales tax could form a solid platform. Both central and local government revenue would also be enhanced considerably if the informal economy could be 'persuaded' to pay its share of taxes.

The argument about public expenditure has to be put openly and fairly, it must not be fudged or obfuscated. The proponents should not be ashamed of it, or of what they wish to do with it; the opponents must demonstrate how they will run society without it. Public attitudes will be forged in this overall conflict. It is probably the most fundamental and important political debate that the UK, indeed all industrialised countries, will have over the coming quarter century.

People, that is to say the electorate, may well have to instruct politicians, rather than be instructed or lectured by them; this applies more to local and regional levels than to the centre. There is a British attitude of deference which gives a status and credence to people because of their position, not because of what they have to say. This helps maintain our class system relatively unchanged. Politicians are a beneficiary of this weakness; they can make silly speeches in Parliament or on a radio or TV chat programme and be listened to with rapt attention, while the same argument made in the bar by a neighbour would invite ridicule. Such deferential treatment must stop. Authority should only be respected if it proves itself worthy of it, and in any event politicians only hold their authority by virtue of the electorate in the first place.

This is not a populist argument, nor is it an attempt to weaken the power of politicians. It is, however, a warning to politicians to stop using meaningless slogans and outdated rhetoric because they have little relevance to the problems of today's ordinary people. Our attitude towards politicians must be based upon supportive criticism. We have a right to demand from our representatives open rather than closed minds to bring us fresh ideas on how to cope with the new problems – even if this might signal the death of the 'whipping' system in Parliament. We also have a right to expect that politicians should take on board any reasonable ideas that might help cope with the unemployment and employment problems. For example, Guy Dauncey, a writer and worker for the unemployed, has suggested that each time a voluntary group takes a positive action which removes a person from the unemployment register that group should receive a subsidy of six months' unemployment pay. This would enable them to continue their work. To date no one in authority has picked up this particular ball, let alone started to run with it, yet it does not sound as silly as the YOPS or YTS schemes did initially.

This reflects well the attitude of politicians to voluntary groups and new ideas. Both are considered of marginal importance. The media tend to take the same view though there is a perceptible growth in the number of 'alternative' groups which are producing programmes to deal with today's circumstances. They cover a very wide range of activities and philosophies and are attracting a significantly larger number of people with their new and often radical ideas. Most are apolitical and concerned with the quality of life rather than the application of power.

Their importance lies in two separate areas. These kinds of group have been in existence over the years but the current climate of instability, and the apparent impotence of the Establishment to deal with it, is giving them a new potential credibility. 'Why not try something else, there's nothing to lose,' is the argument. Some of the new groups are based on communities, like the Easterhouse Festival, and have a practical and limited purpose, though their most important achievement may well turn out to be the example that they set of actually being able to do something other than just talk. Some of the groups are based on self-realisation and fulfilment, practised either in communes or in the world at large. Some have a wider perspective, often of global concern and with an environmentalist tinge. Some sound a little eccentric, others perfectly sane and eminently sensible; The Fourth World and the ETHOS Harmonic School of Venice rub shoulders with the National Centre for Alternate Technology, Financial Initiative and networks like Turning Point and the Business Network. Religions are well represented, many based on the gentler Buddhist philosophies. While political action is almost never debated in these circles there are political undertones; each of these groups would provide a challenge to the existing and established order of things if they were to grow sufficiently. They are tolerated because they are insignificant; getting little publicity except of a sensational or mocking character. This lack of media interest applies to the growth of alternative economics too, though this is far more of a direct challenge to the *status quo*.

The Other Economic Summit was held in London in June 1984. It was intended as a direct challenge to the conventional economic approach of the London economic summit held at around the same time. The basic assumption underlying TOES was that most resources are non-renewable and finite, the physical environment is precious and individuals are capable of infinite self-development. Some ideas are staggering in their simplicity and boldness, although their practicality has not been tested. For example, Peter Rae of the Centre for New Economic Studies has suggested that there should be a new universal value system. Money backed by gold is of course the existing, but arbitrary, system and it works to the disadvantage of the LDCs. His answer is to use energy measured in joules. Every country has a potential energy source, even if it is only under-utilised solar power, energy is measurable, energy can be renewable. It may not work, but as an idea it certainly deserves to be explored in a serious manner.

The network system works well in these areas. BURN, the British Unemployed Resource Network, links together some of the local, community and self-help initiatives. There are networks which link together people who want to get more humanity, even spirituality, into business, and others which include trade unionists and politicians. Ideas are flowing and spreading, but few are taken seriously by those in power. It could be that this is the reception they deserve, it could be that the communication system is not good enough, or it could be that our attitude is all wrong – we are too unreceptive, too hidebound by our dogmas. I would suggest that it is a combination of all three, but the last reason provides the most intractable block. There is an arrogance behind this, based on the principle that 'if we have not thought of the idea then it is not worth thinking about'.

It is very important to overcome this. Conventional politics is all about collective responses, collective decisions and collective actions; in some senses it has to be. Taxation, legal processes, defence and welfare policies – indeed the art of government itself – all rely upon categorising people into arbitrary groups, each comprising millions of people. The Conservative party, which declares that it is for the individual and family against the big battalions, has allowed precious little extra freedom to individuals, as indeed have most of their predecessors. Capitalism gives people the freedom to exploit others, and success is measured by an individual triumphing over a large group of others. It is the politics of greed, envy and ruthlessness – certainly not of fulfilment, mutual help and self-respect, which I have been arguing are necessary.

The Labour party bases its approach on the collective ideal; problems are dealt with collectively, advances made on a broad front. There is a need, however, to add an individual dimension. Alternative economic theory preaches that each individual is unique and should be allowed to develop as such. Given that no one person can operate outside the constraints created by the existence of other people, this synthesis could be approached in such a way as to make collective and individual responses perfectly compatible.

The opportunities for personal development have never been greater, paradoxically as a result of there being less employment. Employment, the disciplines that surround it, and the monotony within it has had a deadening and stultifying effect on most people. This is where the challenge exists, to make the most of the opportunity afforded by fewer jobs. Before they can even begin to grapple with this concept, politicians, especially those on the left, will have to temper their ideals of collective humanity with a recognition of individual choices and needs.

Yet another set of attitudes needs to be modified: our attitude to the 'golden ages' of our ancestors. They were of course rarely that golden to the people who had to live through them, but the point is that they divert attention away from the task of working for the future. We are continually pining for the crispier bacon of yesteryear instead of looking forward to tomorrow's fresh bread. The golden age of full employment really only existed for that very aberrant post-war period of the fifties and sixties; the golden age of merchant adventurers and robber barons was one of unrivalled misery and squalor. Golden ages are not what they seem. Even if they were, they are not recapturable; circumstances are never precisely the same again, and people are unlikely to react in the same ways. We will be far better off not comparing our situation with the safety of the fifties, or indeed with the slump of the thirties, and instead we should put our efforts into working out an approach for the eighties.

Over the past decade the word 'plan' has become a disreputable four-letter word, but quite why this should be so is a mystery. People expect to plan their budgets, businesses are encouraged to plan their future sales and output, and everyone agrees that this is a good thing. Why then is a government supposed not to plan? There is really no good reason at all. Above all else, this new industrial revolution screams out for planning. Manpower, training and education, industrial production, research and development, urban development, leisure facilities and provisions, transport, housing, energy policy and foreign policy all need to be planned so that we can pre-empt problems.

Again, our attitudes to this will have to change, but planning should not be carried out exclusively from the top downwards as it so often is at present. It should be decentralised and democratised as far as possible. It is true that there needs to be a central strategy, but this must be flexible enough to allow for structural changes at local levels and to be superseded at these levels if local circumstances dictate that this should be so. The planning process should involve as many people as possible; the results experienced in community work show how valuable this can be as a motivating force. If you exclude people from a decision-making process, you will clearly get less commitment to the project, whatever it might be.

In any country there are certain people and groups who have a vested interest in maintaining the *status quo*; the most casual reasoning will suggest that they must be those in the upper echelons of the 'Establishment', as widely defined as this can be. These people and the groups they represent often use every means in their power to oppose reform, but they will have to think seriously about what they are doing and question their attitudes in a severely critical manner. The three groups which will need to do this more than most (other than politicians and civil servants) are the industrialists and senior managers, the trade-union leadership and those in the professions.

Senior people in industry and commerce work on the principle that they must take decisions in the best interests of their organisation, which is on the face of it perfectly rational. The problem arises when these decisions are taken in aggregate. If each company decides to introduce new technologically based systems and, as a result, cuts its future demand for labour, where are next year's jobs? Each decision can be defended logically, but the cumulative result is summed up in the June 1985 OECD report on the UK – 3.25 per cent growth coupled with an additional 100,000 unemployed over the coming year. As I have attempted to explain, the mechanisms for converting profits and wealth into jobs do not function at all well in the UK as growth is no longer the key to increased employment. The social disruption that could well ensue from unemployment, especially amongst the young, could actually kill the goose that lays the golden egg of profits. Industrialists will have to face some unpalatable choices over the coming years, and their long-held attitudes will be put to the test.

They could carry on as they are now and hope that, as in *Candide*, 'all is for the best in the best of possible worlds', urging only that 'law and order' be strengthened to prevent too much disruption of production or markets. They could decide to stop introducing new technological systems or to use them in a way that did not result in job losses. They could lower their expectations to silver-gilt eggs, and reduce returns on their capital by either promoting job-sharing or improving services and standards with the employment of more people. An example of this was when Japanese TV firms changed their technology and reduced the number of people needed to assemble a TV set by half. Some of these were retained in 'bottom-warming jobs', others retired early, while others were re-trained, and many former assembly-workers became TV servicers. In Tokyo it is now possible to pick up a phone and get a set repaired within half an hour, traffic permitting. So former employees continued to be employed, and clients' needs were met. At no time was there a loud clamour for this improved service – the companies just went ahead and provided it. In the UK our 'wait and see' attitude will probably prevail until disaster strikes, despite the fact that the Japanese example would clearly allow for the most stable growth; unless of course that change in attitude comes about.

Trade unions represent workers in employment; the unemployed and the retired can be members but little can be done on their behalf. It is therefore in the best interests of trade unions to attempt to maintain as high a level of employment as possible. This has to be qualified, however. Unions find it easiest to recruit new members from amongst men who work full time in large organisations; secondary employment poses great problems, as do co-operatives and the growth of self-employment. But in the future unions are going to have to come to terms with the fact that an increasing number of their members and potential members will be working in precisely these areas.

This implies a great shift in attitudes. The male-oriented organisation will have to amend itself, not only to recruit women but also to represent them properly. Trade unions will have to master the intricacies of part-time and contract work, accept the existence of agencies and temporary-help companies (indeed recruit their clients), come to terms with an overall concept of income which may come from many sources (including the government) and allow members greater input into decision-making, perhaps from their homes, by using the new technologies. Without these changes there will be a vast diminution of trade-union influence at both a bargaining and at a national level. This would be in nobody's best interests in the long term. At one level the only independent representative body that workers have would be gravely impaired, whilst at another a force for stability against the revolutionary Left will have been weakened. This will happen, however, unless unions develop an awareness of how to represent members who will be working, employed or unemployed (perhaps all in the same week), and realise who their new members must be.

The professions have developed superb representational bodies. They are skilled at defending their members' positions, as well as taking advantage of changes in circumstances. The changes around the corner will depend on all the newer technologies with a leavening of expert systems. These could be used for the benefit of patients and of clients, but a combination of extreme caution and self-interest may prevent this from happening fully. Fears about para-professionals being used to replace professionals, of expert systems showing up their inadequacies and of the possible legal complications about responsibilities that may arise could halt promising lines of action. The danger signs are evident even now and, again, a basic change in approach and attitudes is needed.

We shall also have to change our attitude to international relations. Overseas aid has to be given in a spirit of cooperation, with the expectation that it will be used for structural development. At present we give it reluctantly, if at all, or as a result of a tragedy of epic proportions, like Ethiopia. *Aid, in both kind and money, has to be treated as the seed corn of the next world trade boom.*

In a world that is steadily shrinking as a result of new communication technologies the division between East and West and the resulting arms race becomes even sillier than it was when it started. Hunger, poverty and disease are still with us to be eradicated or controlled, yet billions of pounds and the most highly skilled expertise are spent and used on armaments. Jobs are created by the arms industry, but there is more than enough work and employment for people to do without such a trade. Most of it has a very limited spin-off into the civilian sector, so that a thousand pounds spent on a military item will have fewer multiplier effects than the same thousand spent on curing several sick children. Attitudes here should have changed years ago but did not; perhaps this new industrial revolution will do the trick.

It may do so, because all the old ideas should be up for grabs.

No avenue should be declared out of bounds, no institution too sacrosanct. This does not mean that they will all be under threat, let alone disappear, but it does mean that the changes in society will be so great that each institution and each practice and habit will have to justify its existence again. This must apply to all the basic systems that we work within. Is the monarchy a suitable constitutional form for a country where we may be trying to devolve far more of our lives down to local community levels and attempting to involve as many people as possible in decision-making processes? It may well be, but the question ought to be asked. Is capitalism a suitable economic and political philosophy for a country where capital intensity has been expanded so considerably? If it is not, what is it that we do want? Is it communism à la Soviet Union, is it a modified capitalism, is it some form of socialism, anarchy, fascism or some new and exciting philosophy? The conflicts and pressures that are starting to emerge, and will no doubt increase over time as the technologies start to be implemented in earnest, are making this re-evaluation inevitable.

We need to ask ourselves what we are prepared to allow to happen in this, the second industrial revolution. Technologies do not determine what happens, at least not entirely; *people* have the ultimate control. It must be admitted, rather grudgingly, that microelectronic technology dictates more of its own uses than almost any other technological development. It creates its own momentum in that it is essential to the development of other technologies, as well as opening up avenues of thought that were hitherto closed. Nevertheless, human beings have the last word; at the end of the day they can shut off the power – providing of course that we do not allocate this function to a robot controlled by a fifth-generation artificial intelligence computer. This is not an idle jest; it could be a feature of a fail-safe system in the future.

Microelectronics, like most other important technologies, can be used for good or evil. The car can be used as a weapon, gunpowder to bore a well and morphine to kill rather than relieve pain, but microelectronics have such a length and breadth of applications that their effects could be incalculable. They could be used to kill on a more massive scale than ever before, or to relieve suffering around the world; they could be used to bring in a wider democratic system or to perfect totalitarian control; they could be used to liberate employees or enslave them, divide people or unite them. The choices are always ours, we cannot blame the technology for any bad decisions that we make. This means that we have to take responsibility for our actions and to do this we will have to change our attitudes. Cynicism, attractive though it may be on a superficial level, will have to be replaced by other virtues.

Imagination, perseverance, honesty and, more than anything else, confidence in our own abilities are the virtues that will carry industrialised countries through to the year 2020. This is a significant year. It is as far away from 1984 as 1948 (when George Orwell wrote his book), and the current crop of futuristic writers appear to believe that life will be as awful in 2020 as Orwell thought life would be in 1984. The technology exists for these writers to be proved correct, but people must have the confidence to prove them wrong. Confidence to challenge the vested interests, confidence to say that the received wisdoms are no longer valid and confidence to put all that imaginative planning into practice.

The worst thing that can be done is to congratulate ourselves on our national characteristics, whatever they might be, and wait for our renowned sense of fair play and moderation to enable us to muddle through. This was not sufficient in the first industrial revolution and it will not suffice in this one. The future could be far rosier than the past, there could be a liberation undreamt of with the older technologies. It requires planning, it requires positive and imaginative thinking, it requires positive action and that intangible gift of confidence. Optimism rather than pessimism must be the guiding principle, because a break with the past is not a terrible thing if the future is going to be better. We can lose the worst elements, retain the best and create new good ones. Our children, grandchildren, and greatgrandchildren will not thank us if we shirk these responsibilities and miss the new opportunities opening out before us.

Index

Alcoholics Anonymous, 179–80
alcoholism/drinking, 5, 11, 232, 270
Alliance (SDP and Liberals), 92, 151, 180, 181, 214, 246, 247, 248, 250, 259
alternative lifestyles, 237–8, 284–6
amended products, 73–4
AMT (advanced manufacturing technologies), 47
Anderla, Georges, 49
arms race, 290
artificial intelligence (AI) computers, 50, 54, 55, 107, 164, 260
arts and culture, 113–14, 191–2, 212–13, 217–19, 266, 272
Arts Council, 212–13, 217–18, 272
Association of Metropolitan Authorities (AMA), 210
Atkinson, John, 129
automated factories, 46, 47, 48

balance of payments, 29, 32, 118, 151, 177, 244, 245
banks, banking, 38, 49, 51–3, 59, 61, 66, 78, 112, 265, 275, 276
Belgium, 31, 76, 81, 86, 100
Biffen, John, 82
'black' economy, 128
Brandt Report ('North-South'), 185, 274–5, 276
'Brass Tacks', Hackney, 167
Brenner, Dr Harvey, 8–9
British Leyland, 44
British Telecom, 137, 173
BTX teletext system, 52
BURN (British Unemployed Resource Network), 286

cabling, 39, 50, 53, 107
CAD (Computer Aided Design), 47, 49, 60, 123
Callaghan, James, 89
CAM (Computer Aided Manufacturing), 47, 60
Canada, viii, 22, 146–7, 211, 242
caring services, 173, 174, 176, 245, 270; voluntary, 178–82
Centre for Alternative Industrial and Technological Systems, 258
chemicals, artificial fibres and non-metallic products, 108
children: abuse of, 232, 270; employment of, 117, 121; malnutrition, 233
CIM (Computer Integrated Manufacturing), 47, 48, 58

civil service, permanent, 89–90, 94
class system, 280–1, 283–4; and leisure, 191–4, 201
clerical and administrative employment, 50–1, 59–60, 61, 93, 107, 129
The Collapse of Work, viii, 106, 252
communes, 237–8, 285
communication satellites, 60
communications technology/employment, 90, 100, 112, 115, 116, 119, 290
communism, 253–4, 291; and employment ethic, 15–16, 253; and new technology, 253, 254
community, 87, 260, 278; entertainment, 214–16, 266; expenditure, 283; growth of, 260, 264–7; involvement in leisure, 213–16, 272; and schools, 261, 265, 269, 270
Community Enterprise, 86
Community Industry, 182
community schemes/service, 10, 32, 166–7; voluntary, 180–2
Community Service Volunteers, 180
computers, computerisation, 38, 39, 40, 41–2, 46, 47–8, 54–61, 71, 116, 164, 165–6, 190, 259; artificial intelligence, 50, 54, 55, 107, 164, 260; chess-playing, 56; fifth generation, 54, 55, 60, 107, 259–60; personal, 40, 49, 50, 59, 73, 74, 165; and politics, 87–8; production, 48
Conservative party/government, viii, 75, 80–1, 82, 86–7, 93, 96–7, 151, 180, 242, 243, 246, 247, 248–9, 251, 259, 264, 282, 286; political philosophy of, 240–1, 242
construction industry, 110–11, 118
constructive demotion, 138–9
consumer goods, 11–12, 21, 27, 39, 173
contract work, 121, 133, 234, 278–9, 289
Cooley, Dr Mike, 184
cooperatives, 238, 249, 265, 278, 289
core or primary workers, 130, 268
Cork, Sir Kenneth, 64
credit cards, 52
crime and vandalism, 148, 195, 232–3
Crosland, Tony, 28

Davidson, Ken, 131
Dauncey, Guy, 284
defence industry, 53, 112–13, 116, 175, 177
democracy, concept of, 87, 97
Digital Equipment Corporation, 50
DIY, 10, 128, 189, 201, 219
drugs, drug addicts, 179, 237, 238, 270
Durham, Bishop of, 252

293

INDEX

INDEX

296